SERVICE

MPERATIVE

THE PAST, PRESENT AND FUTURE OF THE LINEN SUPPLY INDUSTRY

BY
WILBUR CROSS
AND
JERRY STEINMAN

With a foreword by Dr. Ralph M. Hower

CONTENTS

PREFACE

During 1965 the Board of the Linen Supply Association of America authorized this history. Since I had originally proposed the documentary project, I have been asked to prepare a brief rationale for this book.

Like a person, an industry has a beginning as well as a continuing history. Unlike that of a person, however, its span of life can reach far into the future, if it adequately meets the needs of the community. And I hope that our industry, now nearing its centenary, will function effectively for many years to come. Its origin and development are meaningful not only to its pioneers and present personnel, but also to teachers, students, and others who grapple with the future in terms of the past.

Memories of past events will rapidly dim if they are not recorded. We of linen supply are proud of the accomplishments—and, therefore, wish to preserve them in print—of the many people who in a relatively few years have contributed so much to American health, employee morale, and customer goodwill. We are proud of the growth of this industry to nearly a billion dollars in annual sales in the United States and Canada.

While similar books have been commissioned by very large corporations and by other industries, to the best of our knowledge this is the first time that a major service industry like linen supply has engaged in such an activity. We hope that it will clarify the significant role of the linen supplier in our national economy.

RICHARD R. STEINER

ACKNOWLEDGEMENTS

The authors take this opportunity to thank the Board of Directors of LSAA for reviewing the manuscript, and especially Arnold R. Knapp and Alvin S. Gross for devoting part of a week to a painstaking page-by-page review of the book in its nearly final form. The authors are indebted to so many individuals and firms in the linen industry for suggestions and information that is almost impossible to compile an acknowledgement list. However, at risk of slighting many whose names are not included, they would particularly like to thank the following for their interest and help:

Martin Abelove, C. G. Badham,* Michael Barsky, Morris Bonoff, Daniel Bruni, Nicholas Bruni, Victor Bruni, Dr. Fritz G. Burkart, P. L. Carpaneto, Nat Chonin, Jack Chernikoff, Edward J. Clarke, Nathaniel Cohen, James Connors, Donald M. Counihan,* W. B. Dean, N. L. Dehn, Eric DiStanislao, Bernard H. Ehrlich, Daniel Fitzgibbons, Hilda M. Folkman, Louis Friedman,* Roy J. Friedman, Mike Ginsberg, Herman Gitlow, B. B. Goldstein, Louis Gordon,* Murray Gordon, Alvin S. Gross, J. R. Hagan, Robert B. Hartless, Alan B. Hazard, Brace Helfrich, Sr., Roy Hiroshige, Edward V. Hudson, William Hurlbut, Howard Kahn, Morris I. Kaplan,* J. P. Kielland, Joseph B. Kirshbaum, Walter W. Knuckols, Sam Kornfeld, George Krantz, Ole Laursen, Guy Leatherwood, Daniel F. Marini, Michael Marini, Roy L. Maryatt, Jr., M. Maschke, Jr., Lester Maslow, Robert Maslow, E. F. Merritt, Frank Miller, Joseph H. Miller,* Sydney Miller, John A. Morgan, William Niemi, Jack Orlinsky, Brooke Petray, Richard S. Pollock, William R. Pollock, Jr., Stanley I. Posner,* Max S. Powell, Jack A. Quigley, Gordon L. Rayner, Saul Riebman, Joseph A. Robertson, Sr., Carl H. Rohman,

*Deceased

Howard Rosenfeld, Leighton A. Rosenthal, Clarence Roskoph, Ralph Roskoph,* Wilbur A. Sale, Joseph G. Schuh, William Schumer, Donald T. Smith, Harry Spero,* Leslie W. Spero, Richard R. Steiner, George N. Strike, A. L. Stromberg, Sheldon Stromberg, Hugo Swan, Otto W. Thoma, A. J. Weinberg, Milton Weinstein, Stanley A. Weiser, Ellis Whitehead, Wayne Wilson, Dan Ziegler, Louis Zipperman.

* Deceased

FOREWORD

In recent years the American public has become increasingly aware of the possibility of renting equipment to meet occasional needs: cars, trailers, power tools, skis and ski clothing, and so on—the list grows longer each month. Much of it goes to do-it-yourself customers to meet a temporary situation, with the consequence that it is often being used by relatively unskilled amateurs, yielding only fair results and taking time that the renter could put to better use. The rental firms are in the service category of economic activities, distinct from manufacturing, communications, retailing, and other classifications. The services industry group has been growing in importance for a number of decades, as this book discusses in some detail, and it currently constitutes approximately ten per cent of the gross national product.

To its customers linen supply service is important because they do not have to do it themselves! A linen supply company delivers clean towels, garments, and other textile products on a rental basis and takes away the soiled items for processing—done by skilled operators using the best technology and equipment available. Thus, the customer is relieved of an investment not only in the items rented but also in the space, special equipment, and labor that he would otherwise have to provide for himself. And also (perhaps more important today) he is relieved of the technical knowledge, special skills, and expert management required to do the job satisfactorily and at reasonable cost.

This book sets forth the history of one service industry—the linen supply business, delivering a large variety of textile products to customers on a rental basis. The significance of this study lies not in the size of the industry, for the total sales volume of the linen supply business in the United States barely exceeded $800,000,000 in 1968, handled by something less than 1,600 plants. It is neither a large nor a glamorous industry. In part, this history takes special significance from the fact that the linen supply business is one of the oldest of our service industries, and, having started in the late 1870s, it antedates by at least forty years the earliest of the other rental businesses with which we have become familiar.

This historical account is significant for still another reason. So far as I can find out from historians and librarians, this is the first history of a service industry to be published. In addition to being intrinsically interesting, it will, I think, be useful to students of economic and business history as well as to those in the linen supply industry itself and in other service industries. For it sets forth patterns of development, showing how the industry arrived at its present state and giving clues as to where it might go from here. The professional historian will recognize that the treatment, although seriously executed, is somewhat more journalistic than scholarly. But anyone who has attempted to produce a business history which meets the professional standards of the serious scholar knows how difficult it is (in some respects impossible, because of the lack of adequate documentary material) and how time consuming. I am sure I am not the only one to be delighted to have this publication now, rather than to have to wait years for a more painstaking treatise.

It was not until the second half of the nineteenth century that environmental conditions made the linen supply business feasible. Thanks to the Industrial Revolution, relatively inexpensive textile products became available. The growth of cities, with their aggregation of barber shops, hotels, restaurants, offices, saloons, and butcher shops, created a laundry problem which could only be met by the emerging commercial laundries. Moreover, hygienic standards in public and private life were rising; hand towels, napkins, and aprons were beginning to be recognized as desirable, even necessary. These conditions provided the opportunity for linen supply service to operate on a profitable basis.

Although no reliable information has survived about the very first linen supply companies established in the United States, the typical way of starting is evident from the recollections of men who began operations in the 1880s. A man, or even an enterprising teen-age boy, would contact prospective customers, somehow raise enough money to buy some linen, arrange with a commercial laundry for the washing, and then go to work, using the family kitchen as a base of operations. He delivered the towels and brought back the soiled linen by hand or handcart. If he succeeded and the volume grew too large for manpower, deliveries would be made by a horse-drawn vehicle and he might eventually acquire his own laundry facilities.

To enter the business required little capital, great energy, continuing determination, and the ability to sell. Relative ease of entry guaranteed stiff price competition for many years to come, until advancing technology made necessary a substantial initial investment in special-purpose equipment. To stay in business required something more—the ability to manage production and delivery operations, control costs, and maintain profits. Often a salesman joined forces with an experienced laundry operator to strengthen the entrepreneurial team, or he acquired as partner a businessman with financial acumen and money to invest as a means of solving the monetary problems resulting from growth.

Apparently in the early decades good management was more important than scale of operations. A man or partnership, having achieved success with one company, often expanded the scope of operations by acquiring or establishing a plant in another city, adding others as circumstances permitted. By 1900 what we would now call chains were already in existence. During the 1920s a number of fairly large mergers took place, several combining a score of separate plants and a few involving the sale of stock to the public.

In the meantime the line of items offered to customers had greatly expanded to include hand towels; napkins; aprons for bartenders, butchers and other workmen; table cloths, sheets and pillow cases, and so on. Some companies concentrated at the outset on barbershops, others on doctors and dentists, others on restaurants or hotels. Once launched, the companies usually expanded sales by soliciting new categories of customers and by adding items to their line, often to meet the particular needs of new customers. Investment in linens increased as a consequence, and good inventory control became essential.

When health officials began to condemn the public roller towel about 1913, many operators saw hardship or ruin ahead. Others quickly recognized the move as justified from the public's point of view, at the same time sensing a good opportunity for additional linen supply business. Out of efforts to exploit this opportunity came the continuous towel device in wide use today. In the 1920s, when the concept of colored or color-trimmed items began to attract interest, the linen supply business had to grapple with still larger and more complex inventories in addition to the problem of fading. Again, while some firms resisted the trend, many operators saw in color, as in other merchandise innovations, a chance to win new business. In subsequent years more and more items were added, including work clothing, uniforms, dresses, blazer jackets, and even shirts for executives as a means of increasing volume and possibilities for profit.

The idea of forming a trade association emerged shortly after 1900, first on a state or regional basis and later nationwide in scope when the Linen Supply Association of America was formed in 1916. By that date there were more than 900 linen supply firms in the United States, from coast to coast. Those responsible for formation of the national association had already recognized the opportunities to discuss common problems, exchange ideas and information, and expand the image of the linen supply industry. Perhaps equally important, the Association brought together socially men who needed group support. For we must remember that many of its members, some of them refugees from persecution in Europe, had come up the hard way, with little formal education. They all wanted to better their position in the community, as well as to learn what they could from the experience of others about an industry which had little standing in the business world.

Even as they were forming the national association, members were discussing competition from paper towels. Paper products, indeed, have kept the linen supply industry on the alert from that time to the present, forcing it to work constantly to keep even on a comparative cost and advantage basis and, in some cases, to undertake the distribution of paper products when its delivery system made that profitable. In the twenties and thirties members debated whether, and under what conditions, they should meet the growing demand for color in the products they delivered. They were just moving into more organized and constructive approaches to major problems when the Depression forced retrenchment. In 1937 the Association took a great step forward when it employed a consulting firm to survey and analyze the customers, actual and potential, for the linen supply industry. The results were revealing, but World War II intervened to prevent members from acting upon the clear conclusions drawn from the study.

In 1945 the Association began to move into its current highly sophisticated stage of operations. The national officers appointed a full-time executive secretary as a necessary step in increasing and integrating the activities of the organization. They took an additional and highly significant step in 1946 when they appointed as research director Samuel B. Shapiro, now executive director of the Association. Progress took time, but during the next decade the Association established an impressive program of technical research into fibers, garment design, washing and sterilizing processes, market and merchandising studies, cost and financial studies, automated conveyor and processing equipment, delivery scheduling, and other projects. Along with these utilitarian efforts, the Association began to sponsor seminars and work clinics dealing with the managerial functions in a concerted and continual effort to upgrade middle and top management personnel in the more important and hard-to-specify aspects of their work. Week-long institutes were organized at some of the nation's leading universities to expose top management to the significant and rapid basic changes taking place in our environment, and to start them thinking more deeply about their social and public responsibilities for participating more deeply in such problems as public education, urban redevelopment and the ghettos.

Many who have watched these efforts, including myself, have been tempted to attribute the impressive results to two or three persons— quietly, patiently, tirelessly and skillfully pushing the members of the Association to outdo themselves on many fronts. Yet one also must give full credit to the rank-and-file members who have recognized the need and importance of the total program, made the necessary appropriations of money, and given generously of their time and energy to support the effort. Not every trade association achieves such cooperation or aims so high.

Members of the linen supply industry now recognize (in varying degrees, to be sure) that their role is to purvey cleanliness, sanitation, convenience and comfort, and that at the management level their task is problem-solving. The problems they must solve, however, are not confined to their own internal operations. Rather, their task is to work with the customer on solutions to his problems, planning for new situations with new materials (natural and man-made fibers, plastics, and paper), new items, new processes and labor-saving and cost-reduction methods all aimed at better service to the customer at an economical price.

Gone are the days when mere glibness could obtain larger orders. The linen supply requirements of a modern hospital, for example, are impressive in sheer bulk and variety, but verge on the impossible in their exacting need for sterile textile items in surgery. The man who wishes to induce the hospital administration to shift its linen supply problem from its own stockrooms and laundry to his firm must be able to deal with the technical aspects of materials, processing and comparative costs in detail. And so it goes with many other customers as they, like the linen supply industry, try to cope with rapid technological change. The linen supply business has come a long, long way from the one man-or-boy-with-an-armload-of-towels stage of the 1880s. That is why it responds so readily to forward-looking leadership, and that is why it still appeals to men who like tough challenges and are willing to work.

RALPH M. HOWER

Soldiers Field
Boston, Massachusetts
May, 1970

CHAPTER 1

SERVICE
....SERVICE
....SERVICE

**THE GROWTH OF
SERVICE INDUSTRIES
IN MANY FIELDS**

The dinner party in the attractive New York apartment on Fifth Avenue near Central Park was stimulating. Not only was the food lovingly prepared, the wine elegantly served and the decorations imaginatively designed, but the atmosphere of unobtrusive culture was just right for the types of guests present. The original paintings in the living room were admired and commented on in subdued voices, while in the background an accomplished musician played on an antique spinet. But the high point of the evening was the introduction of a late guest, who arrived only in time for after-dinner cordials and an hour of lively discussion before having to depart.

A slight, distinguished man, with a pencil-thin mustache and a pronounced but indeterminate accent, he was introduced as a European duke—a title he backed up with unquestioned authenticity as he recounted his experiences abroad and friendships with notables on several continents. The dinner party was a great success and the host and hostess retired that evening with a sense of real accomplishment.

That they had been able to achieve this social milestone could be to a large extent credited to one of the most important business and economic phenomenons of our day: the growth and development of the rental service industries. Through one service, the hostess had rented original paintings to hang on the wall; through a second, she had obtained the spinet, complete with musician, for the evening; and through others, she had rented place settings, linens, and decorations. To top it all off, she had brought off a real *tour de force* by "renting" the duke, a man with an authentic title who was at the moment a bit pressed for funds.

If this case history is perhaps on the unusual side, it does serve a purpose in focusing on the ingenuity of the service industries in meeting all kinds of needs, common and uncommon. The rapid growth during the post-war period springs quite logically from the times, a period in which Americans look to outside service to replace the internal help that is becoming more and more difficult to engage. The variety of goods and services available in the latter half of the 20th century is unparalleled in the history of civilization, beyond the ken of even the wealthy of a century ago.

In today's democratic society, where people are more aware than their grandparents were of the multitude of things they can enjoy, there is a mounting demand for goods and services that fill definite needs, offer convenience and contribute to better living. Thus, the service industries in general are broadening their scope of operations. And functioning within this field of service, the rental businesses in particular are meeting the growing needs.

We have, of course, long been a service-oriented economy, with various types of services playing increasingly prominent roles in business and industry, the more so as product competition stiffens. Yet the increase of independent operations and the variety of services offered are of relatively recent origin.

As fields of expertise become more and more specialized, there are certain functions which the generalist—though still very much in evidence—cannot handle. Thus, many businesses turn to the specialist who alone is qualified to keep abreast of the rapid pace of product innovation and the tools, techniques, theories and methods that constitute his particular stock in trade and that grow more sophisticated day by day. The multitude of public-oriented service operations that have come into being have been designed for the purpose of relieving the individual of the frequently monotonous and invariably time-consuming tasks of life, in order that he may be free to pursue more profitable or productive endeavours.

Similarly the current trend in business is to consign certain peripheral activities to independent service operators rather than expand company personnel or facilities to include specialists whose skills are required only on a temporary, occasional or part-time basis. Another vital aim, of course, is to acquire competent service without adding to the ever-increasing cost overload for personnel benefits and other employee programs.

Employing the services of an independent real estate broker, law firm, or public relations or advertising agency has often been more expedient than creating a new or expanding an existing department within a company. But the needs of people have transcended the traditional services. Agencies offering every conceivable human skill or talent—telephone-answerers, typists, stenographers, models, artists, interpreters, writers, researchers, and a variety of temporary help, to name only a fraction of the diverse specialists for hire—have steadily multiplied. And unprecedented services have emerged in response to the varied, sporadic and highly specialized needs of contemporary business, industry, and the professions.

The rental rationale is similar to that for services. It is often wiser for the individual consumer or business concern to rent or lease equipment or goods that may require a large outlay of capital to purchase or that may not be used often enough to warrant the cost. The principal distinction between the rental and other service industries, often lumped together indiscriminately, is the difference between purveyors of tangible commodities for rent and the carrying out of specific functions. A service operation such as a contract maintenance company assumes total responsibility for the care and maintenance of offices and building, while a rental operation would supply only the equipment, to be used by the customer himself.

Nevertheless, many firms do combine service *and* rental and many operations that began as the one have expanded into the others. Limousine service agencies, for example, provide a chauffeur along with an automobile. And the linen supply industry has continuously been testing new products and services and adding to those it offered. The shirts, uniforms and other products that were once innovations have long since become commonplace, as completely new offerings came along.

Data processing services offer another case in point. It has customarily been desirable to lease computers because of their cost as well as the uncertainties of technological change. However, many companies such as IBM and ITT have subsidiaries which provide data services on their own premises for those businesses that have only occasional need for computers or lack the trained personnel to use them or facilities to house them.

A somewhat more novel example is the distinctively panoply of services offered along with office space by New York Offices, Inc., a firm founded in 1962 and described in an article in *Business Week* aptly entitled "A New York V-P for Everybody." The business of this firm is based on the belief that status can be derived from a fashionable address. New York Offices, Inc., rents desk space along with telephone-answering, mail and secretarial services, plus a versatile executive who bones up on each client's business to convince callers that he is an authentic company representative.

As *Business Week* comments, "To an out-of-town company, a New York office can be a convenience and a status symbol." But office space in New York is as costly as it is prestigious. New York Offices President Ira Schwartz cites the case of a midwestern manufacturer whose New York office cost about $30,000 a year. The manufacturer closed his office, availed himself of Schwartz's services, and now receives the same benefits at an annual cost of only $6,000.

Prestige is a factor also in the limousine rental business. Corporations constitute about 75 percent of this market largely because, as one industry spokesman observed, "Picking up a client by limousine is replacing the credit card as a status symbol." Classic Coaches, Ltd. offers a super de luxe chauffeur-driven 1932 Graham-Paige Land Yacht complete with kitchen, bar, lavatory and carpeted lounge at $25 per hour for those who can afford (and who have the inclination) to indulge in such conspicuous consumption.

National Cleaning Contractors, Inc., previously one of the leading contenders in the contract maintenance business, recently merged with Kinney Corporation to become Kinney National Service, Inc., a combined multi-service and rental empire. This company offers a mosaic of services, in addition to car and truck rental, that includes maintenance engineering, exterminating (a $350-million a year industry in itself), carpentry and cabinet work, painting and decorating, data processing, product testing, parking facilities, cleaning and maintenance of homes and office buildings, and even funeral directing.

In 1966, prior to the merger, National daily employed some 5,000 round-the-clock cleaners and maintained about 65-million square feet of commercial, institutional, plant and residential space in nine major U. S. cities. In New York City alone, 75 percent of the office buildings erected since World War II employ contract maintenance services—a statistic indicative of the impact of technological change on service. In the era of the small, family-owned business, an employee or even the boss might have stinted on the cost of a charwoman by sweeping out the premises himself. The skyscrapers and sprawling plants of today have not entirely made the mop and bucket obsolete, yet they have created many new maintenance problems.

These problems have been met with a sophisticated approach that includes research and development, testing laboratories, industrial engineering; computerized inventory systems; specialized vehicles; and other transportation facilities; broad educational programs; and the screening of specialists and multi-lingual personnel for almost any type of client service required.

The current rental explosion, while its roots go back many years, was triggered in California in the mid-1940s when John Wanamaker of Burbank rented out power tools which he stored in an army tent behind his gas station. Wanamaker plowed profits back into low-cost government surplus machines, laying the foundation for a profitable new business and setting up a prototype for other enterprising young men. The housing boom and the do-it-yourself trend gave impetus to the movement. According to figures issued by the American Rental Association in 1966, over 8,900 general rental equipment stores have sprung up across the nation, with more than 1,200 of these located in the industry's original stamping ground of California.

The lure of a new business frontier has attracted a horde of latter-day rugged individualists into the rental business in which the franchise system, in many service fields, plays only a minor role. Recent statistics indicate that about nine out of ten rental dealers operate independently. Many of these businessmen began on a shoestring, and those that survived managed to do so largely through the hard work, family cohesiveness and perseverance of those who ran them. The subsequent entry by department and chain stores into the rental arena has been viewed with trepidation by some small operators, but according to the American Rental Association, the resultant step-up in advertising and promotion has generated increased business for all rather than, as was feared, serving to squeeze out the small entrepreneur.

Hertz Corporation, largest in the highly competitive automobile rental field, is one giant that invaded the rental business with the opening of three Hertz Rent-All stores in Chicago in 1960. Hertz rose from modest beginnings in 1918 when founder and current President Walter L. Jacobs rented out a 12-car fleet of Model T Fords. Within five years the fleet swelled to 565 cars, at which point Jacobs, staying on as company president, sold out to taxicab manufacturer John Hertz.

Another Horatio Alger story in the annals of rental history is Sam's U-Drive, a lucrative and diversified rental operation that began with a nucleus of five trailers purchased in 1950 for $500 by founder Sam Greenberg of Van Nuys, California. Today, Greenberg's rental facilities located in four cities stock a medley of items ranging from screwdrivers to behemoth-sized cranes, and gross about $1,500,000 a year.

For companies and individuals alike, the determination of whether to buy or rent depends upon many factors. The reason for renting rather than buying is given in a *Better Homes and Gardens* article:

> Frequency of use is the key to whether it pays you to rent or own. Obviously you shouldn't buy a $700 floor sander that can be rented occasionally for $6 to $8 a day. You may find it economical to rent a good electric hedge clipper which costs over $50 but rents for about $1.50 an hour up to $7.50 a day. It usually pays to rent such an item if you need it no more than two or three times a year.

A recent American Rental Association show offered a profile of rental trends and indicated that rental equipment operators constitute a valuable outlet for a wide diversity of products, including household and lawn equipment; adding machines and typewriters; wallpaper steamers and papering equipment; beds, cribs and highchairs; trucks and trailers; stage props and other theatrical equipment; equipment for doctors, hospitals and clinics as well as the homebound invalid or convalescent; poodle clippers, squirrel traps, and champagne fountains.

Stimulated by the trend toward a more youthful as well as more mobile population and an expansion in apartment construction, furniture rental companies are making steady inroads among newlyweds, young "singles," and transients whose jobs are tentative or whose residences are temporary. A Philadelphia company that has already franchised six furniture rental operations states that it receives 25 inquiries a week from persons interested in entering the business.

Rental trends also reflect the contemporary interest in recreational and leisure-time activities. The availability of a wide selection of sporting goods for hire permits would-be sports enthusiasts to find their game before investing in expensive equipment. Bicycle rental shops have long been common in some communities, going back to a day when many children could not afford to buy their own bikes. In the more prosperous 1960s, the renting of expensive camping equipment, for example, began catching on because it enabled urbanites to test the wonders of nature without risking too much money.

The party equipment rental business affords the housewife a happy alternative to the traditional begging, borrowing or buying to supplement an inadequate stock of festive items. The status-conscious hostess can rent at reasonable rates the finest china, linen, silver and crystal which in the marketplace would be priced in all likelihood beyond her budget. Interestingly enough, in a wealthy Chicago suburb, renting of party items has become a mark of extreme chic among the community's social set.

The conflict between man's age-old acquisitive instinct and his more recent experience with the convenience and economy of non-ownership is evident even in the landscaping business. Landscape Leasing, Inc., a California firm, has a 6,000-tree olive grove, three nurseries and some 20,000 varieties of trees, plants, flowers, and shrubs to back up former President Raymond E. Page, Jr.'s boast that "we lease everything from a blade of grass to a 90-foot palm tree!"

While most orders come from party-givers requesting a $50 orchid display to decorate an outdoor barbecue, Landscape also supplies municipalities wishing to dress up their streets. A luxury apartment project in Santa Ana, California, recently signed a lease for $200,000 worth of the firm's verdant commodities. Leasing terms stipulate Landscape's responsibility for complete maintenance of both pots and vegetation as well as insurance against damage and vandalism.

The array of glittering wares and esoteric services for hire in the 1960s conjures up a rental-spree fantasy in which women, resplendent in hired jewels and minks, escorted by husbands impeccably attired in their rented tuxedos and frilled shirts (supplied, laundered, starched and pressed by a linen service operation), step into rented limousines driven by hired chauffeurs.

The party-goers speed off to their host's rented manorial home, its facade ablaze with the lights of a thousand rented Japanese lanterns that cast their illumination upon the magnificent rose gardens and potted palms—leased of course. The interior of the house has been tastefully furnished by a furniture rental agency, and a cultural atmosphere is achieved by the rented art collection and the rental-library books that line the rented bookshelves.

Temporary help serves catered food in the finest china which, along with the crystal and sterling, has been supplied by a rental store just as the damask cloth and napkins have been supplied by a linen service.

Whether offering trivia, exotica or fundamentals, the service industries, according to one estimate, account for 60 percent of the nation's work force and an estimated expenditure in 1967 by American consumers of $205-billion, or roughly $.42 of each consumer dollar. Although these figures have not been broken down into their component industries and may be somewhat high, they illustrate the fact that the upsurge in services, and particularly in renting, has given a real boost to the American economy.

Moreover, the boom reflects an underlying revolution in the life-style of contemporary Americans to whom such factors as convenience, economy, luxury and status determine to an increasing degree where and how they spend their dollars.

Equally important, although giants are already emerging, the rental and service explosion has proven a last Klondike for the small businessman who, whether franchised, independent or of the Mom and Pop variety, is making his reappearance on the American scene.

While many of the foregoing examples may seem far removed from the linen supply industry, one of the first rental institutions in the world, they are nevertheless highly significant. The individual pieces fit into an overall broad sociological trend. People and their organizations are receptive—as never before in history—to rental goods and services. It is all part of the growing philosophy that service is not just convenient, it is imperative.

CHAPTER 2

A LOOK AT ANTIQUITY

ORIGINS OF
PRESENT PRODUCTS
AND SERVICES

Today, Linen Supply operates in virtually every city, state and civilized country of the world, a fact which is especially impressive when it is realized that such a service did not even exist less than a century ago. However, the imperative of providing reputable products and dependable service is by no means peculiar to the modern world, and artifacts which provided convenience, comfort and general well-being—including linens—can be traced back, if only in primitive form, to the earliest civilizations.

Archeologists uncovered fabrics woven of flax, wool and various plant fibers in the ruins of a Lake Dwellers' civilization which flourished during the earliest era of the Stone Age in what is now Switzerland. Evidence suggested that these fabrics were not only used for clothing, but as bath towels or crude hand napkins as well.

The ancient Egyptians manufactured soap made of fats and oils blended with ashes and boiled until it formed a soft mass. They also used terry towels remarkably similar to today's bath towels, one of which was found in a tomb of one of Mentu-hotpe's soldiers near Thebes. Two other towels measuring about 20 inches by 18 inches were also found in the tomb of Djar, custodian of Mentu-hopte's harem. Apparently, when the towels wore thin at the edges, the frugal Egyptians cut off the frayed selvages and hemmed them.

The Incas also used towels, and a poncho made about 400 A.D. of fabric closely resembling a rough terry cloth is on display at the American Museum of Natural History in New York City. Towels were used as well by the ancient Greeks and Roman patricians who fastidiously washed and dried their hands both before and after they ate. Baths, of course, were elaborate day-long rites in the early days of the Roman Empire, but such luxurious ablutions disappeared with the fall of the Empire. Hand washing, nevertheless, continued, and the nobles were presented by a servant with a towel (probably woven though not as soft as a terry or Turkish towel) and a metal basin of water upon awaking, as well as before and after meals.

Both the Old and New Testament reveal that washing had great symbolic significance among the Hebrews in Biblical times. When Abraham was visited by the three angels, he gave them water and towels with which to cleanse their feet, and Jesus taught his disciples humility by washing their feet in a basin and drying them with a towel.

Although the Stone Age people probably had some crude form of cleaning materials, the art of laundering seems to have been developed by the Egyptians and Chinese. Egyptian documents of the fourth century B.C. refer to laundering methods, and at least one stone engraving dating from that period actually depicts an Egyptian washday in progress.

The sixth book of Homer's *Odyssey* describes laundering in ancient Greece around 2000 B.C. In this tale, Ulysses, shipwrecked off the coast of the island now known as Coffu, met a royal laundress, Princess Nausicaa, who led him to the court of her father, Alcinous, King of the Phaecians. The story is so appropriate, and the heroine so delightful, that London's Company of Launderers, a modern counterpart of the old English craft guilds, has immortalized Homer's royal laundress as a symbol on its coat of arms.

Commercial laundries existed in Rome as early as 1500 B.C., and it is believed that some enterprising Romans supplied freshly laundered towels, napkins and garments as a form of paid service about 1900 years ago. There is no question that the Romans manufactured soap, bars of which were uncovered in the ruins of Pompeii. Dating back to the eruption of Vesuvius in 79 A.D., many of these bars of soap were reported to be still usable. While the Egyptians, who wore linen, and the Chinese, who wore silk, had methods for cleaning, the Romans were the first to cope in an effective way with the laundering of wool. Out of their skill came the art of "fulling," cleaning and fluffing wool in such a way that it retained its size, shape and softness after repeated use. The fullers, or *fullones,* took in the family wash of typical households throughout Rome. Almost all literature from that time on contains considerable reference to laundering, as well as to the various types of products that were frequently cleaned. Chaucer used the word *lavinder* to describe a person who washes clothes, apparently deriving the name from the French word, *laver* to wash. In his time, the 14th century, laundering was a crude method of wetting, rubbing and beating. Strangely enough, although soap existed in the days of the ancient Egyptians and the Romans, the Europeans of the Middle Ages were reluctant to use it. Soap, as a commercial product, does not appear on the British scene until the 17th century and was not generally in use until the 18th century.

Laundering began to come into its own in Europe when ingenious inventors devised ways of overcoming "washday drudgery." One of the first crude inventions, the dolly, looked like a three- or four-legged stool with a long handle rising from the middle. By plunging this device up and down in the tub, the user avoided bending over or wetting his hands. Eventually other attachments were added so that the dolly could be operated by a hand crank or an animal on a treadmill. John Tynacke patented a machine for washing clothes in 1691, but probably the most important invention of the period was Henry Sidgier's rotary washing machine which, patented in 1782, was based on a principle still in use today. William Tucket in 1817 gave directions for making an effective dolly in a book entitled *The Family Dyer and Scourer.*

In the early 1830s, a Frenchman named Seyrig patented another important device, an extractor that separated moisture from fabrics through centrifugal force. He worked with two British engineers, Edward Manlove and Alexander Alliott, in perfecting the device for commercial use, using the now familiar name "hydro-extractor." The firm that developed from the marketing of this invention, Manlove, Alliott & Co., Ltd., also pioneered in the manufacture of a power ironing machine, invented by another Frenchman, de Coudon, in the 1830s. Since the original machines were of the single-roll type, the term "decoudon," after the inventor, is applied to single-roll ironing machines.

While these and other developments were taking place in Europe, little was happening in the United States. Hamilton Smith had patented a belt-driven washer with a reversing movement in the U. S. in 1832, but it had not gone into general use commercially. The volume laundry business, in fact, was launched almost by accident. The story goes that a man named "Lucky" Davis joined the California Gold Rush in 1849. Having no success (despite his nickname) in finding gold, he turned to washing clothes in a barrel for customers, in a tiny laundry he founded near Oakland. Sometime later, Charles Mattee designed a crude wooden wash wheel for him which evolved into a 12-shirt washing machine, powered by a 10-horse-power engine. The first commercial American laundry was in business.

While there were many laundering devices in use in the early 19th century, the concept of linen supply as a business would not come into being before the 1880s. The main reason was that linens themselves—meaning in this sense mass-produced towels, napkins, garments and other products—were not readily available for business and industrial use. While the Industrial Revolution had gone a long way toward the development of mass-weaving techniques, the products of the looms were still cherished as hard-to-come-by family treasures, to be laundered and used at home. Craftsmen, businesses and industries made little attempt to supply employees with such luxuries as towels, and only the best restaurants served napkins. Mankind, for all of its advances, had an odd reluctance to acquire habits of cleanliness.

Sanitation for the average man still was far off, according to another leading authority, Vincent Brome, author of *We Have Come a Long Way.* "Sanitation in the modern sense," he points out, "was virtually nonexistent."

The water closet was not invented until the close of the 16th century and even by 1690, baths were not taken frequently. Describing life in the late 17th century, Brome states, "A bath can be taken in a wooden tub, but it is not advised by the best physicians before the fire is lit and even then it may be weakening."

By the 18th century, though, some of these conditions had improved even for the masses of London. Brome pictures a tenement house:

"There is one outside lavatory of very primitive construction for the use of 25 tenants of the house."

But other conditions had not improved much at all. Describing an 18th century London woman, Brome says:

> She has six children and . . . the whole family of eight not only sleeps in this one bed, but every night it eats and lives around the bed like castaways on an island. The blankets are washed or crudely cleaned three times a year, and the children may get washed once a week, but all this talk about washing, soap and cleanliness are out of place. The family has lived like this for years. True, the wooden frame of the bed is alive with vermin and what pass for curtains are never free of lice, but they are as natural a part of life as emptiness in the belly at some time of the day.

Obviously, down through the ages, the average man did not know how to keep himself as clean as he does today. For one thing, he did not have the implements. Soap was not in abundance, and those towels that were made were so expensive that they were beyond the means of the average man. If he washed his hands, he either dried them in the air or on some old cloth, possibly a worn-out garment.

Certainly he did not dry his hands with paper, which is a comparatively recent invention, and the papyrus used until the 15th century was much too expensive to squander on hand-drying.

Towels were a luxury of the wealthy, and many were so beautifully made and decorated that they have become collectors' items. The fabrics used were coarse, however, and more like modern dish towels. Soft terry towels were unknown in America and most of Europe until about 1850 when an Englishman, Henry Christy, who had a fabric-weaving mill, was surprised while travelling in Turkey to find towels that were soft though crude. These were made by women in Turkish harems who took rough loose cloth and made loops by picking up threads in a kind of decorative pattern. The word "terry" derives from this process of drawing the thread, from the French, *tirer,* "to pull." Back to England went Christy, with samples of the towels in his luggage, intent on finding some way of producing this soft cloth on a loom and looping the threads on a machine the same way the Turkish girls had been doing by hand. He and his colleagues in his weaving firm showed the looped cloth to Samuel Holt, an expert weaver and mechanic.

"Can you make a loom that will manufacture this cloth?" they asked. Fascinated by the towels, Holt replied, "We'll certainly try."

After many experiments to produce the cloth on a loom, he finally succeeded. He employed two warps—one to form the looped surface. In 1851, W. M. Christy & Sons displayed Holt's improved version of the new towel in the celebrated Crystal Palace exhibition. Queen Victoria was so pleased with it that she awarded Holt a medal. The new towel quite naturally came to be known as the "Turkish towel" by 1877 when the power loom was invented and these products were being mass produced.

Like towels, such items as tablecloths, napkins, sheets and pillowcases were used for thousands of years only by the wealthy. Sixth-century patrician Etruscans decked their tables with cloths whose geometric multi-colored designs rival modern art works. An Etruscan tablecloth dating from 480 B.C., with criss-cross red, white and blue lines, was an artistic achievement. Within the next few hundred years, however, clothmakers used less and less dyes. Tablecloths depicted in paintings of the third century A.D. on religious subjects are invariably white. A third-century fresco of a celestial banquet of angels also shows a white tablecloth, as does a fifth-century fresco at Ravenna.

By the 15th century, painters of the Last Supper, such as Leonardo da Vinci and Tintoretto, always portrayed tables covered with white cloths, but strangely enough, not a single napkin is evident in any paintings until the late 16th century. The Italian painter Veronese shows Christ and others in *Christ in the House of Levy* with napkins clutched in their hands, but this is his only work in which napkins appear in any form.

The word "napkin" is used by Shakespeare: "I stained this napkin with the blood that valiant Clifford, with his rapier's point made issue from the bosom of the boy." (*Henry VI*) "Here, Hamlet, take my napkin, rub thy brows." (*Hamlet*) "And dip their napkins in his sacred blood." (*Julius Caesar*)

It is, however, unlikely that Shakespeare was using the word "napkin" in the modern sense. A napkin in the 17th century was really a kind of towel. The King James version of the Bible, for example, refers to Jesus being "bound with a napkin," and elsewhere describes a ". . . napkin that had been about his head."

As napkins came into wider usage, tablecloths also became more commonplace, if still less functional than decorative. Maerten van Haemswerk's *Family Portrait* (1530) and French artist Louis le Nain's *Peasant Family* (circa 1600) document the fact that tablecloths in the 16th century were reserved for special occasions and festivities. Tablecloths were so uncommon in colonial America, even a century later, that they were seldom used by even moderately well-to-do families.

The history of bedsheets can also be traced back to earliest times. An ancient Roman painting of a wedding groups people around a bed covered with green sheets hanging loosely over the side of the bed. In the Biblical Acts there is a description of "linen sheets, let down by four corners."

The earliest bedsheets, used exclusively by the affluent, were popular with artists of the 14th and 15th centuries who invariably painted madonnas and goddesses from mythology reclining on beds and couches draped with white sheets, their heads on pillows in white cases. Mary, in Lorenzetti's 15th century *Nativity of the Virgin,* lies on a white sheet; a pillow in a white case appears in Titian's *Venus of Urbina* (1538); and the 14th century *Saint Ursala's Dream* shows the holy woman reclining between two white sheets. Master Flora, who painted the *Birth of Cupid* in 1540, was 500 years before his time in that he depicted aquamarine sheets instead of white ones (although 2000 years earlier aquamarine sheets were made in Tuscany).

Shakespeare also referred to sheets in the *Winter's Tale* (". . . my traffic is sheets; when the kite builds, look to lesser linens.") and in *All's Well That Ends Well* ("I have laid these those sheets you bade me on the bed.") By the 17th century, sheets were becoming more commonplace, though still confined to the wealthy.

When Florence Nightingale went to the Crimea to care for hospitalized British soldiers, she found them in a building far too small, with an indescribable stench and insufficient bedsteads. "The sheets were of canvas and so coarse that the wounded men recoiled from them, begging to be left in their blankets," wrote Lytton Strachey in his biography of Florence Nightingale, indicating that many of the men had indeed known what sheets were.

Centuries passed before barbers protected their own clothing from obvious occupational hazards. A painting found in the tomb of User a Het, a royal scribe, depicts a barber at work. Neither barber nor customer wear anything save the traditional Egyptian loincloth, and obviously the artist neglected to include the shorn locks and shavings which surely must have covered both of them.

By the 16th century, barbers had at least learned to protect the customer's clothing. A barber portrayed in a painting of that time by Jost Amann is dressed in street clothes, although the customer is protected by a haircloth. In an engraving dated 1650 the same situation is depicted, and a 19th century photograph of a barber shop interior in the United States indicates that even at that late date barbers persisted in this singular disregard for their clothes.

In all these pictures, the barber draped the haircloth over the customer's chest so that the open part was in back. But in one photo made in the late 19th century, two barbers—one a woman—one shown cutting the hair of customers whose shoulders are draped with haircloths hung like capes, the open ends in front. Where that notion started and where it ended remains a mystery.

Uniforms for waitresses have been in use much longer than barber's uniforms. As early as the 16th century, waitresses wore long cover-all aprons, some blue, some white, some gray, hanging down to their ankles. In 19th century America, waitresses in a famous Boston restaurant wore sleeveless smocks over sleeved dresses, but the man behind the counter wore neither jacket nor apron. About this time, however, waiters were beginning to wear aprons.

Similarly, craftsmen have probably worn aprons or some covering over their clothes since antiquity, as in the case of blacksmiths, carpenters and glassblowers. In 1826, an American blacksmith was pictured in an apron. By the 1880s butchers also wore half-aprons over their street clothes. On the other hand some construction men of that period wore street clothes without protective garb while building houses.

As the Industrial Revolution gained pace, however, there was a trend toward wearing aprons inside factories. By the middle of the 19th century, workers were already wearing aprons, which they probably owned and brought with them to work. Men working at the Singer Sewing Machine plant in 1857 wore them, though women in a shirt factory did not. Wearing aprons was obviously voluntary in other factories. At the factory of McCormick Reaper, for example, only a few workers wore protective aprons, whereas at the disassembly line in a slaughterhouse, everyone did, presumably because of the nature of the work.

Protective garments for workers did not really come into widespread usage until the Industrial Revolution. With the introduction of the cotton gin and power loom, cotton goods of all types—not only aprons but towels, tablecloths, napkins, bedsheets and uniforms—could be mass produced and brought within the means of the average working-man and working-woman.

Like thousands of other industries, linen supply was spawned by the Industrial Revolution. With cotton goods both plentiful and inexpensive, a ready market sprang into being, first for the goods themselves and later for commercial laundering services to process the goods.

The first hand laundry in the United States was not opened until 1832, in Jersey City, N. J., followed in 1835 by the Troy Laundry, Troy, N. Y., and in 1840 by a Cambridge, Mass. business. Other hand laundries opened elsewhere, but commercial laundering did not become widely accepted until after the Civil War, when pioneers like Davis of Gold Rush fame began to take advantage of situations where there was a need for service in great volume.

Laundries then began to spring up in every city, and kept pace with the rapid increase in the use of cotton goods. In 1870, for example, 28 laundries served Chicago, but by 1879, there were 267. About the same time, laundries in New York City increased to about 500.

People were becoming accustomed to having laundry done outside their homes. To a growing number it made sense, and it remained only for someone to take the next logical step. If it were smart to have your laundry commercially washed, it might also be smart to rent the items instead of owning them. Ownership of certain cotton products meant inconveniences to the owner—more trips to the laundry, extra costs, time lost. What with the new machinery being put into laundries that speeded up washing and ironing, an enterprising person could see that he might wash some items more economically and better than anyone could in a home. The more he thought about it, the more it made sense to offer to "rent" to someone the use of cottons and to guarantee to wash them. The idea was natural enough so that it may even have occurred to several people simultaneously in different places. But, as in the case of many concepts that seem so obvious in retrospect, the development of the working idea was to depend upon singularly gifted people.

The formula, in its basic form, appears remarkably simple: Find an area of human activity where there is a *need* for a special service. Develop the idea for performing the service, including the necessary equipment. Launch the service and continue to perform in a dependable manner.

Thus was linen supply born.

CHAPTER **3**

AN "ENTERPRISING CONCERN"

**BEGINNINGS OF
LINEN SUPPLY
IN AMERICA**

"One man can completely change the character of a country, and the industry of its people, by dropping a single seed in fertile soil." *

As with enduring societies and great cultures, significant industries are built on people who, generation after generation, nurture the seeds planted before them. These are the same people who are constantly pioneering and seeking out challenges, rather than easing away from them. Through their continuing efforts, the seeds become fields, the fields towns and the towns cities. Yet many of the original concepts remain unchanged.

In an absorbing book, *Life Is With People,* authors Mark Zborowski and Elizabeth Herzog explore, among other things, one of the more simple microcosms of society, the ancient Hebrew *shtetl,* or "little town." In a poignant way, talking not of great deeds or ambitious planning, they show how the life of the *shtetl* is held together by daily needs and services. The market place itself is a catalyst, bringing everyone together. There, many needs were satisfied, not all of them simply, the need of a housewife for fruit or meat and the need of the seller for money.

There was, for example, the element of bargaining between buyer and seller—the communication back and forth, the opportunity to register, in a serious and yet often placating way, various degrees of approval, disapproval, surprise, dismay and satisfaction. To have simply paid a set price, without the customary bargaining, would have deprived the participants of a deep-rooted need. The life of the village was based on interlocking services, with subtle, underlying motivation. Perhaps shopping for groceries today, in modern American cities, would be less wearing on the feet and exhausting to the spirit if supermarkets could somehow, miraculously, provide a little of the ancient interplay of the *shtetl.*

This, then, is one concept of service: to provide something that meets a need. Another important concept is dependability of time and place. *Life Is With People* describes the ancient custom of honoring each man's place of business, if only an unmarked section in the market place where his customers can count on finding him:

> To trespass on a place of a customer that belongs to a competitor is despicable. One can be called to the rabbi and condemned formally if he violates the "established hold" of another.

Service—or the concept of service—is a word with complex meanings, far more so in today's world than in the days when it could be simply defined as "the supplying of utilities or commodities required by the

* John C. Gifford

public." Service in itself implies reliable availability in a specified location or locations, and by an established organization, group or individual known to the user of the service.

Man has down through the centuries been concerned with land, not only for sustenance, but as a symbol of security and well being. The concept of service is also closely concerned with the land, and the relationship of the service to the territory within which it is offered. A significant and absorbing study of territorial concepts has been made by Robert Ardrey, a noted anthropologist, who expressed himself in two thought-provoking books, *African Genesis* and *Territorial Imperative.*

To some extent in the former work, and to a great extent in the latter, Ardrey examines both the broadest and the most narrow implications of man's concern over territory. He ranges from the territorial clashes that push great nations, and groups of nations, over the brink and into war, to the innate territorial needs of the howling monkey and the yellow bunting. Even for a reader with little knowledge of animal habits, it is fascinating to note that many birds, mammals and fish acquire territorial rights and never violate the domains of others. Many theories are discussed, some relating to the sexual compulsions of the animal world, others to the need for food. One of the most interesting concepts is that, while food and sex drives do play some part in the process, nature itself has provided animals with a strong territorial instinct because "insuring the proper spacing of individuals will not only protect food supply but will provide a check against the spread of disease." Such spacing also brings about certain benefits to the young, including their safety and the training needed to cope with the world beyond. Thus, nature itself has provided a built-in *service* to meet the needs of continuity of the species. When territories collapse and service deteriorates, the species themselves may die off within a matter of time.

Territory is also an insurance against overpopulation. "Nature, by instilling in the individual a demand for exclusive living space, insures two consequences: First, that a minimum number of individuals in any populations will be enabled to breed in relative security and pass on in fair certainty the conformation of their kind. And second, that the surplus will be cast to the wolves; to the owls, to the foxes, to the plagues and famines and lonely, unfamiliar places, there to make the most of perilous conditions or to die."

There are significant parallels here, broadly in the life of another animal, man himself, and more specifically, in the development of business and industry. Most men have trouble existing without roots in one place or another, where they possess a certain amount of secure real estate and adequate shelter. And most businesses cannot provide service without a substantial understanding of what they are providing and when and where.

The problem becomes more acute in the service industries than in those which produce raw materials or that manufacture and distribute tangible products. For one thing, an organization supplying "service" offers what in many cases can neither be described nor seen. Definitions are not always clear and often the client, customer or patron may expect one thing and get quite another, in which case, he turns to the salesman or representative who sold him the service, or who is now handling it.

While the long-standing concept of the "salesman's territory" has consistently applied in the service industries as well as in those which manufacture products or goods, there is an important difference. Firms which provide services that are more or less intangible are understandably more concerned with the critical requirement of being at the right place at the right time with the right supplies, counsel, manpower or other elements necessary to meet the customer's needs.

The linen supply industry has sometimes been mistakenly thought of as basically a supplier of products or goods. That is what the name itself implies and to a certain extent, of course, what is delivered. However, the effective linen supplier is also a management consultant, counseling his customers on the more proficient and productive use of his services. He is sometimes, too, a psychologist, for he has to see beyond the immediate demand for supply to the "people problems" his customers face. In some fields of work, for example, the very idea of wearing a uniform is distasteful. Perhaps it makes people feel they are losing their individuality. The problem spreads from the public through the customer and ultimately to the linen supply service that offers the uniforms in the first place.

The linen supplier is, furthermore, a public relations practitioner. Once he has analyzed the problem psychologically (e.g., "The employees of the XYZ Company don't like to wear uniforms!"), he can often solve it through effective communications, thereby helping to reduce the resistance to using the product or services in question.

Today's linen supply industry is far from the simple, uncomplicated business it was in an era not so many years ago. Yet, since it did start from rather simple beginnings, an examination of those early origins—remote though they may seem in the Space Age—is of considerable value in understanding the industry as it is today, and as it will be in the future.

No one can put his finger on the exact birth date of the industry in the United States. There is one reference, but little information, on the founding of an "office towel service business" in New York City in 1883. About that time a firm was founded by Alfred Mulford

Wood under the name Empire Towel Supply Company, on Tenth Avenue. But for a detailed and factual account, it is realistic to say that a story in *The Boston Evening Transcript* on Thursday, August 6th, 1885, is a good place to start—at least for purposes of studying the early beginnings. On that hot summer day, an energetic reporter uncovered an interesting story which, at the time, seemed far less important than it actually turned out to be. Entitled "How an Enterprising Concern Furnishes Clean Towels to Hundreds of Subscribers," the article related how a "Boston man," Henry M. Davis, had begun "providing towels for regular customers," and continued:

> The Boston Towel Company furnishes its patrons with a certain number of clean towels on a specified day of the week, replacing them with others on the following week. The company has been in operation only a fortnight, but already has orders for a weekly delivery of fifteen thousand towels. The charge is five cents for each towel, the price usually paid for washing them. No orders have yet been received from families, the customers being business firms, banks, insurance offices, etc. Whenever desired, the name of the customer is stamped on the towels supplied, and he receives the same towels each time. The towels are of good quality of linen, and are about four feet by two in size. Most of the orders received have been for delivery on Monday, and already it has become necessary for customers to select other days, though with the increased laundry facilities which the company will soon have it will probably be able to deliver a very large number of towels on any day that customers may select.

Some four decades later, the Linen Supply Association of America was to cite Henry M. Davis as the man to whom "the industry owes its inception." Mr. Davis, who died in November 1920, was recognized as being "always assiduous in promoting the welfare of the towel supply industry and did much to foster the idea of co-operation and friendly competiton. . . ."

So began the linen supply industry. Unheralded, its birth was otherwise unnoticed. Like Henry Davis, men in other cities recognized the same need, and thought they saw an opportunity to profit through providing a new service. They pioneered in an entirely new field, not knowing its pitfalls and its problems, unable to foresee how this small service would transform itself into a major service industry during the next eighty years.

Prior to the emergence of linen suppliers, businessmen had towels in their washrooms, but the towels were their own, laundered by their wives or by a family laundry down the street. There was no system for providing *clean* towels or garments for employees in any office or factory. Restaurant owners, physicians, innkeepers or barbers either troubled an employee to take linens to the laundry or had their wives or maids wash them.

Anyone who wanted a clean towel in his office, brought home a dirty one, and took a clean one back. To impress customers with cleaner service, a barber would ask his wife or a laundry to wash and iron the linens he needed most often. There was a problem of cost, since the system called for the purchase of at least two complete sets, so that one could be in use while the other was being washed. The process was never-ending, with a constant flow back and forth, necessitating some form of transportation to maintain supplies and occasional trips to the store to renew worn or damaged stocks. In not a few cases—as in the offices of physicians—the users often wondered whether the towels had really been cleaned properly.

So it was an ingenious coup when Henry Davis recognized that this was a cumbersome way of doing things and that there had to be a more convenient method. In New York City that very same year, 1885, one Charles Maurice, 25 years old, took the same step into towel supply in the Wall Street area, serving the ever-growing needs of the offices of the financial community. It is recorded that he had decided on starting the business "after watching a similar operation in Chicago." Yet no one has been able to document the facts. Just what was the firm that provided the inspiration? Chances are that the Chicago proto-type was a very small one-man business that never prospered.

Maurice began with a single pushcart, graduating as the business grew to horse-drawn wagons and eventually to motor vehicles. Within ten years of the birth of the firm, Economy Towel, about a dozen others had sprung up in New York—among them Mutual, Empire, Fowler, Independent, Star, Crescent and New York Towel.

In 1886, some 1400 miles further west, in Lincoln, Nebraska, then a town of less than 20,000, similar events were taking place. A 12-year-old, George A. Steiner, heard from his uncle that a Mr. Johnson who owned a laundry in town was looking for a boy to deliver towels for a supply route which he was then starting. Steiner later recalled

> My uncle went with me to apply for this position, and largely through his influence and acquaintance with Mr. Johnson, I secured the job of delivering towels to the business houses and offices in Lincoln. My salary was $3.00 per week, which seemed to be the prevailing wage for boys at that time . . . the delivery of these towels was a simple matter and was performed by placing clean towels on one arm and delivering these before and after school. The soiled towels were carried on my other arm and delivered back to the laundry office.

Several years later Mr. Johnson suffered a business blow when the place where he had been having his laundry washed, the nearby State Penitentiary, decided not to renew its contract with him. Discouraged, he told young Steiner, "you can have this towel business for $25 if you also pay the $25.80 drug bill I owe your Uncle Clements."

Young Steiner was a thrifty young man, with some savings of his own.

"I'll buy it," he said. On August 15, 1889, Johnson wrote out a short bill of sale and George Steiner became a businessman, beginning a linen supply organization that would in time become international in scope. Young Steiner later went on to college and received a law degree.

Like other suppliers of those early days of the industry, Steiner daily went about his business of delivering clean towels, picking up soiled linen, and having it washed in a nearby laundry. On typical mornings, he walked to the laundry, gathered his supply of clean towels and started along the route. The mornings were pleasant. Steiner later recalled a feeling of exhilaration, of performing a worthwhile service, of building a business, of meeting people. The fresh, early-morning air of Lincoln seemed all the more alive and vibrant as he hurried from customer to customer.

In store after store, office after office, wherever Steiner went, he brought in clean white towels with a bright "good morning," chatted a while, and picked up the dirty towels, which he carried out on his arm. Many of the towels he delivered were roller type, 9 feet long, 18 inches wide, and sewn on both ends so they would hang over wooden rollers without slipping off. Each towel could be rolled up or down on the roller when a part of it became soiled, thus bringing a clean section to the front.

Several times each day, Steiner went back to the laundry for clean towels. Then when he had delivered all he could for that day, he returned to the laundry, counted his towels and money, checked his records, left the dirty towels to be washed and, if time was still left that day, went out in search of new customers. In the meantime, he knew that his towels were not going to be washed immediately since laundries did not work during the night. Yet the towels needed the next day had to be counted, inspected and placed in the basket for delivery. Already, the linen supply business was becoming complicated.

Early in his business career, Steiner found that he always needed more towels than he delivered each week. For every towel that he rented out, there was another one at the laundry, either being washed, waiting to be washed, or already washed and awaiting delivery. Besides, since he always anticipated getting new accounts, he had to

have extra towels on reserve. As business grew, he found that he had
to reinvest a great part of his earnings in replenishing and expanding
the stock. A minimum of two items to be purchased for every one
rented required a big investment.

Wherever Steiner went, he alertly watched for new towel rental
customers. But one day, as he was delivering a clean roller towel to
Nisley's grocery and department store, he noticed a clerk who wore
a badly torn apron—one which was indeed in worse condition than
any he had laid eyes on before! He started to walk away, then stopped.
He looked back at the apron. Its condition perplexed him. He had
not noticed the situation before, and he began to wonder whether
other store owners or clerks were also having trouble acquiring clean
aprons. Here was another need to be filled, another chance to render
a service and build new business! He walked up to the clerk.

"We can deliver a clean apron every morning for a dollar a month,"
he said.

At first, the clerk did not understand. Whoever heard of renting
aprons?

"What do you mean, George?" he asked.

"Well, just as I said," Steiner replied. "You know a lot of people
rent towels instead of washing them. You could rent your aprons from
me just the way everybody rents towels."

"What for? My wife can do them herself," the clerk replied.

"Sure, but look what happens," Steiner said, pointing to the apron
the clerk was wearing. "With good service, you'll always have a neat
apron."

To Steiner's surprise, the offer was accepted. But he did not have
any aprons—yet. He trotted across the street to Fitzgerald's Dry Goods
Company, where he bought enough unbleached drill to cut a dozen
aprons. After sewing half the night, he delivered his new product
with considerable pride, and not a little excitement.

"I later secured a price of ¾ cent each for the laundry work on
the aprons," young George wrote. "This left us a gross profit, not
counting wear and tear on aprons, nor delivery costs, of practically
2½ cents per piece. The price for laundering towels was ½ cent."

With that delivery, there began, as far as we know now, a new
kind of linen supply service that eventually developed world-wide.
No longer was the business one of towel supply alone, but rather a
linen service.

The kind of alert thinking that resulted in the rental of the apron
in Nisley's grocery, the kind of salesmanship that sold the idea, and
the attitude of being ever-watchful for new business sparked Steiner.
Finding new accounts everywhere, he soon had too much work to
deliver, too much to inspect, too many records to keep. He enlisted

the help of his younger brother and together they formed a new company, the Lincoln Towel and Apron Supply Company. They owned no laundry, no wagon to carry the towels and aprons, no horse to pull the wagon. Their sole assets were their innate Yankee business aggressiveness, their alertness to opportunity, the good will that George had already created, and the towel and apron inventory on hand and at customers' premises.

These were assets enough so that together the brothers created new opportunities. First, they expanded into another market. If a grocery clerk could rent an apron, why couldn't a bartender or restaurant owner? The Steiners approached some local businessmen, who promptly agreed to take the apron service.

So many local businesses became customers of the young Steiners that they soon faced a new problem—what to do about the growing volume that made the towel and apron burden heavier and heavier on the arms as the day progressed. They needed a means of transporting the towels and aprons, both clean and soiled. Their first equipment investment was a "hand wagon" which resembled a push cart.

The wagon enabled them further to increase business, since now they had more energy and more time to sell. New accounts came in, and the mountains of soiled linen grew so huge that they were scarcely manageable at the laundry. Steiner explained:

> So we asked Uncle Charles Rohman if we could use the back part of his store to deposit our soiled linen and receive our clean linen from the laundry. It seemed that everyone wished to extend a helping hand to a young fellow those days, so Uncle Charlie welcomed us to his store. This arrangement made quite a mess on and under his rear counter, but he did not complain and always treated us as though we were good tenants, when in fact we paid him nothing for this valuable space.

As business expanded, the young Steiners bought a horse named Flora and a wagon was obtained by trading a bicycle with solid rubber tires. Just as prospects looked most promising, the bright picture was clouded by the arrival of competition in the form of Quincy Martin, a man from Denver who had different ideas about linen supply. His concept was that proper service to a customer should also include an oak cabinet, with a mirror, a comb and a whisk broom. Putting this marketing idea to the test, he immediately started to lure away customers from the Steiners who had to make a decision: Should they continue as they had been doing and ignore the threat, or should they fight Martin directly by giving away cabinets of their own and thus taking a real financial risk?

They decided to take the risk. They approached the Hardy Furniture Company in Lincoln and asked for a supply of cabinets that were more attractive, slightly larger and with better hardware than their competitors. As each lot of new cabinets came into their hands, they approached the lost customers and found to their great relief that this tactic won back most of them.

The Steiners brought many outstanding men into the business. One of the most memorable was the firm's first employee, William R. Pollock, who answered a newspaper advertisement in his home town, Salt Lake City, for "a good honest boy." He joined the new branch of American Linen in that city in the late 1890s and watched the company grow from a pushcart operation (the original pushcart, a valuable piece of Americana, is now on exhibit at the company's Salt Lake City plant) to a chain of plants throughout the world. Pollock's mother had walked 1,200 miles in 1851, from Council Bluffs, Iowa, to Salt Lake City. He had the "sterner stuff" that enabled him to get started every morning between five and six, currying his horse, "Turke," hitching it to the wagon and starting the long day of delivery and selling.

"Just taking care of the horse amounted to what would now be considered a half day's work," Bill Pollock said when he was eighty-one years old. "After starting at five or six in the morning, I generally got home at eight or nine at night."

At the age of eighty-five, reflecting on his long, successful career, self-made Bill Pollock sent a memorandum to his three sons, all linen supply managers, listing his twelve rules for good business:

1. Always have a good personality
2. Take good care of customers
3. Without them there would be no business
4. Have good quality in ironing, washing, folding
5. Have bundles nice and neat for customers
6. Get good routemen, in fact all employees
7. See that your employees have nice uniforms
8. Keep your plant good and clean
9. Keep your trucks clean and neat inside and outside
10. Get good salesmen for new business
11. Treat your employees good—and learn to like them
12. Keep the outside of plant clean and nice.

The Steiner story is representative of what was happening in parallel ways—or would soon happen—throughout the young and growing industry. There were many others like the Steiners in the early days who started in an unsophisticated new business, and quickly found that they had a tiger by the tail.

Notable among these pioneers was John Alden Spoor, a director of the Pullman Company who had already achieved eminence in the great era of railroading. Spoor's enterprise was conceived as a solution to one of the Pullman Company's major problems. The generally poor service and delivery failures of laundries servicing Pullman were jeopardizing the company's contracts with railroads. Fed up with the situation, Spoor organized the American Steam Laundry Company on January 10, 1887, in St. Louis to serve exclusively the Pullman Company in the Midwest.

A year later, the laundry was in trouble. Not only was it losing money, but it also failed to provide the kind of service the Pullman company needed and for which Spoor had hoped. Stockholders in the laundry and executives in Pullman were equally disenchanted, but Spoor was not ready to throw in the towel, in any sense of the term. Having worked his way from a manual laborer in the railroad yards to company director, he was not a man to give up easily. Waiting in the laundry office for the other stockholders to arrive for the annual meeting, he turned to the pages of the Sunday edition of the *Chicago Tribune,* which he had brought with him to the train. The first page was devoted entirely to advertisements: Schlesinger and Mayer at State and Madison Streets were offering children's suits, all sizes, at 35 cents (worth 50 cents to $1); ladies' camel hair pants and vests, reduced to 83 cents. A 4000-acre Iowa ranch was offered at $15 an acre. Room and board—$5 a week. The Columbia Theater billed Fanny Davenport in a repertoire of plays, including Shakespeare and Dickens. Admission: 50 cents.

Rumblings of the Haymarket Riot of 1886 were still reverberating in the Chicago paper. Adventists in Battle Creek, Michigan, were saying they would not be surprised if the world were to come to an end soon. The end of the world! Spoor remembered talking as a child with his favorite cousin, Amanda Alden Emmons, about such terrifying ideas, and he suddenly recalled that she had married a young attorney, Kendrick Ebenezer Morgan, who had a practice in Little Falls, N. Y. Too bad he was a lawyer and knew nothing about the laundry business! But why not? Morgan had a good head, drive and ambition.

"Gentlemen," he said, when the stockholders assembled. "I think I know who can do the job for us, if he'll take it."

On July 13, 1888, Spoor introduced to the dubious stockholders K. E. Morgan who was destined to become the founder of one of the major chains in the industry. Within a few months, Morgan effected many changes in plant operation. The flow of work was scientifically scheduled, and schedules were strictly followed. Equipment was kept operating at peak efficiency. Morale was boosted. Pullman schedules were being met. As the laundry operation improved, Morgan became convinced that here was a business with a tremendous potential. He bought more stock in the company throughout 1888 and 1889.

As the St. Louis laundry operation began to improve, Spoor and a friend, Charles Leonari, who headed the Wagner Place Car Company, broadened ideas for better service to the Pullman Company. In 1890 they started the Eastern Steam Laundry Company in Boston, followed in 1891 by the Niagara Laundry & Manufacturing Company in Buffalo which, in addition to laundering linens, also manufactured them for railroads, steamships and hotels.

About the same time that Morgan was consolidating the St. Louis Steam Laundry, James Plew was finishing dental school in Chicago. Once he began to set up his practice, he discovered that the only way he could provide his patients with towels was to purchase and launder them himself which, to his mind, was no way to practice dentistry. It then occurred to him that other dentists must face the same problem, and that a service which supplied them with clean towels might be very much in demand. The idea so intrigued him that, abandoning all interest in a dental practice, he approached the Chicago dental community to sound out there interest in a linen supply service. The response was sufficiently enthusiastic to convince him that such an enterprise did, indeed, have potential.

Plew, along with a partner, Thomas A. Soper, set up the Chicago Towel Supply Company to supply linen to dentists and other medical specialists. Business prospered, but Plew, who had other irons in the fire, sold out his interest in the company to a wealthy socialite, C. H. Chadwick.

Under Chadwick and Soper, the firm expanded its clientele to include businessmen as well as dentists and physicians. As customers multiplied, so too did the workload and bookkeeping, ultimately forcing Chicago Towel to open an office building on South Wabash Street in Chicago in 1900, although at the time the company did not yet have its own plant.

The United States just before the turn of the century was growing too. Four new states had been admitted to the Union in November, 1899: North and South Dakota, Montana, and Washington. According to records kept by the Morgan Company and later published, the average price for a horse in the 1890s was $71.89 and, as the firm cautioned:

> One had to be careful in buying horses to draw the laundry wagons
> not to get stuck with an ancient, spavined, wind-broken nag that some

smart horse-trader might foist off on an unwary buyer. The word 'automobile' was not yet in the language . . . Horse-drawn vehicles and bicycles were the only practical means for delivery . . .

As one prophet of the day expressed it:

> Nobody has managed to antiquate the horse in the past one thousand years of history. 'Gas Buggies' are for playboys and idiots. If anyone tried to use one of those contraptions for delivery purposes, he'd end up with his products so shook up you couldn't tell one from another. . . . and all stinking nastily of gas fumes.

One other economic aspect of the day: "It costs 2¢ to mail a letter, so letters are mailed only when necessary."

In various cities other dauntless men ventured into the challenging new field of service with varying degrees of success and inevitably a number of failures by the wayside. Conspicuous among those who made it was Abraham Pierce Shupe, a descendant of President Franklin Pierce, who arrived as a young man in 1888 in Cleveland from New York City. He rented office space in a small store room on the old Superior Street Viaduct, near what was later West 25th Street. In those days, most of the Cleveland offices were located in modest brick buildings, none over three stories high.

Once installed, with a proper address and evidence of professional dependability, Abe Shupe canvassed the industrial and business sections of the city, offering the "novel idea" of renting clean towels each week. The plan was considered "an unnecessary frill" by many of the hard-headed businessmen yet Shupe made so much progress in his selling efforts that shortly he required the services of an assistant. Deliveries were at first made in what was described as "a half-bushel market basket." But, as orders increased, a two-wheeled pushcart was bought and placed in service, soon to be followed by a cart and horse (supposedly not one of those "spavined, windbroken nags" earlier warned against).

In a modest little historical booklet published 40 years later, entitled "From the Acorn to the Oak," the Shupe firm, by then called The Cleveland Toilet Supply Company, was able to boast of an inventory of "nearly Fifty items." These were supplied to offices, banks, stores, industrial plants, clubs, and "Tea Rooms and High Class Restaurants." By that time, the organization had acquired a large fleet of trucks, was employing some 100 workers, and was serving practically all of Cuyahoga County.

One interesting early observation, which must have been typical across the nation, was that there was something "sissyish" about cleanliness. Much of American 19th century literature, particularly some of the works of Mark Twain, reflect this idea that to be a real man you had to have hands that were not afraid of the soil and a brow that was perhaps smudged with evidence of sweat and toil.

Abe Shupe discovered that once he had cracked the market and broken down consumer resistance, demand exceeded supply. Customers began to insist upon cabinets with mirrors, known brands of quality toilet soap, hairbrushes and combs, and other accessories "that were mainly used by the 'dudes' of the early Nineties."

Business progressed from a service of convenience to a service of necessity, a pattern of development that has emerged repeatedly in individual histories within the industry. Restaurants and other businesses in which sanitation was essential began to recognize the psychological value of clean linens in attracting customers and patrons.

On its fortieth birthday, the Company noted that "some of the customers, or their successors, who were first to patronize this business in 1888 and the years subsequent to its founding have been and still are regular patrons. . . . Whether large or small, each account is assured painstaking and prompt service."

True to form, Abraham Pierce Shupe, described in his obituary as one of the industry's "most colorful characters," died at work, while seated behind his desk at the office. He was 70.

The oldest linen supply company in Chicago, Garden City Towel Supply, was not Shupe's firm, however, but founded in 1887 by Jacob H. Friedman, who was not to live to see the real success of his entrepreneurial venture. When he died five years later, the business was inherited by his wife. Later, his son, Roy J. Friedman, who was to become a president of L.S.A.A., in 1920, became sole owner.

Another pioneer was Frederick Doam Martin, founder of the Martin Linen Supply Company in San Antonio, Texas. Born in Adell, Iowa, in 1873, he started the original firm, the Martin Towel Company, in Lincoln, Nebraska, in 1889. In the early days of his business, about 90% of his service was in roller towels, with the remainder in hand (or "side") towels, mostly distributed to retail establishments rather than offices. In 1909 he and his brother Frank founded the present firm. A vigorous and healthy man, Fred Martin lived to be eighty-seven, long active in linen supply matters and honored as the "Oldest LSAA Ex-President."

The name of Frank H. Hartless became prominent in the 1890s. He started his career in unorthodox fashion, joining a small circus as a trapeze performer and tumbler at the age of thirteen. After two years with the circus and further experience as a locomotive fireman and a laundry driver, he opened his own business, the Austin Laundry, in 1892. Later, he founded the Hartless Linen and Towel Supply Company, of which he was president at the time of his death, January 5, 1946. He served for thirty-five years as secretary of the Tri-State Linen Supply Association and later the Linen Supply Association of America, both of which he helped to organize.

On November 17, 1943, an interesting full-page advertisement appeared in the Hartford Times. It was headlined FIFTY YEARS AGO JOSEPH H. GOWEN CAME TO CLEAN UP HARTFORD. Gowen worked in a candy factory in the year 1893, when it failed because of a bank panic. Out of work, he happened to talk to an old friend whom he had not seen for some time and who was having some success renting coats, aprons and towels in nearby Springfield, Mass. Gowen decided that the business climate ought to be the same in Hartford, Conn., which had no such supply service. He invested in a nag that "was only a few jumps ahead of the tallow factory" and an equally woebegone wagon located in the back yard of Jensen's candy store in Springfield, for which he paid $20, in tiny installments over many months. Combining hard work with Yankee thrift and ingenuity, Gowen built Hartford Apron & Towel Supply Company into the largest such firm in the city by the time it was ready to celebrate its fiftieth anniversary.

The success story was not without its setbacks. Gardner Clafflin, who said he had $3,000 and would help establish the business, was several days late showing up to purchase the needed supplies, and when he did arrive turned out to have only $300. Gowen had by then borrowed enough money to buy a few yards of white duck, with which his wife made up some aprons. He had managed also to buy up a few coats on credit in Springfield, after which he set out for Hartford and a new career. Half way there, the horse gave out, and he had to stop at the home of a relative overnight. After paying a stable charge of 50 cents, Gowen was penniless but still continued on his way. Since Clafflin still had not appeared by the time Gowen reached Hartford, he had to borrow $10 from a friend to start operations.

Those were the days in which a young entrepreneur had a better chance of starting on a shoestring than today. One of the classic stories of the industry is that of Charles A. Bonoff.

"If Horatio Alger, Jr., were alive today," wrote a reporter in Brooklyn in 1929, "we would like to give him the plot to a new story. The chances are that he would name it *Charlie the Bootblack, or An Immigrant's rise to Wealth*". He then went on to recount the story of Charles Bonoff, owner of the Brooklyn Coat & Apron Supply Company, Brooklyn Napkin Supply Company, Cascade Laundry System, Modern Barber Towel Supply Company, Nu-Way Family Laundry Company and General Linen Supply Company.

Charles Bonoff could remember clearly the days of the Russo-

Turkish war in the 1870s. As a child, he lived in Elizabethgrad, Russia, where his father was in the laundry business. ("That's where I got the flair for the game.") He watched the womenfolk taking the garments down to the river, stretching them on antiquated mangling boards, pressing them with crude irons, and going through the continuous process of scrubbing, rinsing and ironing. After surviving some of the bloody pogroms of the Czarist regime, the Bonoff family fled to America, settling at first in New Haven, Conn. There young Charlie had the good fortune to come under the wing of an aunt, a shrewd and hard-working woman who said to him, "Charlie, today is Friday. Today I feed you. Tomorrow I feed you. Sunday I feed you. But on Monday, you go out for yourself." She then furnished him with a bootblacking outfit, and he was off to earn his living.

Bonoff tried his hand at a number of pursuits in several cities—from doing odd handyman jobs to peddling tinware, farming and clerking—before winding up, like his father, in the laundry business and eventually in linen supply. In 1898, he founded the first of his companies, later referring to the business with justifiable pride as "The House that Cleanliness Built." Some 30 years later, he employed about 550 people at his main plant, General Linen Supply Company. The later head of this company was Carl Troy, and when his son, William B., became president in 1962, the company employed 1500 persons and was the largest textile-laundering plant under one roof in the world.

One of the other great success stories of the early 1900s was that of the four Miller brothers—Sam, Joe, Mike and Maurice—of Cleveland, Ohio, whose firm, founded in 1899, developed so steadily that right after World War I it was described as second to none in the United States in supplying linens and towels. Sam Miller, general manager of Independent Towel Supply Company, became one of the most widely known and respected figures in the entire industry, serving for almost half a century as treasurer of both the Linen Supply Association of America and the association that preceded it. Initially Sam and his brother Joe did their own driving and delivered linen supplies to a small group of customers. After eight years, during which time the business had grown considerably, they hired their brothers, Mike and Maurice, and established their own building. Within twenty years from the founding date, the company had a payroll of more than 250 people and handled over a million items a week, from towels and napkins to table covers, barber linens, coats, aprons and frocks.

Sam Miller attributed the growth and development of his company to organization, and the constant supervision and evaluation of every operation. It was his belief and business philosophy that each individual procedure and process could be steadily improved upon by cutting costs, making work more efficient and providing better customer service. Sam Miller knew exactly how things were running and he could be counted on to confer with foremen and department heads at least once each day. Organization, in the Miller manner, was the heart of good service.

Perhaps because of strong family relationships, religious beliefs, and Old World traditions of helping the less fortunate, the linen supply industry has long been noted for another from of service: participation in community affairs, philanthropic programs and other dedicated activities.

Joseph H. ("J.H.") Miller is known not only as one of the pioneers of the linen supply industry, but also for his stellar role in medical history. This co-founder of Independent Towel and Supply received the first successful human blood transfusion on record. It was performed in 1906 by the late famed Dr. George W. Crile. "J. H.", was bleeding internally and it was believed only a miracle could save him. The entire Miller clan, including his late brothers—Maurice and Samuel—were the donors.

Sam, the donor at the first transfusion, was at J. H.'s bedside when Dr. Crile, still in a dinner jacket from a party he had left minutes before, entered the room.

Taking a chance the two brothers would have compatible blood (blood types had been discovered four years before), Dr. Crile decided to transfuse the patient with vein-to-vein surgery. It was a daring, desperate idea since previous transfusions had been performed only on laboratory animals—and even some of these had been unsuccessful.

All the surgical needles were too large for the delicate job of sewing together an artery in Sam Miller's wrist and a vein in J. H.'s wrist and the whole project was a standoff until one of the nuns at St. Alexis Hospital, where the transfusion was performed, produced a hair-thin needle she used in embroidering delicate linens. Dr. Crile took more than three-dozen stitches in an 8-inch area. Then the clamps were released and blood from Sam began to flow into J. H.'s vein.

Dr. Frank P. Corrigan, then a young intern at the hospital (later a U. S. ambassador) is one of the few living witnesses to the history-making medical feat. He recently said:

"The effect of the fresh blood flowing into the dying man's system was like a miracle. He recovered consciousness and his skin became a lovely pink. He opened his eyes and smiled and began to take note of his surroundings.

"We were lost in wonder and admiration at the sight of this man coming back to life, until the head nurse said, 'Doctor, the brother has fainted.' "

It seems that Sam had had more than he could take and had passed out cold. He was as pale as J. H. had been a short time before. The

entire operation had taken more than three hours, although the flow
of blood had encompassed only a few minutes. The third Miller
brother, Maurice, gave blood in two other transfusions. They were
needed before J. H. was fully on his way to recovery. Today's medical
fraternity feels that Crile took a fantastic chance, since little was known
about blood types.

Another pioneer of the day was Frank W. Means, who in 1901 began
the operation of a small but increasingly profitable linen supply service
in Davenport, Iowa. His Tri-City Towel Supply Company became so
successful that the young man decided to try his hand at bigger game.
He moved to Chicago, where he opened a similar business, and then
interested the management of Chicago Towel Company in a unique
plan. He would, he said, use the Davenport operation as a prototype,
and found a chain of linen supply firms throughout the Midwest.
Jointly, F. W. Means and Chicago Towel formed what was to be the
Clean Towel Service with branches throughout Illinois and bordering
states. The growth and expansion from then on constitute a well known
story covering numerous mergers and new businesses, and reaching
a climax in April, 1960, with the establishment of the name, F. W.
Means & Company, with Chicago Towel Company as a corporate
division.

During the history of the linen supply industry—even today, but
especially in the early days—female executives have been greatly out-
numbered by the males. One of the lady pioneers, however was Mrs.
Ida B. Bacon, who in the 1930s, as president of Union Towel Supply
Company of Jersey City, N. J., was introduced at a testimonial dinner
as "The Fair Queen of the Linen Supply Industry." Born in Newark,
she was taken by her British parents to England at the age of one,
and later educated in the Episcopal Girls College at Exeter. In 1898,
she came back to the United States, to begin what was to be a lifetime
career at Union Towel Supply (then Hudson Laundry Company). She
was such an astute business woman that she rose from a subordinate
position to the ranks of general manager, treasurer and vice president.
In March, 1925, she married Edgar B. Bacon, and when he died in
1928, she assumed the presidency.

Speaking out during an interview in 1939, Mrs. Bacon criticized the
linen supply industry for being backward:

> Am I right in feeling that very little real constructive effort is being
> put forth by our industry, as a whole, to keep our service abreast of
> the times? Other fields of industry are seeking and adopting improve-
> ments that make for better service, but towel service equipment is
> practically where it was a quarter of a century ago. Why? Because we

are educating the public to *price*, rather than to quality, by furnishing much for little.

Very little general thought is given to the appearance or cleanliness of delivery equipment and its personnel, to the manner in which the service is rendered and how it is operated, to the style and condition of the cabinets and its furnishings.

If paper is more favorably considered than fabric, are we not to blame? In the past, towels were brought from home, but by education, we convinced the public that for a few cents daily we could save them this annoyance. Why cannot similar arguments be used to good effect against paper? We might rightly say that this is being done, but are we in a position to offer an adequate service at a reasonable price and, in addition, stress the advantage of fabric service? We have had to fight very hard to hold our ground during the past decade, but who among us does not enjoy a real fight? It has meant for all of us closer application to the problems of our business, harder work, and, perhaps, longer hours than have heretofore been necessary. I feel confident that, with wise planning and consistent thought in the right direction, our industry will regain its footing, for it is built on a public need just as surely as is any public utility.

Although Mrs. Bacon was ahead of her time, she was soon to see steps taken that would launch linen supply on its way to becoming one of the most resourceful and progressive of all service industries.

CHAPTER 4

THE TURNING
TIDES

**OTHERS ENTER THE BUSINESS,
BRINGING INNOVATIONS
AND VITALITY**

"It is one of the maxims of the civil law," wrote the celebrated Samuel Johnson in *The Rambler* in 1751, "that definitions are dangerous."

It might with equal conviction be said that the lack of definitions can also be dangerous. This was aptly demonstrated during the early period of the linen supply industry, when it was taking a place in the American economy. Linen supply was so poorly defined that many businessmen continued to think of it in terms of nothing more than towels and jackets. The other products and the growing range of services were either associated with some other business activity or overlooked entirely.

Although the time would come when linen supply would bring to mind uniforms, tablecloths, shirts, napkins, sheets and pillow cases, hospital linens and a long line of other products, the linen supply industry had too weak a voice. Intensifying the problem was the economic recession just after World War I. While many businessmen bemoaned their fate, Thomas A. Edison was admonishing his contemporaries:

> Hard times come in recurring cycles and are nothing new . . . the country always recovers from them and goes forward with greater strides than ever before. We will get over it now too. The tide has begun to turn. A restoration of confidence will do more to restore us to normal than any other factor. . . . we have the best transport system in the world, with more miles of railroads, more automobiles, more and cheaper methods of getting our products to market and a normally free buying public to consume products.

The situation was not much different from recessions of other years. The companies and industries that were strong managed to survive and even thrive, while those that were weak or without adequate goals and policies faltered and failed.

The linen supply industry, unlike many other long established businesses with considerable histories to look back upon for precedents and long-standing associations to rely on for counsel, was still a fledgling in which even the oldest members could barely boast, "Look, we have passed our first quarter century!"

For one thing, the idea of service had not yet matured. It was still an unsophisticated term signifying a variety of items supplied at a specific time or involving a number of deliveries weekly, or a cleaning process at the laundry plant. The most knowledgeable men in the industry would have been surprised had anyone referred to them as business or economic counselors, experts who could sit down with clients and discuss the applications of services to current and future needs. Few of the leaders of the industry gave much thought to the nature and problems of the customers they served. It was enough to know that Restaurant X required 500 napkins and 100 tablecloths a day, or that Joe's barber shop used 100 towels a day. Who would be so brash as to suggest a review of the business with a restaurant or hotel owner, to discuss over all economics and procedures?

During the years from the turn of the century until World War I, many of the entrepreneurs who entered the business did so because linen supply was one venture they could start with little capital. Quite a number of these new starters bounced in, then out, building routes to bring in temporary income, then leaving for other pastures. Those who remained found within the industry the opportunity they had hoped for in America.

As young men, somewhere they had heard that here was a service business that you could enter with comparative ease and that you did not require much capital. Then somehow, too each of these young men had been smitten by that great American Go-Into-Business-Yourself desire, the belief that a future is best built by the man who has the gumption, fortitude, and ability to go it alone.

There was a similarity between all the men who entered the linen supply business before, or shortly after, the turn of the century. They believed ardently in the free-enterprise system. Most were young. They were ambitious. They knew what a good day's work was, and they drove themselves hard. The stories that filter down from those years, of the seven-day weeks, and the 16-hour days make it clear that the linen supply business was not for the lazy.

Clarence Roskoph, as a 16-year old, started trudging the sidewalks of the Cleveland garment district in 1903, a basket of roller towels on his arm, the wolves of hunger snapping at his heels. The grandson of a Bohemian immigrant who had arrived in Cleveland in 1834, Clarence worked for his brother-in-law, Sam Goldberg. The two plodded around among the cloak and suit houses of the city, furnishing towels to the workers for a nickel each a week.

"I guess," said Roskoph, "that 3 cents out of every nickel went back into the business."

Getting the towels cleaned at a family laundry was too expensive for the young firm.

> We did our washing at home, in the kitchen, in a big wash bucket. My mother made the towels. We'd buy a big bolt of cloth and she'd cut them and stitch them up. And we did the washing after having been out all day. We woke early in the morning, then went on the routes

to pick up the soiled linen. Then back we'd take the towels for laundering. Those we washed at night we delivered the next morning. We didn't have any inventory of towels on hand. Who could afford it?

Roskoph's business expanded. Soon, he was not only serving towels, but he had added aprons—six for 25 cents— for the Cleveland barkeeps and butchers, and coats and bar mops, and finally a full line of rental linens. Roskoph and Goldberg were finally able to take their wash out of the kitchen and get it done elsewhere. They were also able to buy an old horse which they promptly mortgaged against the price of a rickety wagon. Union towel was finally rolling, but being on wheels sometimes had disadvantages. When winter storms piled up snow in the streets, the ancient animal could not pull the loaded wagon with Roskoph on it. So he would climb down, and trudge beside the nag. As he once commented:

> I remember one day in particular. I reached a certain restaurant whose proprietor started to give me hell because I was late. There he was, bawling me out for being late and I had just walked six miles through the snow to get there! I blew up and told him where he could go for his towels—a place a lot warmer than Cleveland!

On another wintry day, when the snow was not yet deep enough for Roskoph to get off the wagon, he may have become the inventor of the windshield. The swirling snow blinded Roskoph. The wind cut his face. His tears blinded him. So he climbed down, found a tarpaulin, cut a hole in it, placed a piece of isinglass over the hole, and rigged the tarpaulin in front of him on the wagon.

Roskoph's partner, Goldberg, was also an inventor—designing a towel server that came into use in the second and third decades of this century. Noticing the old-style water closet with its hanging chain, he decided that this kind of arrangement could be used to supply towels. He added an elbow to the overhead part of his device, and anchored the chain to a soiled linen basket on the floor. Patent possibilities were being explored when the cabinet shop that was turning out pilot models burned to the ground.

Union Towel became noted in Cleveland prior to World War II for something other than supplying linens: company-sponsored clambakes. While the subject may seem far removed from this book, the account is a commentary on the business climate of that time.

"Back in those days, relations with employees were pretty much on a 'one big family' basis," Ralph Roskoph recalled. "Everyone, including the plant caretaker, plunged wholeheartedly into anything considered of common good."

He recounted that the plant supervisor was a specialist in staging clambakes and that every year, come the season, he was relieved of his regular duties for two weeks to stage one. These were not strictly internal affairs. The top echelon of people from Cleveland and its suburbs were invited and, almost without exception, attended. The clambakes were held in the laundry. Employees spent an entire day moving pieces of equipment out of the way and installing tables and benches in their place.

Since Union Towel's plant was located in one of Cleveland's economically depressed neighborhoods, Bob Roskoph still recalls with a chuckle the look on the faces of mink-clad dowagers attending one of the functions for the first time. Dinner in a laundry plant—oh, no! Yet, he says, "The clambakes were so well directed by our plant supervisor, and the good fellowship that pervaded the affairs was so infectious that, when even the most finicky lady left the party it was always with the question—'When are you going to hold the next one?'"

In 1902, in Cincinnati, a young man, Daniel Ziegler, arrived in town from a Kentucky farm where he and his five brothers and four sisters had barely found subsistence. In Newport, just across the Ohio River from Cincinnati, he first found work in a macaroni factory. Soon he was courting a girl who worked at what was then known as Colonel Patterson's Kentucky Laundry. They decided to get married and on the day selected for the wedding, Ziegler, said to the foreman of the macaroni factory:

"I'd like to get off early as I'm getting married tonight."

"You can't go," the foreman replied. "You know we always got to clean those kettles before we leave for the day."

Ziegler dutifully cleaned the kettles, but a whisk broom in his right hand snagged in the whirling machinery. By the time he extricated his hand, he had lost three fingers. Two fellow employees rushed him to a doctor by street car, standing in its vestibule all the way. After the doctor had treated the wound Ziegler went home, dressed for his wedding, and called for his bride.

"I've had a little accident," he told her, but the ceremony went on as scheduled.

Ziegler searched fruitlessly for another job, until he realized that linen supply could have a promising future. In Newport, Ky., a suburb of Cincinnati, he solicited the renting of roller and barber towels and made deliveries along the route of the Newport trolley line. His customer list grew, and Ziegler borrowed a friend's horse and cart, before finally buying his own red wagon. He recalled:

> Later, I had a chance to buy a horse from a hardware store that had discontinued making deliveries. The owner wanted $75 for her, a real

nice mare, and I sure wanted to buy her. I told a friend about it, and
he said, "Go ahead and buy her, Dan. I'll lend you the money." So
I did.

By 1907, the three-year-old business swamped the Kentucky Laundry,
where Ziegler had his wash done. So he and another linen supplier,
Adam Doering, teamed up to buy an old printing shop where they
installed laundry equipment and hired two girls at $3.50 a week to
process the towels and bar aprons. Three years later, Dan sold his
interest in the plant and moved across the river to Cincinnati, where
he rented larger facilities.

Ziegler also remembers buying his first automobile.

"We took her out the first Sunday on a spin down to Alexandria
and back without meeting another machine. It could never happen
again."

Ziegler saw one big change in the linen rental industry in his lifetime.
The day is past, he commented, when the little fellow could get into
it, because the small stops don't pay out any more.

"Today," he observed, "it takes a lot of money to go into business—any business. Everything is so blamed high! And you have to
go after the big quantity stops. The little towel customer costs you
more to make the delivery than the stop is worth."

A lot of towels have flowed over the flatwork ironer since that
eventful day in 1904 when an injured bridegroom boarded the Newport trolley car with his first deliveries of roller towels, and the 1960s
when Ziegler Towel Supply Company was an old-line company in
the industry. Yet Dan Ziegler, sitting at the age of eighty-seven in his
sun-dappled back yard in Southgate, Ky., was more firmly convinced
than ever that the secret of success in the linen supply business was
dependable service: "Be honest with your customers and see to it they
get the service you promise them. That way, every one will be satisfied
and the business will flourish."

To the north of Cincinnati, near Cleveland, at about the time Ziegler
was getting started, two other young boys, eighteen-year-old Harry
Spero and his new partner Manny Friedman, were also going into
business.

Three dead horses helped to found what was destined to become
one of the larger linen supply companies: Penn-Ohio Towel Supply
Company of Youngstown, Ohio. The incidents took place in 1905, but
founder Harry Spero said before his death in 1968 that it seemed as
though the problems involving the horses happened "only yesterday."

In 1905, Spero was ending 18 months of employment as an $8 a
week bookkeeper at Independent Towel Supply Company in Cleveland. He had been approached by a casual business acquaintance about

opening a linen supply business in some other, as yet undetermined, Ohio city. Neither Spero nor the prospective partner, Manny Friedman, had much money to invest—the most they could muster between them was $250.

Little money or no, they began to look around for a likely location for the venture. Youngstown was chosen because a railroad running out of Cleveland has a $1 roundtrip fare to the northeastern Ohio steel city—the best excursion bargain in the state.

The partners entrained for Youngstown, made a large number of calls on linen service prospects in record time, and returned to Cleveland with assurance of immediate business from at least fifty of them. So Youngstown was chosen for their enterprise.

Stock was the next problem—towels, combs, hair brushes and cabinets—into which went almost all of the $250 capital (along with substantial credit commitments secured by Harry Spero). What cash remained was little more than enough to buy a thoroughly used, badly battered Fleischman's Yeast wagon for making deliveries once Youngstown was reached.

Since a horse was also needed, Harry Spero went to a glue rendering plant in Elyria, Ohio, just southwest of Cleveland, and rescued one for five dollars. After this purchase, a $10 bill remained as the partners' total capital.

They set forth for Youngstown, 70 miles southeast of Cleveland, on a fine but chilly Sunday morning, coaxing the animal into activity. Although neither of the partners knew much about horses or how to drive them, all went well until they reached Garretsville, Ohio, midway between Cleveland and Youngstown. Just outside that town, the horse gently laid himself down without warning and as quietly died, blocking the road.

Spero and his associate walked to the nearest farmhouse where, in response to their knock, they were greeted by the business end of a 12-gauge shotgun. It took fast talking on Harry's part to convince the farmer they were not highwaymen, but were in need of help, including a place to sleep that night. Finally convinced, the farmer bedded them down on the kitchen floor, promising to take them to a horse dealer the following morning. He lived up to his word, but the deal turned out to be two old horses for $25, or nothing at all. Spero used his persuasive powers to induce the horse merchant to accept the $10 they still possessed, along with a bale of towels as security for the $15 balance.

And thus it was that they optimistically continued the trek to Youngstown, one horse pulling the wagon, the other limping idly behind. When they reached their destination, dead broke, they were fortunate in contacting an acquaintance who agreed to put them up overnight and to stable the two horses. Up bright and early the next morning, eager to get the new business underway, they found both horses lying dead on the stable floor.

Once again, they had to float a small loan: $10 to get the dead animals removed, and 75 cents to rent a horse for the day.

After a few additional setbacks, the Youngstown Towel Supply Company was finally in business, with some fifty customers. Even this small amount of business, however, kept the partners frantically busy. Since they were low on stock and had no funds for increasing the inventory immediately, they had to service most customers six days a week and others every other day. After floating a few more loans, in more substantial ranges between $100 and $200, the business finally began to make the expected profit.

After more than sixty years, from this shaky start, the business has grown into a large organization (United Service Company), with the basic Penn-Ohio Towel Supply Company and fourteen subsidiaries. Operating in Ohio, western Pennsylvania and part of New York, the company employs over 1,000 people and has a number of strategically located laundering plants with major installations in Youngstown, Cincinnati, and Erie, Pa. Much of the expansion has come through the acquisition of existing linen supply businesses, which usually retained their original names and local identities but were improved with respect to plants and facilities.

The early history of linen supply forms a tapestry of individual entrepreneurs: Andrew D. Bonanno, who started in Boston in 1898; William H. Clarke, who started in Washington, D.C., in 1900; William T. Moore of Baltimore Towel Supply & Laundry Company in 1897; Charles A. Sellars, who began in Indianapolis in 1900. We cannot ignore another memorable distaff member of the industry, Mary E. Sweeney, who started with Wheeler Clean Towel Company in Boston in 1900, or Bernard A. Ruwe, who entered the industry in Cincinnati in 1901, or Samuel K. Wilson who started the same year in Wheeling, West Virginia. These, too, were among the pioneers, as was Barney Abelove of Utica, New York, 1904; Abe Papp, of Roxbury, Massachusetts, 1904; George B. Freeman, of Peoria, Illinois, 1904; Lee Matthey, of St. Louis, 1905; G. Russell and Harry P. Hovey of Worcester, Massachusetts, Allen, of Pawtucket, Rhode Island, 1906.

"It was quite a year, 1903," began a recent magazine profile of linen supplier, John DeNormandie—a profile that is in effect a tribute to his father, Joseph. That year, the Wright brothers had achieved a notable step forward by keeping a "mechanical kite" suspended in the air for fifty-nine seconds. And in Detroit, a "reformed bicycle manufacturer" named Henry Ford was about to open a shop for the manufacture of horseless carriages.

In Chicago, young Joseph DeNormandie was engaged in less dramatic pursuits. He had just quit his job as a driver for Peerless Laundry, purchased four dozen butcher aprons, two coats and an apron box from Peerless. Having left the laundry route with the understanding that if his venture failed, he could return to Peerless, DeNormandie began soliciting the bar and tavern business, featuring "Fentons," a type of sleeveless vest the bartenders of the day wore, and which his mother made.

"I was eleven then," DeNormandie's son, John, later recalled, "and I worked after school as my father's helper. A couple of years later, when I graduated from grammar school, I remember I went to work full time the same day. I was even wearing my graduation suit, blue serge knickers and a white shirt."

While the elder DeNormandie solicited the bars and taverns, young John hunted for other customers, zeroing in on butcher shops and markets:

> In those days, butchers bought their own aprons and their wives used to wash them at home. But I was able to build up a complete route by the time I was 15 by convincing them that it was cheaper in the long run to let me supply them with aprons and spare their wives the drudgery and inconvenience of washing and ironing.

Then disaster struck. A competitor moved in on the fifteen-year-old linen supplier, offering apron customers cut-rate service. John supplied aprons for a nickel whereas his competitor offered six for 25 cents.

"It was the blackest day of my life," young John mused. "I had worked for two years to build up my route and I saw it stolen away overnight."

Disheartened, he returned home that evening. "Don't give up," his mother told him. "You can do plenty."

"Like what? The business is all gone," he answered.

"No, it isn't. You can get the business back."

"How?"

"Can you get hold of a couple of that fellow's invoices?"

"I think so."

The next morning he went out and canvassed the old route. From two customers he obtained billings showing the cut-rate prices.

When he brought them home, Mrs. DeNormandie put them in her purse, put on her coat and hat and went directly to all of the competitor's regular customers.

"What do you pay for aprons from him?" she asked.

"A nickel apiece," each answered.

"So-o-o," she said, "look what he's charging new customers," and she whipped out the invoices. Not long after, the competitor withdrew from his attempts to undercut DeNormandie and the young man was back in business.

Joseph DeNormandie continued to develop his growing business until his death in 1925. At that time, his son took over the firm, working with his younger brother Grant. As was characteristic of the growth of many companies in linen supply, a third generation entered the business and eventually a fourth. "Apparently," reported the magazine published by the Linen Supply Association of America, *Linen Supply News,* in the mid-sixties, "there will never be any shortage of young DeNormandies and their kin to keep the wheels of their growing route fleet turning."

Around the turn of the century, another name to become recognized in linen supply appeared when the Gitlows arrived in New York from their native Russia. By 1909 the eldest son, Abe, then in his early teens, was working to help meet family expenses as a driver on a laundry route, when he met a young man, somewhat older, named Silver who was working his way through dental school.

To pay your own way, you have two choices: Either you work for someone else or you start a new business. Silver chose the latter course because he knew enough about the needs of the professionals, especially dentists and physicians, to see that they could use a towel service. While still in dental school, he started a towel supply business.

In no time the business had grown so much that he needed an assistant—and who could be a better choice than young Abe Gitlow, a hard-working, pleasant kid? Abe worked for Silver until Silver graduated from dental school. Silver then said to Abe, "You can buy this business if you want to. I can't run it while I'm a dentist."

Abe, barely fifteen years old, went home and that night talked the proposal over with his father and three brothers, Al, Max, and Sam.

"How much does Silver want," Abe's father asked.

"About $900."

"We don't have it. How . . ."

"But it's a good business, Pop. It's the only one supplying dentists and physicians in the city."

"Can you make some arrangements to pay him?"

"I think so."

Abe went back to Silver, and the young dentist agreed to accept the $900, paid out over a long period. Since the business itself would not bring $900 profit in the allotted time, something else had to be done to pay off the debt. Back in the house, Abe sat with his brothers, Al and Sam.

"I'll get another job," he said.

"How will that help?"

"Well, we'll earn extra money that way. You two and Pop can run and build this business, the Silver Supply Company, and keep money coming in from that so we can eat."

"And with what you earn, you mean, we'll pay Silver. Then we'll have the business ourselves," Al agreed.

Without signing any formal agreement, the Gitlow brothers and their father entered into a linen supply business that would in time rank among the leaders in the nation.

The industry then was a far cry from what it is now. The small linen supplier had to be a jack of all trades. He had to sell and deliver. He had to purchase linens. He had to sew and make repairs. He had to get them washed. And he had to provide some means of transportation.

"We rented a horse and wagon for $2 per day," Abe Gitlow recalled. "We paid $6 per week, because we rented it three days a week. It was a lucky thing I had lived in the country once. I knew a little about horses."

When in time, the Gitlows were covering the five boroughs of New York City, they began to broaden their services, supplying towels and linens to restaurants, barbers, and other organizations.

"The early days were days of specialization," said Abe Gitlow. "Some suppliers specialized in serving saloons; some firms specialized in supplying butchers. There was no industrial business. The gasoline stations—the few there were then—didn't have rest rooms. So no one did any business with them."

Another important family in the industry is Maslow, although its roots do not go back quite as far as in the case of some of the others. Charles Maslow, then a twenty-four-year-old immigrant from Russia, launched his business in 1914. With a partner, Sam Spatt, who had been in linen supply since 1909, he founded Best Coat & Apron Manufacturing Company, and simultaneously tied in with Spatt's original firm, Central Coat and Apron Supply. The latter was to rent and service the products manufactured by Best which today represents one of the larger companies in the industry. Lester, the oldest son of Charles Maslow, heads Best Coat, while his other sons, Robert and Arthur, own a multi-plant linen supply firm called Bugle Linen Service. Joe Maslow, one of Charles Maslow's two brothers, is represented in the industry by his sons, Lawrence and Norman, and by grandson Steven, a son of Lawrence. Their company is Stanlinco Ltd. Herman, the third brother of the first generation, has a son, Larry, who is with Stanlinco.

Prior to World War I, the products offered to customers were plain and utilitarian. There were, of course, exceptions. Harvey Carl

Wheeler, a colorful physical culturist who even into his seventies was able to perform chinning and other physical demonstrations headed the New System Towel Supply Company which offered franchise offices from coast to coast. As an enticement, he offered fancy cabinets, gold-plated mirrors and towels embroidered with customers' initials. As Wheeler shipped his goods into one town after another, a string of small linen supply businesses was built in Chicago, Memphis, St. Louis, Kansas City and other cities.

In the meantime, Fred Martin, earlier mentioned as having started successfully in Lincoln, Nebraska, had moved into Kansas City, gradually building routes there as well as in Muskogee, Oklahoma, and Beatrice, Nebraska. He had established his business without cabinets, installing only a shelf and soap bar in each location. The day of reckoning finally came, however, when the Wheeler New System Towel Supply opened in Kansas City in direct competition with him. At first, Martin lost many customers, until he fought back by having a Mr. Mikkelson, a cabinetmaker in Chicago, turn out the latest design in new cabinets. Using these as a selling tool, he won back much of his business.

In Muskogee, Oklahoma, where Martin was trying to build his new branch business, he met one day in 1910 a young man passing through town on his way to a farm in New Mexico, Brace A. Helfrich, who recalled the event:

> I saw his wagon and I asked him for work. I was almost broke, and I wanted to conserve my funds. Fred Martin talked big business. He smoked big cigars. He thought that no one could beat him at selling. So one day I went out and got more orders than he did, and he took me on as sales manager in Kansas City, at what was, for those days, the magnificent sum of $15 a week.
>
> When I reached Kansas City, I was disappointed. Fred had a building across the street from a big laundry. When the laundry finished cleaning his towels and aprons, they just pushed the handtrucks out into Martin's building, which wasn't much to look at. It was one-story high, there was a hole in the floor, and the gold lettering on the front window had peeled off. Mrs. Martin was working on the books.

After Helfrich helped to develop the Kansas City business, Martin sent him to Oklahoma City to help establish another branch. But building branches brought only limited satisfaction and income. Why should a young man work for someone else when the vista was clear and limitless? The newly married Helfrich and his bride talked it over, and finally they too made the big step, going into business in Wichita.

"I borrowed from friends and from Fred Martin, and put in some myself. We started with a stock capitalization of $4,500 but we sure didn't have all of it." he said.

Helfrich did not pick his location out of a hat but chose Wichita for a definite reason. Through towel supply salesmen Helfrich had heard that here was a town of good size that had linen suppliers who were not, according to the reports, doing the job the right way.

Helfrich then went to Wichita to survey business conditions:

> First, I went to real estate, insurance companies, and other offices to see what kind of linen supply they were getting. In those days, almost every office had a washbasin in it. So I'd walk in, see if there was service, and if there was a cabinet. Then I asked if I might use the washroom. This was mainly an excuse to see what it was like, and what was in it. If the office or the washroom didn't have towels, you knew darned well the field wasn't covered. We did a lot of detective work this way, and we kept notes. When we finished we felt Wichita would be a good place for us to start.

When he first investigated the market potential in the town and decided to start his business there, he made clandestine arrangements to receive merchandise. A few weeks later, the freight office in Wichita, then a sleepy town of about 65,000, received unmarked crates of towels, without identification, numbered according to a secret code for bills. No one knew whose crates they were until Helfrich came to pick them up in person at the office.

As he related:

> We started off completely in secret. I didn't let anyone know I was going to start the business. Fred Martin even rented the building for me. Then, when I was ready, I came into town, carrying all our money in $100 bills. We opened the business with a blast, soliciting all of a sudden. Martin and I went out selling. We carried cabinets, brushes, and towels, and demonstrated with a flair. To obtain entry into an office, we gave a soft blotter and then tried to give an ad lib sales talk—too many were already using canned talks. We didn't ask for an order at first, acting as though it was a demonstration, just as free as the air you breathe.
>
> Then we made the sales, Later, during World War II, I also started the system of collecting in advance. No one had done that before. When the industry met at conventions, everyone was astounded to hear that I was able to institute this system. Most customers accepted this innovation readily. The percentage against it at first was relatively small; in due time everyone agreed to it.

To implement this system, Helfrich gave each route salesmen a bonus of $10 for the month if he obtained 80% of the advance money; a $20 bonus if 100%.

Helfrich's business flourished. By 1914 he had done well enough to buy one of the first trucks in the linen supply business, a 1914 Ford chassis without body, for $425. Then he went to McKenzie Carriage Works, where he drew a picture of the truck body he needed.

"I want mirrors on each side of the truck," he said, "and I want them put on in such a way that they're waterproof."

"Also paint the whole thing in cream color." Every other car or truck at that time was painted either black or dark green.

"And I want our name on it, in gold leaf letters, shaded. Use the name KEEP KLEAN."

Keep Klean it was—and Keep Klean it remains today.

In the early days, many of the men who set themselves up in linen supply came from eastern Europe, where they had fled from persecution. Such a man was Harry Alpert, who arrived in 1910 in the United States with only a half dollar to his name. At first, he lived in Grand Central Station in New York City on bread and water, until he happened to encounter a fellow immigrant, who directed him to a cousin's home. He started off with the usual round of part-time jobs, taking whatever he could get.

Shortly after he arrived in the United States, young Alpert worked as a painter until one day when a rope on his scaffold broke, throwing him to the sidewalk. When he regained consciousness, he vowed he would never be a painter again. But what could he do? A cousin, Aaron Hyde, told him about a new frontier: the coat and apron supply service, which a man could enter without a lot of capital.

He and his cousin bought some cloth, and a seamstress, young Alpert's wife, sewed the aprons. Alpert worked on the outside, selling in many parts of Brooklyn, while cousin Aaron worked on the inside, mending the aprons, taking care of the records. Soon they had gained many customers. Business was better. They were able to do more than they had planned. Typically, they invested in a horse and wagon.

"The best horse I ever had," Alpert used to say, "was a retired fire horse. I had one problem with him though. Whenever there was a fire in the neighborhood, he'd take off after it."

Three others with similar nationalities and backgrounds were the brothers Reuben and William Sandler and Louis Gordon, all of whom had escaped from Russia early in the 1900s. The Sandlers found themselves in Detroit in 1910 with what, in a classic understatement, was described as "little capital to invest," yet sufficient to buy basic equipment and rent enough space to establish Reliable Linen Service, a firm which has continued to this day.

Louis Gordon was born in the central part of Russia in a small town called Oshmino:

> My father, a wounded veteran of the Crimean War, could hardly earn a living by himself, and my mother helped to support the family. I had only an elementary school education, for during the Czar's regime, Jews could not attend higher schools, with rare exceptions. I can recall the Cossacks raiding the town in which we lived. There was always fear of the pogrom.

In 1904, when a wave of terrorism again swept through Russia, an uncle arranged for Louis, then fifteen, to go to America. It took three months of hardships and hunger just to reach a Baltic port. Further months went by, as he lived in barracks provided for refugees, until he was finally able to board a German vessel, the *Blucher* and take steerage passage to New York. Working as many as 80 or 90 hours a week for mere subsistence, he cleaned and oiled machinery, made iron products and worked for a painter.

Five years later, Gordon unexpectedly, got the break that was to mold his career:

> I met a man by the name of Fleischer who was then in the laundry business, washing towels for dentists and physicians. He used to make his deliveries with a horse and wagon. He approached me one day and told me that he had taken a liking to me and asked whether I would be willing to work for him as driver of his wagon, for he was sick and could not walk up stairs. I went to work for him, and I recall that my wages were $20 a month. He became very ill and asked me to take over the business, which then had a volume of about $20 a week. He offered to sell me the business, as I recall, for $350. I had no money at that time, but I borrowed $20 from my uncle as a down payment. It took me several years to pay off the balance. That was the beginning of my career in the linen supply business.

Shortly after he bought the modest little laundry route, Gordon had the good fortune to meet a colorful character, a dentist who practised under the name of "Painless Parker." Parker travelled about in a horse and buggy and rented 4,000 towels weekly, suggesting to Gordon the tremendous potential of the linen supply business. Gordon initially purchased towels from Ben Bimberg, a close personal friend, and had his laundry washed at local plants in the Bronx. Within a few years, business began to increase rapidly. Realizing that he and several partners he had subsequently acquired were building a substantial business but did not have their own plant, Gordon affiliated with the four Gitlow brothers. Out of the Gitlow firm, Silver Towel Company, and the Gordon firm, Modern Towel Company, came the new corporate heading, Modern Silver Towel Supply Company.

In Philadelphia, Sam Kornfeld who had a "gents dry goods store," and who was seeking to supplement his income, conceived the idea of making aprons for butchers and bartenders, planning to sell rather than rent them. But as he went around selling the aprons, he realized that he was taking the wrong approach. Since rentals seemed to be in greater demand, he began to spend more time developing a coat and apron rental route, while Mrs. Kornfeld remained in the store. He found a place to have his soiled garments washed and pressed—at the Pennsylvania Towel Supply Company, an old-line hand towel company serving offices, and one of the two important linen suppliers in town, the other being White Duck Coat & Apron.

Meantime, other pioneers were developing the linen supply industry on the West Coast. One of the early leaders was Joseph Burroughs, who in 1905 founded the Oakland, California, Towel Supply Company, and who later became one of the first active western members of the Linen Supply Association of America. Burroughs came from Reno, Nevada, the seventh child of an itinerant preacher and the only boy in the family. The linen supply business was not totally new to him when he started. He had a laundry route in Reno, working for an uncle there, and he saw in Oakland the chance to start in a new rental field. There, he and his sister, Mrs. Carrie Hall, incorporated their business. A penciled notation in the minutes states that the corporation was capitalized at $50,000, but probably most of the stock remained outstanding.

Business did not go well at first and Burroughs had to spend time in other work to support himself. Whenever it became necessary, Burroughs took a train to Los Angeles, remaining there awhile, selling real estate and peddling hand paintings from door to door. By 1907, though the fledgling Oakland Linen Supply Company had ten employees, the highest paid among them being the stable man, who worked a nine-hour day, seven days a week, for $3 a day. Mrs. Hall as partner, bookkeeper, and general office manager, drew $13 a week.

With the same missionary zeal that his father had shown, young Burroughs continued to enlarge his linen supply business. The firm grew slowly until World War II. when it became one of the larger plants in the West.

By the beginning of World War I, the linen supply industry in the United States was on its way to becoming a significant part of the American economy. A list compiled on June 8, 1917, indicates that there were 948 linen supply firms in the United States and Canada, with the latter country accounting for 37. New York, as might be expected, was far in the lead, with 162. In second place was Illinois with 75. Ohio had 62; Pennsylvania 57; and California and Missouri 53 each. Next in order were Massachusetts, 46; Texas, 42; Indiana, 31; Iowa, 23; Washington, 22; and Michigan, 21. Only Vermont and the territory of Alaska were listed as having none.

Linen Supply was well on its way.

CHAPTER 5

FROM GLOOM
TO BOOM

**FLUCTUATIONS IN THE
PATTERN OF ECONOMICS**

The year 1918 marked not only the end of the war in Europe but the beginning of a period of economic self-examination which was to be anything but cheerful to many U. S. industries. Americans, who had been welded together in a great common cause, now found themselves fractured into many groups, each striving to find and hold its niche in the stark postwar scene. It was difficult to retain a proper sense of values, both in the economic world and in the social affairs of man. The public was much more likely to be enthralled by the Sacco-Vanzetti trial of 1920 than it was to see any great significance, beyond that of an interesting "stunt," in the flight of the Navy seaplane NC-4 from Newfoundland to the Azores or the 1919 flight of Alcock and Brown across the Atlantic from Ireland to Newfoundland. The Wall Street bomb explosion of September 16, 1920, made a far bigger impact on Americans than had the founding, some nine months earlier in Switzerland, of a controversial organization called the League of Nations.

Businessmen too, had difficulty assessing economic values, determining which was firm ground and which was quicksand. Some industries had one advantage: they could look back historically to the aftermath of other wars and note the patterns of growth and change. Not so the linen supply industry. It did not go back even as far as the Civil War. It had no precedent to study in other countries after their wars, because linen supply was almost non-existent abroad, at least as a recognized industry. Nor could an answer be found in the post Spanish-American War era, when linen suppliers were few enough.

More linen supply would be needed, in an ever-climbing spiral of demand—of that there seemed little doubt. Yet there were big questions.

Seeing this demand, some linen suppliers reasoned: why not expand, like other industries, into other cities? Why be confined to one location? A chain of linen supply plants might cover an entire region, or, who knows, possibly even the whole United States.

But where, and how?

The Steiners had faced this problem early. They had competed with Quincy Martin in his offer to supply oak cabinets with the towel service. They had managed to keep their accounts, building and cultivating them as did the farmers with their nearby fields. Both corn and linen supply prospered for a while in the Nebraska prairie.

But in 1892 the rains that fed the corn and provided the water for the linen supply wash ceased. The corn on the farms burned in the hot sun; and with the heat and drought, all business wilted. Because farmers had no corn to sell, they earned no money to buy anything in town. When they bought nothing in town the merchants sat around listlessly. Business dropped off as a result of the unfortunate chain of circumstances, and it became apparent that linen supply was—and always would be—tied in with the general economy of the regions it served.

Was there a pattern in the successes and failures of some of the individual pioneers—Fred Martin, Sam Miller, George Rohman, Charles Sellars, Sam Wilson, Barney Abelove, Dan Ziegler and others? The Steiners had entrenched themselves firmly in one territory and then looked around for other regions where service was non-existent and the need looked substantial.

If there was any lesson that emerged from a study of the Steiner organization, or those of Ziegler, Martin, Abelove, Miller or the others, it was not so much one of markets and potential as it was just plain hard work!

A graphic example of the process of growth is seen in a calendar outline recently typed up by The American Linen Supply Company in Seattle, Washington:

1907—Started by W. E. Maryatt—one route. (Mr. Maryatt died in 1925)

1911—Son Charles W. Maryatt (died in 1960) joined with W. E. Maryatt—still one route.

1921—Enterprise Laundry purchased—Two family routes—one linen supply route.

1921—Son Roy L. Maryatt purchased Mutual Supply—One route.

1923—Roy L. Maryatt joined W. E. Maryatt and Charles W. Maryatt.

1925—New building—Maryatt Electric Laundry—Two family routes—3 linen supply routes.

1940—Traded ten family routes for three linen routes of Supply Laundry Co.—making eight linen routes.

1946—Bought one route in San Francisco—Acme Towel Supply.
Bought five routes in Los Angeles—Kleen Towel Supply Co.

1955—Bought three routes in Everett, Washington.

1964—Bought Overall Industrial Supply in Portland, Oregon—Twelve routes.

1967—115 Industrial and Linen Routes in five plants and two depots.

One element did begin to emerge, however: the concept of service—the kind of service that had been defined in a partial way by that first memorandum in 1914 from President W. F. Ayers of the Ohio Linen Supply Association. Service was a two-way street. It could not be offered as a mere promotional device; it had to be a working philosophy that would result in a sound and profitable business arrangement for buyer as well as seller. The Steiner firm stumbled upon at least one surprising, and valuable, lesson. Everywhere its management turned it found new linen supply business. Volume was growing daily, in good weather and bad. The time came to build another plant—the third—in Chicago.

Frank and his brother did not count on one development though. After a while their biggest Chicago account, the Wrigley Brothers Chewing Gum Company plant, suddenly shocked them with a request.

"Stop service," Wrigley said. The firm was building its own laundry.

The Steiner brothers wondered how big losses would run now? Would they have to give up in Chicago? A month passed. They watched the books of accounts carefully and studied sales records. Would they have to admit defeat for the first time?

Then, surprisingly, they discovered that instead of losing money they were showing a profit. They had been so intent on providing superior "service" for the large-volume account at prices that were too low, they had achieved nothing but losses!

There was also a valuable lesson to be learned in the history of the Morgan company. In February of 1902 Kendrick Ebenezer Morgan had been elected president of the Niagara Linen Corporation. The date was a milestone in his career, as well as in the history of linen supply, inaugurating as it did a period of consolidation and preparation for future growth. That same year, the Morgan Steam Laundry—the first to bear the Morgan name—was founded in New York, which then had a population of 3,437,202. The firm was established especially to do business with the burgeoning railroad companies, steamboat services and shipping lines. Some two years later, Morgan formally entered into the same kind of linen supply business in which others had already begun to pioneer; he incorporated the Niagara Linen Supply Company to do his laundry work. Three years later he launched the Paris Towel Company in Chicago.

Then, in 1907, the Morgan enterprise expanded in New York. Its capitalization was increased from $100,000 to $300,000 and Hudson Steam Laundry in Jersey City, New Jersey was bought. Morgan started the Cook Laundry Company in Albany, New York in 1910; developed new business in Cleveland; expanded holdings in Chicago and St. Louis, and acquired property in Los Angeles.

But growth was too fast. The Morgan organization could not pay for machinery improvements, new buildings, daily operations and supplies. New capital was needed.

Fabulous Diamond Jim Brady came to the rescue. He joined forces with Morgan, buying several thousand shares of stock. At last there was enough capital to go ahead with planned rapid expansion and plant improvement. The Morgan organization was again on the move. But just before Christmas of 1918, Kendrick Ebenezer Morgan was killed when he stepped from a Chicago bus in front of a passing taxicab.

The future lay in the hands of K. E.'s son, Alden Kendrick Morgan, who was to continue building the firm.

The Morgan Company of that era presents a good case study of some of the changes taking place, not only in the chaotic postwar world on the outside, but in the internal structure of individual companies. Prior to that time, many a corporation lived and thrived because of a single man and went out of business when the man died. But times were changing. Fortunately, Alden Kendrick Morgan and his associates were equal to the challenge and the task or reorganization in the crucial years ahead.

While Morgan had been growing and spreading, so had Chicago Towel during the second decade of the twentieth century. As pointed out, much of the growth can be attributed to the dynamic Frank W. Means, and his expansion from Davenport, Iowa, as Tri-City Towel Supply Company, to other locations throughout the Midwest. His affiliation with Chicago Towel and the resultant formation of branches, all linked together by central management, was part of an emerging pattern for others to follow.

Even as late as the 1920s, however, members of the industry did not have to look at the history of the large companies to find blueprints for their own philosophies. They could emulate the practices of the entrepreneurs who started on shoestrings. There was, for example, the case of William H. Clarke, who started in Washington, D. C., in 1900, as Elite Linen Service, Inc., in "a little room over a building in Georgetown." He stored the clean linens there, but took the soiled ones to another firm, the Star Laundry, to be washed. His father's company was called Clarke's Coat, Apron & Towel Supply Company. When in February 1905, he went into partnership with Edward O. Craig, the name of the firm became C & C Coat, Towel, & Apron Supply Company, Inc.

In 1916, Clarke bought the Eagle Overall Laundry on S Street, with a partner named Fields, with a special purpose in mind which paralleled Morgan's expansion in New York City. Because this was a period when steamboat companies and railroads were booming, he concentrated on supplying linens for them, as well as offering wholesale laundry service for overalls, uniforms and other goods owned by the customers themselves. However, during World War I, Clarke and Craig moved out of the laundry business, dropped the Eagle Laundry name and concentrated on the field they felt had the real future: linen supply.

Many a linen supplier in the old days started out with little more equipment or capital than did the chestnut seller near the White House. A characteristic example is that of Joseph Schuh, who in 1960 received his gold wallet card from the L.S.A.A. in recognition of fifty

years of service to the industry. As a boy of sixteen he secured a
job as driver of a delivery wagon for the Western Toilet Supply
Company of St. Louis, Missouri. Of German parentage, one of twelve
children, Schuh was diligent and perceptive. When the owner decided
to sell out two years later, Joseph Schuh had already saved enough
money so that he could realistically consider going into a business
for himself. Another young man with similar inclinations, John Beck,
who had also decided to go into business for himself asked Schuh
if he would like to invest his money and become a partner in Western
Toilet Supply. The offer was accepted and in 1911 a new company
was born.

The business prospered, but the two owners found they were han-
dicapped by not having their own laundry plant. In 1918, not yet strong
enough financially to build it themselves, they consolidated with three
other companies to amass enough capital to build their own plant.
This kind of consolidation represented another trend in the industry.
The new corporation, with fourteen stockholders, became Atlas Linen
& Towel Services Company, with L. F. Turnbull as its first president.
During the next few years, Atlas bought out several smaller companies
and steadily grew.

Despite the rapid growth of the industry in the first two decades
of this century, linen supply was still undeveloped—and underde-
veloped—in many ways. Louis Friedman bespoke the experiences of
many when he recalled some of his early activities in the business,
starting in 1914 as the first employee of Youngstown Towel & Supply.
At the outset, he rode the old Ohio Interurban trolley cars while
servicing his territory. He would load several baskets of towels on
a car, ride with them (often on top of them) to the end of the line,
then hurriedly rent a horse and buggy to make his rounds to the fifty
or so offices that represented his customers. Even when interurban
trolleys were abandoned in favor of company horse-drawn wagons,
it was a dubious improvement. The Ohio roads were so rutted and
muddy that transportation was the bane of the average linen supplier's
professional existence.

"No one I called on cold-turkey had ever heard of linen supply,"
said Friedman, "and even selling three hand towels, a cabinet with
mirror, a comb and hair brush, and a supply of soap, all for 60 cents
a month took a lot of doing!"

By the time Maurice Maschke, Jr., joined veteran Louis Friedman
in founding Pioneer Linen Supply in Cleveland in 1937, the face of
the industry had changed tremendously. Maschke, who had started his
career in the practice of law, was to find that his background would
be increasingly useful in the corporate structure of linen supply. From

the days when the business was unknown to the public and legislators alike, to the time when he entered the field, more attention was being focused on the industry. There were matters of controversial legislation both Federal and local, more intricate tax structures and increasing government regulations. It was a far cry from hopping a trolley car, delivering a few bundles and trying to get potential customers to listen to the sales pitch.

It was on April 1, 1919, in the postwar era of doubt and change, that one of the giants of the industry, the National Linen Service Corporation, was born. The story goes back, however, much farther than 1919. In 1908, a young man, I. M. Weinstein, went to Atlanta to set up the Merchants Towel Supply Company as a representative of pioneer Fred McGonnigal of Cleveland. In World War I he joined the Army and saw action in France in 1918. He fought in the battles along the Somme River, and was severely wounded by machine gun fire during a combined American/Australian attack at Chipley Wood. Hospitalized abroad for four months before he could be returned to America, he began making plans for founding his own organization.

Thus it was that, on April 1st, 1919 National (first known as Atlanta Linen Supply Company) was started, in a former kitchen 12-feet long by 10-feet wide in the back room of an old wooden residence building on Walker Street in Atlanta. Total capitalization was $2,500, of which Weinstein furnished $1,500 and Herman Gross, an associate from the old Merchants Towel days, $1,000.

Within a few short months, ace salesman Weinstein and his partner, Herman Gross, landed so many accounts that the company outgrew its cramped kitchen quarters and the neighboring laundry became overworked. It was time for expansion.

Weinstein knew what he wanted to do: build a laundry. But that required money, and Weinstein had put most of his life's savings into starting the firm. Furthermore, banks did not generally lend money to linen suppliers. The banking fraternity then looked on linen suppliers as being in the "rag" business, without stability, inventory, good will, or other assets. Money had to be found elsewhere. Who knew how big the company might become if only the right person were to be found who could understand the potential!

One day in downtown Atlanta he stepped into a local shoe store. There, buying a new pair of shoes, was a short handsome man, A. J. Weinberg, who owned a drug store and who was one of Weinstein's customers.

The two talked amiably about the weather, economic conditions, sports.

Then Weinberg surprised Weinstein.

"I'd like to get in another business," he said. "The drug store is all right, but I'm thinking of real estate, or something else. I just don't know what it'll be."

"Look," Weinstein said, "if you're shopping around, think of the linen supply business. You've watched us. You've seen that we're growing fast. Why don't you join us? I'll show you the books and see whether we can work out something."

During the next few weeks, Weinberg, Weinstein and their accountants reviewed the books, talked things over, and finally drew up a contract. Weinberg would become one-third owner of the corporation, buying stock, and lending $6,000, the sum needed to build a laundry.

With the money used as down payment for machinery, a new 35 by 70-foot laundry building was built and equipped. One story high, it had large windows and a huge wooden doorway through which linens could be wheeled to and from the horse-drawn route wagons. The sparse equipment inside would make even modest laundries today look big by comparison. There were two flat washers, one extractor, three pressers, and a flatwork ironer. The plant did not even have a boiler.

"Look," Weinstein had said to his next-door neighbor, a man whose name has been lost in the records, "you have a boiler, and we need steam for laundry equipment we want to install. So let's make an arrangement."

"I'm game," the neighbor said. "That steam is going to waste anyway."

"Okay," Weinstein expanded his idea. "Let's make this deal. We'll supply the coal in order to get the steam." The neighbor agreed and the young company had power for its own plant.

The move into the new laundry and the joining of forces with Weinberg proved to be wise. During the next two years Weinberg ran the business end while Gross ran the laundry and Weinstein devoted himself to sales. The company grew steadily until there were six instead of just two horse-drawn routes and the recently built laundry was no longer big enough to meet production needs. Space had to be doubled and new machinery bought.

At this point there was a change in the organization. Gross, who had seen the Atlanta Supply Company grow, yearned to start his own business and move to Charlotte. He offered the chance to buy into Atlanta to a friend, J. B. Jacobs, who accepted, buying a substantial interest in the business.

The ambitious trio—Weinstein, Jacobs, and Weinberg—pooled energies and abilities to bring their young company into the forefront of the linen supply business. Their first decision was a major one. The three men agreed that local growth was not enough. Linen supply service had not as yet hit the South as it had either the East or the Midwest. The Southern market was relatively untapped. Since there were only a few other supply services, Weinstein, Jacobs and Weinberg saw the potential and went after it.

They contacted others in Atlanta and told them of the frontier in the linen supply field. Arrangements were made. The new men would build and operate businesses in different southern cities, with Weinstein and his partners providing the know-how. Partner Jacobs led off, going to Birmingham. Another Atlantan went to Savannah, still another to Chattanooga. Everywhere they used the same techniques, developing large volume to bring customer prices lower.

Each of the plants succeeded, with Atlanta's volume leading the way so fast that within a few years a new building was erected. Thought of as a "palace" in comparison with the first laundry, the long one-story building, housing a great deal of new equipment, contained some 20,000 square feet. Other plants in the organization were also expanding, and additional ones were being opened.

Weinstein became known for his ingenuity at coping with emergencies and "impossible" situations. On one occasion, during the disastrous 1926 hurricane in Florida, he received a message at the home office in Atlanta that the firm's Miami plant had been seriously damaged and needed immediate supplies. When railroad officials told him that the rail lines were congested and service critically disrupted so that little freight could get through, Weinstein contracted for a freight car and loaded the necessary supplies and repair equipment. Then he rode with the freight to Miami, talking his way through whenever railroad dispatchers were about to shuttle the car to a siding.

Then there was the time when National was to open a new plant in New Orleans. Weinstein had arrived in the city a few days earlier and was shocked upon awakening one morning to learn that floods had swept through the city and his new plant was three feet deep in water. With transportation at a halt, he commandeered a rowboat, and rowed from the hotel to the plant. There he stripped off most of his clothes and waded in. He was so successful leading what employees he could muster in moving supplies and equipment out of danger that National was the first plant in the stricken city to get back into operation.

Running separate operations in Birmingham, Atlanta and other cities had inherent disadvantages. Purchasing was not easy to centralize. One plant followed policies different from those of another. It seemed to Weinstein that the various plants would gain from a more formal organization, just as the Consolidated group had gained by merging in New York City.

So in 1927 the Southern Linen Service Corporation was formed, with Weinstein, Jacobs and Weinberg as its principals. During the intermittent years, plants were added in Winston-Salem, Miami, New Orleans, Mobile and Jacksonville. Jacobs returned to Atlanta, turning over the Birmingham plant to a manager. Gross sold his Charlotte plant to the company, and returned to Atlanta as manager of Atlanta Linen. By 1928 the company operated in ten Southern cities, with a gross volume of $75,000 monthly—almost a million-dollar-a-year business.

"In those days," A. J. Weinberg, now an octagenarian, reminisced "clerks in grocery and meat markets didn't wear aprons. We sold them the idea, and we also sold the barber shops on the idea of renting towels.

"We had come in at the right time. The South was just awakening to the possibilities of having industry in the region. The area was changing, and we tried to pick those cities that were having the greatest industrial growth."

Weinstein and his partners continued to visit cities where there was a possibility for expansion. They carefully considered the city's prospects, payrolls, living conditions and related matters. In some cities, they offered to buy existing organizations, in others, they started new companies.

Most of all they wanted to really consolidate all the Southern operations, and forge ahead on a larger scale. The money now needed was tremendous in contrast to the $6,000 required in 1920 for laundry equipment. Partner A. J. Weinberg contacted Sidney W. Souers of the Canal Bank & Trust Company in New Orleans, one of the first of a few farsighted men in the banking industry to recognize the growth potential of linen supply.

"We want to consolidate all our operations," Weinberg told Souers. "We figure we need $1 million to buy out the other firms and form a National Linen Service Corporation."

Linen supply men who had sought loans at other banks had become accustomed to rejections; the comment was usually, no matter what the sum asked. "That's a lot of money to lend on the basis of dirty towels."

But Souers was different.

"We'll let you have $500,000 to start, then in six months we'll lend another $250,000, and if you need it, another $250,000 six months later." The agreement signed, Weinstein then set about consolidating all the branches, forming the National Linen Service Company.

When the depression came, National Linen Service was in a unique position. Although linen supply companies in other parts of the country felt the pressures of a weaker economy, National Linen continued to grow. Weinberg recalls that in those years people in the South did not have the money to buy linens and towels so instead they rented them.

So fast did linen rental service business grow in the South that by the onset of World War II, National Linen was doing a gross volume of $20 million annually in thirty-four plants, from Florida throughout the South, as far north as Virginia and with affiliates in Texas and Los Angeles. It had grown from a one-room operation with two horse-drawn routes to an organization with more than 500 trucks, whose routes now radiated as far afield as two hundred miles from a plant. Instead of having two stockholders, as the Atlanta Linen Supply Corporation did, it had 1500 by 1944 and was listed on the New York Stock Exchange. To meet its own needs for supplies, it had formed the Empire Manufacturing Company to make all its garments, using over 10 million yards of cloth annually; enough, as one writer phrased it, "to stretch once around the world and then on to New Zealand." It also had established its own cabinet maker, the Alsco Manufacturing Company, its own soap manufacturing plant, its own truck body and repair and painting department, a complete machine shop to repair parts for washing machines and other equipment, and a house organ with a circulation of 4700 for its employees.

In 1943, from its thirty-four plants, National Linen delivered 630,966,648 pieces of freshly laundered linen to 200,000 customers. These linens were washed with more than one million pounds of soap, and the company paid a tax of more than $1,687,000.

In 1969 National Linen Service, whose president was L. V. Ludwig, a Georgia Tech graduate and an NLS employee for 35 years, had sixty-five linen supply plants and twenty-eight other service outlets in twenty-four states, serving 500,000 customers. It was now a division of National Service Industries, Inc. which had eight other divisions. National Service Industries, Inc., reported an annual dollar sales volume for all of its divisions of $289 million in 1969. The chairman of the board of the parent company is Milton Weinstein, son of founder I. M. Weinstein. The son had taken the business where the father had left off and built it into a nearly 300-million-dollar-a-year organization.

Competition in the early 1920s was tough for a number of reasons. It was not easy to turn prospects into customers because, for one thing, the idea of renting linens was not universally accepted. As Moe Struminger, who entered the industry in 1921, pointed out in an interview not long ago, firms tended to specialize. Their fields of opportunity were far more narrow than in later years because they aimed their business at specific types of customers, such as barbershops or restaurants; or they carried only a limited number of items. It started with hand towels, then office towels, then butcher's aprons, barber's towels and barber's aprons. The renting of bed linens and uniforms was not widespread. Only later came full acceptance of such items as colored coats for banks and other institutions, mechanics' overalls or hospital supplies. A company today which tried to do business under the limitations of the early and middle twenties would have rough sledding.

Competition did not always follow the Marquis of Queensbury rules, as evidenced by this typical account, reported in a Kansas City newspaper in 1922:

> The teeming centuries of history . . . reveal no more persistent fight than that being waged daily in the county recorder's office by two rival towel supply companies of Muskogee.
>
> For some reason or other . . . the Martin Towel Supply Company and the Muskogee Company, doing a similar business, have the idea they are each under contract to deliver towels.
>
> The delivery man of one company arrives on the scene at an early hour of the day; removes the towel rack of his competitor from the wall along with the cabinet provided, feeling he has won out. Within a few hours, the other company's man comes on duty and promptly sees to it that the first man's rack and cabinet are taken down.
>
> So far the only casualties reported are a few towels that have been treated with scorn for no reason other than that they belonged to the other company. The cabinets, however, are showing signs of weakening, under the strain of daily removal and replacing and the chances are that the county commissioners will be called upon soon to decide who's in the towel supply business in this particular office.

Growth of the more established firms was constant during the 1920s. The industry was beginning to realize that greater efficiency could be achieved in larger organizations. More linen supply work meant that the laundry could operate at a higher percentage of capacity, routes could be scheduled more efficiently, and the overhead cost per item handled could be lower.

So in the 1920's and ever since, the expansion of firms became commonplace. In the *Linen Supply News* of March, 1923 a small item points out that "Frank Selmier of St. Louis and Indianapolis, operating the Frank Selmier Towel Supply Co., has purchased the business of Louis H. Schaum and the South Side Towel Co. of St. Louis, which he is merging with his own business in that city."

Ads were placed frequently in *Linen Supply News,* offering to buy businesses. An advertisement in March 1929 says:

> WANTED TO BUY—Linen Supply Company, located in the middle west, doing a gross business of $1,000 per week or better. State full equipment, percentage of family laundry work, present indebtedness, terms desired.

All replies will be treated strictly confidential. Also state time convenient to you for survey. Reply Box 315, *Linen Supply News.*

Other notices of merger appeared frequently. Thus, in July 1929, the Peerless Towel Company and the Individual Towel Company in Philadelphia merged.

By the beginning of 1929 the linen supply industry possessed two elements that denoted prosperity: financial stability and substantial real property. The future looked bright, keynoted by the comment of an anonymous participant at the annual convention who told a reporter, "I, for one, am glad to be a member of an industry that is so healthy, so vibrant, and with such a vast and exciting potential as linen supply."

But on the morning of October 24, 1929, the era of postwar prosperity came abruptly to an end. The Great Depression was on its way. It was estimated that stocks declined in value during the course of the next two months alone by about $15 billion. What would happen to linen supply, when the giants on all sides were toppling? Oddly enough, even as the worst of all American depressions was starting, the linen supply industry was optimistic. It was a not locked into Wall Street the way other industries were, and it had a much-needed service to offer, which might be even more in demand during hard times.

Sam Miller of Cleveland sounded the general note of optimism: "While the past year (1929) was a good one, with the exception of the last two months, we are looking forward to a good steady business for the year 1930."

F. M. Steiner, in Minneapolis wrote:

> This is a year for us to see that "cleanliness" is put over big. Everything is being done to broaden the market for use of clean linen. A half million dollar financing fund was recently provided by the American Soap and Glycerine Producers to promote cleanliness. The need . . . is not more business—the need of our business is encouragement, self-control and confidence in one another.

G. A. Steiner said, "I am always optimistic about the future. As evidence of this, the various linen supply companies in which I am interested have extensive plans for improvements already under way."

Al Gitlow wrote: "For the past year business has been fair, but it is rather slow at present. However, I do hope that business will liven up for 1930."

But, as the depression deepened, the linen supply industry also suffered. Prices dropped alarmingly, with many suppliers striving frantically to stay in business, offering prices that were at cost. "Bobtailers" (men who did not have their own laundering plants) sprang up everywhere, exerting another downward pressure on prices.

Collective sales groups were formed. Under this arrangement, companies took all their salesmen off the payroll, and the men were then employed by a central bureau. The business the salesmen obtained was allocated to the various companies. One day a salesman solicited for Company A. The next day, he solicited for Company B. to meet its quotas. For a while this potentially strife-ridden arrangement worked. But after a year or thereabouts, squabbles among suppliers erupted, ending the bureaus. While the system was working, one linen supplier, stood up at a meeting and announced:

"Gentlemen, a year ago I told you, my friends and competitors, how wonderful you are. Tonight, I'm saying the same thing, but I mean it."

By 1932, the effects of the Depression had been seriously felt by all industries, large and small, across the country and even abroad. In an article in June of that year, entitled "Fish—Or Cut Bait!" industry spokesman Abe Papp, who had started with Mechanics Apron and Towel Supply in Roxbury, Massachusetts in 1904, had this to say:

> The time has come for honest thinking and concerted action in the Linen Supply Industry. In the rosy days before the depression struck us, many linen supply dealers were obsessed with the idea that they were really clever because it was so easy for them to pick up new business and make money in spite of competition. It was clear sailing in a buyers' market.
>
> In those days we had what the customer wanted. The customer had the money to pay us for it. The picture is now reversed. Many of these customers have not the money with which to buy our services and we do not know how to find an additional market to replace our lost patronage.
>
> With all the progress made in our organized trade agreements, no progress had been made in developing facts surrounding the linen supply industry, from plant organization, production, finance, management and distribution standpoints.
>
> Through the depression's severe jolts, we have been thoroughly aroused to our weaknesses. We now realize that permanent expansion of our business is to be obtained only through a thorough knowledge of our own business and through educating the public by means of proper publicity as to what our industry as a whole really is.
>
> In those rosy pre-depression days, success made the individual dealer so conceited in his own ability that he held the trade organization representing his special industry in contempt, but now, when he is getting bumped from every direction he realizes that the future salvation of

his business depends upon the help this same trade organization can render. He now wants to get on board and shoud be permitted to do so, providing he is willing to play the game squarely.

It has been twenty years since the founding of the organization that was eventually to become the Linen Supply Association of America, but the Association, shunned by many suppliers and only half-heartedly joined by others still had a long way to go. Perhaps in retrospect the Depression was more of a blessing than a catastrophe for the linen supply industry. Certainly it provided a much-needed shock that was to stimulate later development and growth. But that story will come later. For the moment, let us turn back the calender to the origin of the Association.

CHAPTER **6**

THE IMPERATIVE
OF ASSOCIATION

**IDEAS BORN OUT OF
NECESSITY LEAD TO
NEW ORGANIZATION**

" . . . in the internal workings of natural selection an instinct for order has been found superior to an impulse for disorder. If nature abhors a vacuum, it likewise abhors anarchy . . . "

These words by Robert Ardrey, studying the organizational instincts of nature, ranging from fish to birds and beasts of prey, might well be applied to the society of man and the works he has created under the label of "industry." As the 20th Century entered its second decade, linen suppliers found themselves in a curious state of disorder. Many, individually, were making substantial profits, increasing their business, extending their routes. Yet they found themselves a strange new breed, often without acceptance in the contemporary business world, and generally without a tangible professional concept. The whole idea of service needed a clear interpretation. It was still a muddled concept. And, while service was talked about a great deal and heavily touted as one of the great benefits to be derived from linen supply, even the most astute industry spokesman would admit that the definition was vague.

The idea of association came about largely through necessity and an instinct for order that can be likened to the understanding that Mr. Ardrey much later achieved through his observations of nature. No one in the industry, including the old timers who were involved with the formation of the original association, can recount exactly where or when or how the idea was born. Most agree, however, that the beginnings can be traced back to late 1911, inasmuch as the first meeting and dinner of what was to be the Tri-State Linen Supply Association was held in Cincinnati, Ohio, in June, 1912. Many feel that the late A. Pierce Shupe was the man who sparked the action. At that time he headed Cleveland Towel Supply Company, the business he had started in 1891. It is certain that he was an able organizer and administrator and that he believed in the value of association during his long career which ended with his death in 1939. He not only served as an officer of Tri-State, but later as the first President of the National Linen Association of America (now the L. S. A. A.), as well as president of the old Ohio Towel and Linen Association and of the Cleveland Linen Club.

Other Cleveland personalities involved with the formation of the Tri-State Association were Sam Miller of Independent Towel, Jake Goldman, Clarence Roskoph and Sam Goldberg, of Union Towel. At first, the organization was local, but it began to take on statewide dimensions when Dan Ziegler of Ziegler Towel Supply became a member, followed shortly by firms from Detroit, Michigan and Indianapolis, Indiana.

Just prior to the outbreak of World War I in Europe, events were taking place unsettling to the industry and disruptive of what had orginally been a simple and orderly process of supply. No longer did suppliers face just the normal business problems of soliciting, getting the linen washed, delivering the linens, and collecting the monies owed. Their market was threatened. The roller towel, sewn on both ends and hung around a wooden roller, had been one of their items most often supplied. Its use was being questioned.

The attack came from two quarters. Health officials contended that the spread of disease could be traced to the use of the public roller towel. Any person could dry his hands on the same part of the towel someone else had used. And if germs were on the towel, they reasoned, the second person was likely to pick up a disease.

Without generalship, suppliers in each area where the roller towel was under attack were stunned. The health officials seemed to know what they were talking about, but did their negative reaction mean that towel linen supply would soon cease to exist? Each supplier wondered whether he should continue to supply roller towels. If he stopped, he knew another competitor might supply similar towels to his accounts, because part of the public still wanted them.

A second attack came from the companies which had developed paper towels and found there was a market for them. Executives in that industry had reasoned that if linen suppliers could supply cotton towels, the paper producers could supply paper ones in direct competition. Even though these towels did not have the same absorbency and touch characteristic of cotton, the paper industry began to make substantial headway.

Realizing they faced new problems, but not knowing how to tackle them, linen suppliers in Cincinnati gathered together. Uppermost in their minds was the possibility of imminent legislation against the roller towel. In the midst of this meeting, one supplier proposed, "We're not the only ones facing this problem. What we should do is have a meeting of as many linen suppliers as possible, from many cities around here, to see if we can figure out what to do."

The group agreed. In the name of the Cincinnati Towel Mens' Club, they invited suppliers from Cleveland, Indianapolis, Dayton, Columbus and other cities, as well as a number of manufacturers of laundry equipment.

As one of the men present later expressed it, "We didn't know exactly what we wanted to accomplish at the first meeting, but we thought that the growth of the industry was linked up with our each getting better acquainted with the other and our working on mutual problems."

Men from many cities responded, and some of these were later to play important roles in the Linen Supply Association of America. There was Abe Shupe, of course; Dan Ziegler, whose business was situated across the river, in Covington, Ky.; Sam Miller, also from Cleveland;

Edward Mikkelsen, the cabinet manufacturer who had made those special cabinets for Fred Martin; Frank Selmier, whose business was in Indianapolis; and Carl Aull, from Detroit.

More than thirty-five men gathered at the Palace Hotel in Cincinnati, at 9 o'clock Tuesday morning, February 18, 1913. Considering the difficulty of travel, and that few linen suppliers could afford to take time off from work it was a remarkable gathering. They sat, discussed and argued for two days. On the first day, they decided to form the Ohio Linen Supply Association.

> The object for which this association is formed is to advance the interest of the towel and toilet supply houses in the State of Ohio.
>
> *First*—By bringing about better sanitary conditions.
>
> *Second*—By increasing the efficiency of service.
>
> *Third*—By diffusing among our patrons accurate and reliable information concerning the towel and linen supply business.
>
> *Fourth*—By promoting a larger and more friendly interest among those engaged in this business.

The following day the participants agreed unanimously on a strategy for attacking the roller towel problem:

> BE IT RESOLVED. by the Ohio Linen Supply Association in convention assembled: that—
>
> Whereas, the general dissemination of scientific knowledge, coupled with our practical experience in the toilet supply business, has brought home to us the knowledge that the individual towel is more to be desired from the standpoint of health and cleanliness than the common towel, and
>
> Whereas the members of this organization can, through diligent efforts, educate the users of towels throughout the State of Ohio to a degree where they will appreciate this fact,
>
> THEREFORE BE IT RESOLVED that all of the members of this organization instruct their employees to solicit no further orders for common towels and that their said employees be further instructed to inform all applicants for common towels of the desirability of the individual towel, and to present facts, arguments and literature to all such applicants to the end that they may be convinced that from the standpoint of health the individual towel is the proper thing to use. And
>
> Be it further resolved that the members of this organization shall use their best efforts to replace all common towels, wherever in use, with individual towels as speedily as business conditions and good judgment will permit. And

> BE IT FURTHER RESOLVED that we do hereby congratulate the State Board of Health and its Secretary upon the wise and judicious manner in which they have handled the towel question.

The Association was in existence. It had taken its first step. It had also made provisions for permanence. There would be dues: $5 yearly for each member. Thirty-five agreed to become paying members. The Association's total receipts for its first year of existence were $175. Expenses for that first year totaled $51.01. The secretary of the Association, Carl Aull of Cincinnati, purchased a Proudfit Loose Leaf Secretary Book for $4.21, and there were other expenses such as "$3.80—Alcorn Multi Letter Shop." Net balance for that first year of operation was $123.99. The Association was off to a good start, under the leadership of Abe Shupe, a fiery orator in the William Jennings Bryan tradition.

The following year, the Ohio Linen Supply Association met again, this time in Toledo. Carl Aull, the secretary, filed his report:

> Members reported last report were 36; since then we have received eight applications, making a total of forty-four . . . Remember, fellow members, that the Ohio Linen Supply Association is the first State to organize a State Association for the Linen Supply interests. It is a new movement that others will follow until we have a strong national organization. Remember, when suggestions come to your mind that will help others, send them to the Secretary. We will make mistakes, to be sure, but let us profit by our blunders.

Already the Association was moving into cooperative endeavors designed to aid and instruct members. L. J. Oehler, a linen supplier spoke on "Membership and How to Increase It." Then, in open session, the members discussed ever-present problems, many of which still rank at the top of any linen supply meeting agenda, such as "How to Cut Down the Abuse of Towels."

The following year, 1915, in Dayton, linen suppliers heard D. Frank Garland, Director of Correction & Welfare, speak on "Public Service from the Standpoint of Welfare," and Dr. Light, Chief Health officer of Dayton, discuss "Infection." Now there were fifty-two members in the Association, including significant additions to the roster: the Empire State Towel Supply and the Niagara Linen Supply, members from New York State, and the American Linen Supply and the Memphis Steam Laundry Company. Word of the Association had been spreading and the time was ripe to enlarge its scope.

On March 2nd, W. T. Ayers of Ashland, Ohio, then president of the Association, made a speech which was to set the future tone of Association activities. First he asked that the Association be expanded:

It seems to me that the objects of this Association will be better and more completely accomplished if the field is enlarged and the actual membership includes the men engaged in the linen supply industry in the Eastern and Central States—say, New York, Pennsylvania, Ohio, Kentucky, Indiana, Illinois and Michigan. Such an organization will give a much better opportunity for the exchange of ideas and experience, make a more efficient organization and give us greater influence in our respective committees.

We know that men in other states are in sympathy with our organization; else we would not find them in our midst today . . . There is no doubt in my mind that the broadening of the field will give this Association greater influence and be more helpful to its members.

Second, Ayers pointed out that the essence of a good linen supply business is service in the best and broadest sense of the word: "To me there is no greater word in the English language than SERVICE. This doesn't mean only commercial service to our customers, or patrons, but service to our fellow man, our friends and competitors, if you please."

Expanding on this theme, Ayers enlarged upon a major problem that has continually plagued the linen supply business:

Because a man is your business competitor is no reason why he should not be your friend. Because he underbids you and takes some of your business, don't go about "getting even" with him, or "making him like it." Be patient with him and show how he has injured himself more than he has injured you. Show him where he has made the mistake. Surely the right kind of service from him is worth as much to the customer as is yours . . . Some are more successful than others because they have given the right kind of service, because they have been giving their customers full value in the service rendered, not because they have resorted to sharp practices with their competitors.

On March 2, 1915, the convention acted upon his first proposal, that the Association be expanded, by passing the following resolution:

"Whereas, we believe by changing the constitution of the Ohio Linen Supply Association and making it of broader scope the desired results can be accomplished, therefore be it resolved that the name of this association shall be the Inter State Linen Supply Association."

To broaden the scope of the Association, the members also resolved that "the object for which this Association is formed is to advance the interest of the towel and toilet supply firms in Ohio, Pennsylvania, Kentucky, New York, Illinois, Michigan & Missouri."

Farsighted men, they realized that some day there would have to be a national Association. But, for the moment they held back. The organization was growing, but not yet ready to become national. By now, it had also become evident that the competition from paper would continue to have an effect on linen supply.

Carl Aull, the man who would be president of the Association in 1917, faced the problem squarely. In an address delivered at the 1915 convention, he related the inroads that the paper towel was making, and again pointed to the advantages that the cotton towel presented to customers. The address, titled: "Paper Towels vs. Fabric," was the first of many on this subject to be aired at linen supply association meetings. Frank Selmier, who would become next president, expounded on, "Delivery, Drivers and the Checking of Customers and Drivers," a subject that was, and is, a major cost for all linen suppliers; for if drivers do not check the number of linens given to a customer correctly, costs mount.

The Association was moving toward becoming truly national, providing a forum for discussion of problems of linen suppliers throughout the country. Its interests were no longer just the immediate Midwest. Now there was a growing realization that this was the nucleus of an organization that could provide many services, to all linen suppliers, guiding them through difficult times, sponsoring research, finding methods that would enable them to perform a better service at less cost. In unity there was indeed strength, since few or none of the firms were large enough to develop alone the kind of services and information needed to help them function better. There was a yearning for knowledge, for information on latest developments, for discussions that would enable linen suppliers in all areas to face their problems intelligently.

The time to become national arrived in 1916. Carl Aull had become president. Shupe had been president for the first two years, and Ayers the third year, when the association was known as Inter State. At the 1916 convention, a motion was made from the floor.

"Be it resolved that we amend the constitution to embrace all the towel men and linen supply men of America and further be it resolved to recommend that we change the name to National Linen Supply Association."

What was later to become the Linen Supply Association of America had been formed. It was still small with only eighty-four members listed on the roster. By now, the New Haven Coat & Apron & Towel Company, founded in Connecticut before the turn of the century, had become a member, as had the Spokane Toilet Supply Company, in the state of Washington, and Waterbury (Connecticut) Coat & Apron & Towel Supply. There was the Austin Linen & Towel Supply Company of Chicago, Illinois, owned by Frank Hartless, who was to play a later prominent role in Association affairs. A number of manufacturers had also joined. In addition to American Laundry Machinery Company, there was Best & Company, Troy Laundry Machinery Company, Angelica Jacket Company, Ben Bimberg, Theodore Mayer Company, and others.

Now that the Association was national in name and purpose, it was also decided that the next meeting should not be held in Ohio, where the first three had been held (the fourth had been in Indianapolis). Detroit became the site for the 1917 convention—a decision that in time would have a lasting effect on the future of the Association and the industry. For, at this meeting there appeared a young reporter, Jake Smith, 5'7", thin, dark, and active, who wrote for a Detroit paper, and also for the *Starchroom Laundry Journal,* a magazine devoted to the laundry and allied industries. He came to the meeting to report on its activities. But as he talked to the men in this fledgling industry, he began to visualize the need for a trade publication serving linen supply exclusively. Here was a young business field, with its own problems, in some respects in direct competition with the laundry industry. The interests of the readers of the *Starchroom Laundry Journal* were obviously not always the same as the interests of linen suppliers.

Shortly before the convention ended, Smith approached the executive officers.

"Gentlemen," he said, "I would like to propose to you that a trade magazine be published exclusively for your industry. I think I can handle it. All I may need is a little assistance from you."

Such men as Carl Aull, the new president, Clarence Roskoph of Cleveland, Frank Hartless, the man who would be secretary for many years, Sam Miller, who was in at the beginning of the Association and who would be treasurer for many years, Frank Selmier, a former president and Joseph Burroughs, who had come from Oakland, California, listened attentively.

"It's a good idea," Aull said. Everyone agreed. The Association's officers promised to help subsidize the *Linen Supply News,* a promise they never had to keep because the magazine became immediately self-sustaining.

Throughout his years as publisher of *Linen Supply News* until 1929, when he died at the age of 43, Jake Smith had one goal in mind: Build the Association; work for the Association; the industry needs it. To that end he ran many articles pointing up Association activities, to interest potential members in its activities, and to keep interested members dedicated. He often journeyed to other cities to assist in the formation of local groups or to aid in their reorganization, most of the time at his own personal expense.

The first issue of *Linen Supply News* appeared in September, 1917, in which Smith defined the magazine objective:

> This will introduce the *Linen Supply News.*
>
> It is the only publication in the world devoted exclusively to the linen and towel supply industry.
>
> It will fill a long-felt want because it will be a clearing-house for all worthwhile information relating to the industry.
>
> It has the full endorsement of the National Linen Supply Association. . . .

In that first issue—made up of eight pages, with one picture, of Alex Gammell, of Chicago, the Association's newly elected president, Jacob Smith reported extensively on the Association convention in the firm belief that the more linen suppliers around the country knew of the Association's activities, the more would join. Much of what was discussed at the convention, Smith reported, concerned local conditions, and how linen suppliers had to protect themselves against cut-throat pricing.

In the historic first issue of *Linen Supply News,* major problems were pointed out. Paper, was one. Former president, Frank Selmier of Indianapolis said bluntly: "I am in the towel business, and we will supply any kind of towel the customer wants—whether it be paper, roller or individual." Many disagreed, feeling that the paper towel business did not belong with linen supply, though in time a number of suppliers did become distributors of paper too.

There was also in that issue a letter from L. F. Turnbull, the Association's next president, succeeding Gammell. He told of business conditions in St. Louis.

> Mr. Ralph Kelfer and Mr. Goldstein, operating under the firm name Olive-Boston Barber Supply Company, have gone into the general laundry business. It may be said that St. Louis in the towel supply business is rapidly becoming motorized. Nearly all companies operate exclusively with automobiles. There are forty towel companies operating in St. Louis and only through intelligent Association work has it been possible to prevent a condition of chaos.

The *Linen Supply News'* first advertisement was contributed by the J. B. Ford Company, of Wyandotte, Michigan, manufacturers of soap who had also sent seven representatives to the Association Convention. Although no available records detail that many linen suppliers had laundry or processing plants by 1917, this soap-manufacturing company considered the field worth cultivating. "It saves on the amount of other and more expensive supplies," the ad assured its readers, "and the work it assists the Linen Supply man to turn out pleases the customer. Is it working for you?"

The second issue of *Linen Supply News* moved on to other topics. The convention was over and the big news of the past meeting had become dry ink. But that hardly meant the Association was to lie dormant until the next meeting. Alexander Gammell, in a lead editorial, asked for support for the Association and pointed out its values:

> Long before I was a member of any association, I began to feel the need of knowing my competitor personally. I called on him and found that he could bake a delicious apple on his steam radiator (which isn't a bad thing to know) and also that he was selling a 30-inch towel for the same price I was getting for a 36; That he had a lot of my goods all right, and was using them—but like myself would prefer his own—SO WE TRADED. That when a fellow approached me to launder seventy-five coats in a hurry, on which I found a competitor's name—by communicating with this competitor I discovered the same party had been to see him the day before wanting 100 coats, bearing my name, laundered in a hurry. AGAIN WE TRADED, and the man who was in a hurry was compelled to do business with other supply men who had not yet discovered the benefit of knowing each other.
>
> During this great epidemic of high prices of materials—we must collectively produce a sound business basis on which to stand. The uninformed must be taught the cost of production. When one member finds a good market in which to buy—the opportunity should be extended to other members. Syndicate buying is showing wonderful results in many lines of business. Every supplyman in the United States should become affiliated. If you have not yet sent in your application, DO IT NOW.

The drive was on to expand all association activities throughout the United States. In that same issue, there appeared the first conclusive report on a topic of major concern to all linen suppliers: Soap.

> An investigation of the soap conditions in the country reveals the facts that there is a growing scarcity of raw materials used for the production of laundry soaps. (World War I was imposing restrictions.)
>
> The increased cost of the soap has brought the question to the mind of laundry men that soap is largely wasted and unused by washmen and that its use as a lubricant and detergent is not appreciated by all.

The magazine also contained advertisements from five companies. In addition to J. B. Ford, there was an advertisement from Theodore Mayer & Company advertising "featuring as usual fabrics especially adapted for the hard use incident to the linen supply trade, new accounts solicited;" Angelica Jacket Company—"Buy Angelica Service Linens if you want the best—but contract for them now."

Hackneyed though it may be, the old saying "Necessity is the mother of invention," certainly had its place in the growth of the industry in the critical days during, and just following, World War I: First, there was the necessity for association, to discuss common problems and seek common solutions. Second, the necessity for an authoritative voice that would call out and hold together in a common purpose the men who comprised the industry. Members drew strength from the sharing of trade secrets and procedures and the exchange of constructive ideas, from mutual friendship and understanding and from the inspiration of designating and working toward common goals.

A great deal of refining still had to be done in establishing those goals clearly, and in defining the concept of service. In 1921, in an article entitled "Keep Up the Service," William F. Heissenbuttel urged linen suppliers to provide service in keeping with the times. With the country passing through a period of economic distress, he warned supply men against trying to oversell customers into buying more goods than they needed or could then afford. At the same time, the level of fine service had to be consistently maintained for the good of the individual companies and the industry as a whole:

> Nothing, in my judgment is more essential than that requests for a cutdown on service should be handled in the most dignified way, without endeavoring in any way to belittle the rearrangement, or to make the man feel small who is asking for lowered service at a lowered rate, and that the lower rate should be fair. . . .

This was one of the early definitions of "service" as a give-and-take arrangement with a long-range objective. The industry was becoming more service-conscious. That same year, Jonas Mayer, then of Theodore Mayer & Company, wrote an article, "Lower Prices of Better Service," in which he discussed the necessity to supply better goods and better service, regardless of price. In 1922, Tom O'Connell, of Chicago, said "The Linen Supply Business is strictly a service proposition, and the greatest contributing factor to success is the right kind of service." He suggested that the industry might do well to adopt the motto of the Rotary Clubs of America, "He Profits Most Who Serves Best."

A year later, an article in *Linen Supply News* stated, "I believe that most of us have been negligent in the giving of service to each other, for in my opinion therein lies the fundamental influences of giving better service to the public. . . . let us start by giving more and better service to each other." The author urged linen suppliers to look back on what the industry had been before the days when there was any association, and when there was no medium of communication like the *Linen Supply News*. The difference, he said, lay in the growing exchange of viewpoints and information.

In 1928, at the Cleveland Convention of June 12th to 15th, the Association adopted as the keynote of the convention: "SERVICE—the greatest word in the English language:"

> Service means usefulness. No man is a real, true live member unless he devotes part of his time to the best interests of his local and national Association . . . the Association renders one of its most important "SERVICES" to you, in order to enable you to improve and extend your "SERVICE" to your community.

By the end of its first decade, it was evident that the Association was moving beyond its initial role as a medium for fellowship and a forum for the discussion of problems. It was becoming something which had not been recognized in the beginning: a force that would have an increasingly important impact on linen supply and the country's economy.

"Unsung heroes of linen supply" is a phrase that could aptly be applied to the persons who have served as full-time secretaries or executive heads of local, state, and regional associations of linen suppliers. At one time according to *Linen Supply News* there were over forty-five such groups.

The primary duties of the secretaries embraced public relations, labor negotiations, personnel problems, clearance of textiles that found their way to the wrong plant, arbitration. To help their member companies grow with profit, they were also practicing economists.

In the years when linen service was considered intra-state and when the codes required by the National Recovery Administration provided for joint industry action on pricing practices, the secretaries sometimes acted as coordinators to minimize the possibility of their members entering into ruinous price wars. These men were on call day and night, because as in much association work, especially that done on a local basis, they were expected to cope with the personal problems of members as well as their business problems.

Over the years the number of such associations has dwindled to around sixteen. These groups, of which ten are state and regional, are involved in union negotiations, state and local legislation, personnel work, public relations, and educational activities. Most of the regional and state groups hold sales and production clinics as well as annual meetings.

Secretaries who have been with their associations for ten years or more are Milton R. Durrett of Birmingham, Robert M. Place of California (state), Matthew J. Dooley of San Francisco (local), Gordon L. Rayner of Boston (local, state, regional), Wilbur A. Sale of St. Louis (local), Jack Orlinsky of New Jersey (state), Katherine L. Fay of New York (local), William B. Shaffer of Cincinnati (local), A. L. Stromberg of Cleveland (local and state), James G. Swindells of Portland, Oregon (state), Hugo Swan of Dallas (regional), and William H. Short of Seattle (regional). Stromberg has been with his association for 39 years, Rayner for 36 years and Orlinsky for 31 years. In Canada Norman A. Rill of Montreal has been the secretary of the Quebec Institute of Linen and Industrial Supply Services, Inc. for many years.

The imperative of association had been established beyond question.

CHAPTER **7**

THE RESPONSIBILITIES OF ASSOCIATION

**AS THE VOICE
GROWS STRONGER,
IT IS ALSO HEARD FARTHER**

Many a young man during World War II, elated at having finally won his gold bars as a second lieutenant, was cautioned by his superiors to remember two abbreviations: "R.H.I.P." and "R.H.I.R." The first meant that "Rank Has Its Privileges," certain rights and rewards that the enlisted men could not enjoy. More importantly, the second indicated that "Rank Has Its Responsibilities," and that in return for privileges, officers were expected to discharge duties and bear the various burdens associated with rank.

Those members who initially joined the Linen Supply Association of America in order to derive the obvious and numerous benefits it afforded were likewise soon to learn that although the privileges of affiliation were many, so too were the responsibilities. LSAA, however, was fortunate in that even during its formative period, when the organization was neither large nor affluent enough to employ a full-time staff, there were many dedicated members who gave perhaps even more than they received.

One of these leaders was Frank Hartless of Chicago, who week after week, year after year, traveled through the Midwest, urging linen suppliers to join the national association. Another was Abe Shupe, president again in 1923, of whom in that year, the *Linen Supply News* reported:

> He completed a three-weeks tour of the largest cities between Cincinnati and New York City. . . . Every phase of the linen and towel supply business was discussed at the business sessions, and it was the unanimous verdict of the local dealers that Mr. Shupe's visit accomplished a great deal of good, not only enlightening them, but cementing them closer together.
>
> In every city, the theme of Mr. Shupe's remarks was the importance of good service, quality laundering, national organization and the coming national convention in Kansas City. He emphasized to dealers that the great possibilities of this industry will come only when we have improved our service, when we have served linens and towels of immaculate white, when our national organization is stronger, and when we attend our national convention in greater numbers.

In a typical speech delivered in Buffalo Shupe pointed out:

> If you provide good service, you won't have to worry about the price cutter. You can't grow and develop new business unless you get all your service is worth. No price-cutter can give quality service. The dealer is a poor, deluded fool who cuts prices below cost. More business is being driven away from our industry by poor service than because of its prices.

Shupe not only emphasized the present conditions of the industry, but also focused on future challenges. He forecast that the continuous towel cabinet would be the coming thing, imperfect though it still was, and would ultimately prove to be the most powerful competitive weapon in the battle against paper.

One of the services the Association performed in those early days was to pass along information on successes achieved with the continuous towel. The *Linen Supply News* reported that continuous towels were indeed big aids in sales campaigns.

"The continuous towel cabinet," said George Crawford of Bridgeport, "seems to be the only thing in sight at the present."

Jake Cowen of Hartford also pointed out in the same issue: "I am putting out a lot of continuous cabinets and I have some very large users, one whose bill runs $500 per month."

Steve Howland of New Bedford said he was supplying 800 individual towels per day to a cracker factory.

From Chicago, Frank Hartless reported: "We feel the same in Chicago about the continuous towel. One concern in Chicago has built up a tremendous business with the continuous cabinet, putting out approximately 10,000 rolls per month."

Shupe was not the only one to give so wholeheartedly of himself for the construction of a stronger membership. Wherever one turned, linen suppliers active in the Association made efforts to induce others to join.

Jake Smith, publisher of the *Linen Supply News* steadfastly promoted membership. The cover of the March, 1919 issue was devoted to the coming convention. "For every dollar you spend in going to Buffalo, you will get ten back in business knowledge. Formulate your plans now to attend the coming convention. Let nothing stand in your way . . . Please remember it is YOUR business to go."

The president of the Association, L. F. Turnbull, endorsed Smith's theme. "There is nothing in your particular business half so important as this trip. If you as ONE keep the spirit nationally alive, you as ONE will profit in keeping the spirit alive in your particular locality."

Pre-convention issues of *Linen Supply News* contained items in boldface type: "Secretary Frank H. Hartless of the LINEN SUPPLY ASSOCIATION invites every linen and towel supply dealer in the United States to attend the convention at (whichever city it was being held in).

By May of 1921, just before the Association was to meet in New York, president William F. Heissenbuttel, of Peerless in New York City reported, "Two years ago, New York was without a representative in the LINEN SUPPLY ASSOCIATION OF AMERICA. This year its members have relieved the National Officers entirely of the usual details of the convention and are standing shoulder to shoulder, taking care of every and any detail."

He noted that representatives from the New York Board of Health would be on hand to air their views on hygiene and industry and the role of linen supply in promoting sanitation.

The Association had also grown tremendously, he noted:

> We are fortunate in having 100 new members who will in all probability meet with us, but the doors of the convention are open to those who are not already members. It is true that the doings of the convention will be reported in the trade papers, but the trade paper cannot convey that sense of uplift which comes through rubbing shoulder to shoulder, and the trade paper cannot portray the exhibits of a convention hall. Think of it! At least a dozen devices for the winding and successful vending of individual and continuous towels, the newest thoughts in textiles and the latest prices! New styles of cabinets at after-the-war rates.

The growth of the Association continued under the auspices of a hyper-active membership committee. In June, 1922, *Linen Supply News* reported:

> Fred Martin, as General Chairman, was doing great work: Roy Turnbull of St. Louis, in addition to plugging for new members, has had entrusted to him the editing of a very neat little booklet containing the names of all members of the Association . . . Mr. Turnbull put a lot of time and effort on this "official membership" booklet because Roy never does things by halves. J. N. Burroughs of Oakland, California, has had a busy time securing new members, and so on.

Burroughs and Helfrich developed a series of letters to induce non-members to join. Burroughs' letter began: "Do you know that the Linen Supply Industry of America has one of the best national associations among trade organizations?" It went on:

> The time now seems ripe for those of us on the West Coast who are engaged in the towel and linen supply business to join hands. Several are already members of the national association. We want to make this a 100 per cent membership in a West Coast chapter . . . Dues are a minimum of $10 plus $5 per wagon.
>
> Will you please make this your next point of action? I am sure you are sufficiently familiar with the benefits of this Association. . . .

By the 1922 convention, many linen and towel suppliers in the New York area were actively engaged in the Association. R. S. Rose of Initial Towel Supply, and president of the Greater New York Towel Supply Association, William F. Loehler of Crescent Towel, and P. C. Langdon of Fowler Towel Supply attended the convention. And in the very same year, the Wheeler interests joined. *Linen Supply News* reported:

> When the LINEN SUPPLY ASSOCIATION OF AMERICA was first organized, many large firms did not take it very seriously but took the attitude that they were from Missouri . . . This is only natural with any new thing. The latest to become affiliated is the Wheeler interests of Boston, the largest operators of towel supply companies in the world . . . They have somewhere in the neighborhood of 250 branches located in all parts of America, Canada and Europe.

When the 1923 convention assembled in Kansas City, considerable awareness of growing responsibilities already existed. Abe Shupe, re-elected then as President, commended the tireless work of his predecessor, President Heissenbuttel, and commented on the responsibilities of office. He explained that in his own travels about the country, he was dedicated to trying to "instill the idea of cooperation," and added "I do hope the time will come when the members of this Association, and every man engaged in the industry in the United States, will seek not to see how cheaply he can put his goods out, but how well, how large, and how satisfied a patronage he can establish."

He spoke for many linen supply leaders, when he said:

> There is plenty of undeveloped business in this country. There could be twice as many people in it as there are, and they could all do well and prosper, but they can never do well by cutting prices simply to get business. I never saw a man get anywhere running around in a circle. You can't go out and give your goods an inferior grade service and have your customer satisfied; you are going to drive him to your competitor or to his own goods, and I hope and pray that the day is coming when you will all see that. Don't think that because years ago we put out one line, that that day is going to last forever. You have got to absolutely give a customer what he wants, charge him a fair price with a good profit for yourself, and then your customer will be satisfied and you will prosper. . . .

On September 22, 1929, the industry suffered a severe shock. Jake Smith, who had accomplished so much for the Association, died at Harper Hospital, in Detroit, at the age of 43. A self-educated, self-made man, he had earned much respect and affection from the industry, and many were the eulogies.

Condolences poured in from across the country and within a short time the sorrow had led to action in the memory of Jake Smith. With Abe Shupe as chairman, the linen supply Association set up the Jacob Smith Memorial Fund, one of a number the Association has since supported. Shupe dedicated the fund with these words:

> It seems hardly necessary for us to mention at this time that Jake as a child and a boy only knew as a home the Cleveland Jewish Orphan Asylum, and that he treasured in his heart the greatest feeling of love and affection for that institution which had been to him, mother, father, and home during his tender years . . . It was the thought of the committee, after serious consideration, to use the funds derived from contributions sent in by his friends and associates to endow a room or cottage at the Jewish Orphan Asylum, in perpetuity of his name, feeling by so doing it would not only be liquidating a debt of gratitude to Mr. Smith but at the same time perpetuate his memory and inspire the young boys who are now, and later probably will be inmates in that institution.

In the Detroit building where Smith had published *Linen Supply News,* another man, Bill Hurlbut, also had an office for his film-distributing company. The men had become close friends, and Bill had learned a great deal about the industry from Jake. In the emergency, Bill Hurlbut put together the next issue, for October 1929, and for the next thirty-two years remained the editor of *Linen Supply News.*

The magazine continued the same policies that Smith had established earlier. "Help Build the Association" was its constant plea. There was still no full-time executive director, no dynamic year-round program of research and development, and no book publication and film production program. The annual convention was the major activity, at which speakers pointed to possible solutions for individual and industry problems. A part-time secretary for the Association, Ida May Bateman, sold exhibit space for the conventions and handled routine matters. One subject continuously came to the fore at directors' meetings: the need to make linen supply better known. An intensive industry-wide effort, many felt, could do much to popularize linen supply and spur the growing use of its services.

In 1929 the LSAA Board of Directors decided that such an effort should be made. At the 1930 convention, Joseph Callner of Chicago, proposed that a National Education Campaign be directed to schools which in practically every instance had "no washing facilities," and for other groups. The aim was to install towel service in educational institutions at reasonable prices.

At the 1931 convention, members proposed a fund of $250,000 for the educational campaign. But Joe Callner, now president of the Association, as well as other committee members opposed the idea as impractical. First, the fund should be raised by voluntary contributions; second, industry members, even though they had supported the move, had not yet been educated to its potential; third, this was 1931, and $250,000 was an unrealistic sum when the country was in the throes of depression.

Instead, it was decided to run a test with money obtained by voluntary contributions from companies and local and regional associations.

With almost $10,000 thus raised, the Association developed a broad program, particularly for that time when the art of public relations was still young. The appropriate committee prepared truck posters about the value of linen service, pamphlets on "Uncleanliness Breeds Disease," and "Eat in Clean Restaurants," washroom posters, and a model speech that linen suppliers could give to local organizations.

Herman Cohn, director of the Department of Publicity and Education recorded:

> Some 178 members of the Association, or approximately 41% of our membership, are users of the printed advertising prepared by the department during the course of the past nine months. Of these there are 114 users of truck posters. During the period ended May 1st, the department expended a total of $8,957.16. The users of the materials paid part of the costs. We propose to continue with a second series of display posters and with a complete new campaign of pamphlets and envelope inserts. We are at work on the preparation of a Drivers' and Salesmen's Manual.

It had not been his intention, he continued in an unexpected aside, "to condemn the industry for its failure to cooperate 100% with the department. In a period of economic distress, it is only natural that men should give first attention to their present problems and look with misgivings to the future. This is a time when strong men will survive, and their strength can be found only through the application of sound business principle." But alas, the times were too chaotic. As much as the campaign was needed, it had to be dropped. Other objectives were more important. Survival came first.

At the 1931 convention, Callner reported that he had:

> 1) Prepared copy and distributed 119,450 KEEP KLEAN folders;
> 2) Distributed 223,500 Prosperity Seals in an effort to have members sell goodwill and show their optimism and faith to business . . . during the trying period ahead;
> 3) Prepared copy and sold 50,000 Price Cutting circulars, detailing the evils of price cutting;

4) Distributed to plant owners an article entitled, "Advertising the Laundry";

5) Prepared copy and sold 60,500 START CLEAN folders;

6) Began the use of a press-clipping service;

7) Assisted members on numerous matters.

"I call to mind particularly an incident," Callner said, "where a Portland, Oregon laundry owner, who is also a member of the Board of Education in that locality, addressed my office seeking information that would help him give the school children under his jurisdiction proper drying facilities."

Callner contacted the Cotton Textile Institute, who helped the supplier work out an acceptable plan that brought clean towel service to the school children.

The lack of an effective campaign did not, however, go unnoticed. For example, T. J. Hyland of the Midway Laundry and Linen Supply in Chicago wrote to *Linen Supply News* in November, 1935:

> I hope I am not being sacrilegious in comparing the advertising of Godliness by the clergy to the lack of advertising of cleanliness by the Linen Supply Industry. One advertising firm, Lord & Thomas, has placed 180 million dollars worth of advertising in the last five years . . . How much of this stupendous amount was spent by the linen supply industry advertising cleanliness? Close your eyes. What do you see? You have the correct answer. Strange as it may seem to you and me there are hundreds of thousands of people in this country who know not the meaning of Linen and Towel Supply. There are others who know of the industry, but think of being supplied with linens or towels as an expensive luxurious service . . . Advertising the industry systematically and intelligently either nationally or locally couldn't help but bring results.

During the remaining Depression years, and then the war years, various abortive efforts were made to carry out a cleanliness program, but none succeeded. In 1937 the consulting firm of Williams & Sayler was called in by LSAA to study the industry and make recommendations for a program to make Americans more aware of cleanliness and hence of linen supply. In its review of the industry, Williams & Sayler reported: "The Linen Supply Industry is doing at present an annual business of approximately $104 million. It is supplying towels, garments, tablecloths, napkins and other washable products to approximately 700,000 customers."

The greatest part of this volume, they noted, was in washable work clothing in industry and trade. There were almost 290,000 customers, renting more than $36½ million of laundered garments a year. Hotels and restaurants were, as a group, the second biggest users of linen supply. More than 20,000 such establishments were using $26,758,000 worth of laundered linens a year. Barber and beauty shops accounted for $17,500,000 and hand towel supply for $12,760,000. Professional users of linens and "other services" accounted for the remainder.

Looking ahead, Williams & Sayler pointed to a tremendous untapped potential. In 1937, they forecast as immediately possible $411 million of linen supply annually, and for washable work clothes alone more than $220 million.

> These statistics of present business are, at first glance, impressive, but when they are considered in connection with the fast market that still awaits cultivation they present a different picture—the picture of an industry which, as a whole, has not begun to take advantage of its opportunities . . . In every branch of the market there exists a tremendous reservoir of new business, a relatively small part of which, if obtained, would increase tremendously the present volume of business done. The Linen Supply Industry is in the fortunate position of being able to benefit from a movement for higher standards of cleanliness, which, if organized, would undoubtedly command the support of organizations powerful in the moulding of public opinion. A cleanliness campaign would unquestionably bring to bear upon barber and beauty shops throughout the country the value of higher standards, and thus make the linen supply company's task easier in this field.

> In restaurants the untidy dark-colored coats and uniforms so universally worn, even in good clubs and hotels as well as in many restaurants, present an obvious point of attack . . . The trend toward greater use of women in waiting on tables, both in hotels and restaurants, should be carefully studied by linen supply men. Among food manufacturers, there are many whose practice in regard to uniforms leaves much to be desired, though on the whole this section of the market has high standards of cleanliness.

> Active physicians, osteopaths, and dentists . . . and other healers number 283,000 people. After proper deductions, the group yeilds a total linen supply market of 120,000 offices. Of these fully 50,000 are today served by the industry. The Linen Supply Industry is in a splendid strategic position to launch and lead a movement for greater cleanliness and by doing so add tremendously to its present volume of business.

Such a movement, the report pointed out, would establish standards of cleanliness for the public. It would gain momentum through a national publicity and public relations campaign, awarding prizes for outstanding cleanliness, publishing bulletins, and developing the theme of cleanliness through many media.

But the country was still pulling itself out of the Depression. The linen supply industry was not yet strong enough to expand Association activities beyond the important convention meetings to a year-round program. Many gains, however, were made locally. For example, at the end of the thirties, the original Ohio association was taken out of moth balls and revitalized into a forceful area group through the efforts of Al Stromberg, aided by Sanford Miller, M. Maschke, Jr., Pete Mendelson, Herman Gross, Ward Forrest, and Arthur Edelstein.

Presidents of LSAA from its inception until 1944 were:

A. P. Shupe	Morris Jepsen	George B. Freeman
Frank Selmier	Fred D. Martin	John M. O'Donoghue
Carl J. Aull	A. A. Baumgartner	Leon H. Matthey
Alexander Gammell	E. J. Hogan	James S. McCloskey
L. F. Turnbull	Abraham Papp	Tom Selmier
W. F. Heissenbuttel	Jos. M. Callner	William Ruther
Latimer H. Long	Brace A. Helfrich	Gordon C. MacMaster
Louis Papp	Albert Gitlow	Hugh P. Flynn

As the country united itself, so did the linen supply industry and the Association. But when World War II ushered in other problems for the industry, the Association, on the threshold of bigger and more purposeful activities, did not yet pass through the doorway.

That step had to wait until 1945 when Roy J. Friedman of Garden City Towel Supply Company was president of the Association and in the second year of his three-year tenure, the longest in Association history. He and the Board of Directors made the decision they had long known had to come—to make the office of the association secretary a full-time paid position. *Linen Supply News* announced the decision with approval:

> National officers have for some time been of the opinion that the Linen Supply Association of America could be of greater service to the industry if a full-time trade association executive were employed to conduct the organization. The office of secretary has been filled by the appointment of Herbert V. Hedeen . . . who possesses a fine cultural background, having attended the University of Chicago and the Bryant and Stratton Business College.

Hedeen had previously been Executive Secretary of the Dodge Dealers Association of Chicago and his appointment was only the first of many changes to come. That same year, it was announced:

In line with the plans of the national officers to increase the scope
of activities of the national organization, the executive officers, at the
New York meeting, decided to call a special session of leaders in the
industry to convene at Cleveland early in December. National President
Friedman has prepared a list of members whom he intends to invite
to this meeting. At least one member from each geographical area will
be included to give country-wide representation. Through the means
of this gathering, Mr. Friedman and the national officers will be in a
position to secure an excellent concept of what should be expected of
the organization in the way of services. With the employment of a
full-time secretary, it will be possible to increase greatly the activities
of the national organization and the nature and amount of such enterprise can be determined at a conference called for this purpose.

Friedman and others had more in mind. They knew that an organization could function purposefully only if it knew where it was going,
if it had the right personnel, and if it had the proper financing. Within
the next year, the constitution's bylaws were modernized to reflect
the new broadened purpose of the organization. To find new directions
for the Association, the Board, headed by Friedman, hired another
experienced Association executive, Samuel B. Shapiro, as Associate
Manager and Research Director. Shapiro who had been a professional
association executive, took office in February of 1946.

That July the *Linen Supply News* briefly reported: "Two members
of the national association staff were formally introduced to the convention. Both were making their first appearance before the national
body: Herbert V. Hedeen, Secretary, and Samuel B. Shapiro." The
announcement was momentous. Sam Shapiro—who came to take on
a special four-month assignment to prepare a comprehensive activity
program, and who has been with the Association ever since—was to
be a major force in helping the Association to develop many services
for its members. He was to pioneer also in developing its technical
research and assisting it to become a distinguished trade association.
(He served in subsequent years as president of the American Society
of Association Executives.)

Already, members of the linen supply industry sensed the changing
directions of the Association. At the 1946 convention, an announcement
was made that membership in LSAA had increased almost 20% in
the past year, to 778.

In his first appearance before the Association at that convention,
Shapiro set the tone for the years ahead. There should be, he pointed
out, a far-reaching program. This would include technical research
on equipment and garments, promotional work, studies on conservation of linens, market research that would show linen suppliers where

their services might best be needed, technical studies, in-depth cost analyses to guide linen suppliers, the development of a statistical service, and a public relations program. He also pointed out that such a comprehensive program could not be effected under the old budget of $30,000. Dues would have to be doubled to meet the Association's needs of $65,000 within the next year.

To a man the convention rose, approving the dues increase.

Before the Association set off on its new course, it had been essentially an Eastern and Midwestern group. The West was too remote, travel was time-consuming and difficult, and linen suppliers in that section of the United States, with only a few exceptions, generally stayed away from the Association and its conventions.

In fact, just before the Association decided to become more purposeful, its officers and executive committee were entirely from the Midwest and East, with the exception of Parvin Spencer, a Texan. Roy Friedman, its president, was from Chicago. Vice president Richard Moore was from Boston. Sam Miller, the perennial treasurer, who was to hold office for 48 years, from 1913 to 1961, was from Cleveland. Frank Hartless, Secretary Emeritus, was a Chicagoan. The Executive Committee was comprised of Parvin Spencer (San Antonio), Moe Struminger (New York), L. F. Turnbull, the former president (St. Louis), and Hugh Flynn (Rhode Island).

Through a steady growth in membership services and much deeper involvement in LSAA work on the part of linen and towel supply companies and associate firms, membership became first truly national, and then international. Officers, directors, committee members come from all parts of the United States and Canada.

In 1946 LSAA had 670 members, of whom 575 were linen supply parent firms and branches and 95 were associate. Three of the linen suppliers were in Canada, there were no members in other countries. By 1969 the Association had 1,498 members, of whom 1,206 were linen supply parent companies and branches, and 292 were associate. Of the 1,206 linen suppliers, 1,060 were in the United States, 49 were situated in Canada, and 97 were in 23 other countries.

In 1946 dues income totalled $30,000 and the total budget was around $45,000. In 1949 dues income neared $400,000 and the budget was $851,000. Minimum dues in 1946 were $15.00, and $150.00 in 1969. The maximum dues paid by any one company in 1946 was $2,500 compared with $25,000 in 1969.

The full-time staff in 1946 consisted of three persons; by 1969 it had grown to twenty-two, with twenty in the Miami Beach headquarters and two in the New York City office.

The basic policy of LSAA is that fundamental power resides in the membership. Power is delegated to the elected representatives, a Board of Directors of fifteen which makes its decisions about the course of LSAA on the basis of the expressed needs of members. LSAA's twelve standing committees and its ad hoc and task groups are under the jurisdiction of the Board. Wherever possible activities are directed by a standing or special committee, and staff personnel are assigned to committees. Recommendations for new activities or changes in existing programs are initiated in most cases by committees which make their proposals to the Board of Directors. All activities are reviewed regularly to ensure that useless projects are dropped. The Board of Directors meets at least three times a year; committees meet at least once yearly and frequently more often.

In 1946 major activities were reported as follows: Annual Convention, OPA work, Wage-Hour Law analysis and meetings, and six newly inaugurated projects: a Business Barometer, and Operating Costs Survey, an Advertising Program under the heading Servilinen with appropriate materials, Linen Conservation materials, a news letter for members and a news letter for secretaries.

In 1969 the following activities served LSAA members:

MARKETING
Architects—Folders and Manuals
Marketing Manuals for Institutional Customers—Colleges, Hospitals and Nursing Homes
Disposables—Articles and Speeches
Exhibits at Customer Conventions
Home Linen and Executive Shirt Rental Articles
Marketing Information—Statistics, Trends, Sales Analyses and Decision-making Information
No-Irons—Customer Folders, Articles and Speeches
Articles and Case Studies on Newer Services—Newer Garments and Department Store Manual

SALES
Continuous Towels—Sales and Service Manual
Sales and Service Manuals for Hotels/ Motels, Restaurants and Supermarkets.
Route Salesmen's Correspondence Course
"Ride With the Winners" Sales Manual
"Selling and Servicing Linen Supply" Booklet for Route Salesmen
"Sales Tips" Bulletins

Regional Sales Congresses and Sales Trainers Seminars
Sales Contest Manual
Sales and Service Correspondence Manual

OPERATIONS
"Production Methods for Linen Suppliers"
Production Movies
"Materials Handling Manual"
Test Services to Check Laundering Formulas
"What You Should Know About Laundering And Textiles" Book for Linen Suppliers
Plant Layout Kit
Mildew Control Reports
Delivery Guides
"Processing Polyester/Cotton Blend Garments"

RESEARCH
Washing on the Hanger—LSAA Finishing System
Soil Handling Systems
Sanitation
Washable Disposables
Automatic Inspection
LSAA CARD System—Computer Routing

EMPLOYEE RELATIONS

"Employment and Training Guide"

"Employee Selection" Manual

Route Training Posters

Personnel Tests and Application Forms

Routemen Selection Manual and Forms (Now being prepared)

Safe Driver Awards Program

"Accident Control for Linen Suppliers" Booklet

Labor Relations Seminars

Labor Relations Articles

TEXTILE CONTROL—(LINEN CONSERVATION)

"Textile Control for Linen Suppliers"

"Linen Conservation Ideas" and "Linen Conservation Methods" Manuals

"Textile Control by Route Salesmen" Booklet

Linen Use Ratios

Linen Conservation Posters

BUSINESS MANAGEMENT

"What Every Linen Supplier Should Know About Federal Labor Law"

Regional Management Seminars

Executive Management Institutes

Management Simulation Training

"Preventive Security for Linen Suppliers"

"How to Budget" Manual

Textile Item Coding Glossary

Operating Costs Survey

Semi-Annual Business Growth Survey

Key Business Control Ratio Reports

Truck Cost Record Cards

"Cost Accounting for Linen Supply" Manual

Electronic Data Processing Seminars

EDP Application Descriptions

EDP Articles

ADVERTISING AND PUBLIC RELATIONS

Advertising—Institutional and Advisory Service

Truck Posters for Customer and Public Causes

Magazine Articles about Linen Supply

Master Speech Texts for Member Use

Motion Picture and Sound-Slide Films for TV or Showing by Members

Publicity Releases

History of Industry (Now being prepared)

Linen Supply Promotional Booklet

Promotional Folders for Work Garments, Doctors, Motels, Restaurants, Beauty Parlors, Food Markets, Linen Supply in General

Reprints of magazine Articles about Linen Supply

Reprints of LSAA Advertisements

NATIONAL AFFAIRS

Contacts with Legislators and Administrative Agencies

Analyses of Bills and Laws Affecting Linen Suppliers

"Customer Contracts Service" covering Antitrust, Customer Contracts, Property Marking Laws, Court Decisions, etc.

MEETINGS

Annual Convention and Exhibit

Regional Meetings on Sales, Sales Supervision, Operations Office, Employee Relations, Delivery, Textile Control, etc.

Management Seminars and Institutes

Committee Sessions

Specialized Meetings—Hospitals, Synthetics, etc.

World Linen Supply Congress

GENERAL

"Linen Supply News"—averaging 120 pages is sent monthly to members. It contains in-depth articles on linen supply, news of the industry, and about 15 departments—Marketing, Labor Relations, Washington Information, Research, Operations, Safety, Personnel, Sales Tips, Public Relations, Management Information, etc.

Annual Roster-Buyers Guide

Annual Bound Volumes of Linen Supply News

Problem Clearance—By Mail, Telephone, or In Person

Publications, films, and other materials available to members of LSAA are described in the appendix.

In June 1941 when the linen supply industry was threatened by a shortage of machinery, textiles, trucks, tires, and chemicals, the Association decided to retain a Washington attorney to present their views to the government. LSAA President John O'Donohue, Albert Gitlow, and Joseph Weiss, president of the New York linen supply group, asked attorney Stanley I. Posner to represent linen supply. In the words of Weiss, "he obviously knew his way around in Washington."

Short and balding, even in his early thirties, he asked disconcerting questions that at first puzzled people until they realized that his queries compelled them to think.

Through the combined efforts of the National Affairs Committee and Posner, working with members in the various states, the importance of the linen supply industry to public health and sanitation was established. Governmental agencies became convinced that linen suppliers made a direct and indispensable contribution to the war effort. The prompt removal of infectious agents from textiles was established as vital to community health, and in industry it was soon apparent that personal cleanliness is closely related to efficient production. The need for clean apparel and clean towels, bed linens, and other flatwork was demonstrated to be as vital in a war economy as in peace-time, perhaps even more so. The linen supply industry was therefore provided with the necessities for maintaining its operations.

Through World War II and thereafter, Posner served the linen supply industry with dedication and wisdom. His speeches at the Association's annual convention and elsewhere embodied for the guidance of members his penetrating knowledge of economics, law, linen supply, and the humanities. He represented the industry ably in all of its relationships with administrative agencies in Washington as well as with Congress. His work for linen supply in regard to the Federal Wage-Hour Law enabled the industry to get a needed breather before its employees were covered by the Act.

He was a strong proponent of state unfair practices acts. Based on the material developed by attorney William Hoffberg of New York City, he prepared a special service for subscriber-members of the Association and the Institute of Industrial Launderers whom he also served as General Counsel. This continuing program known as the Customer Contracts Service covered not only federal and state laws and court decisions about customer contracts; but also national and state anti-trust laws and court rulings, the state unfair practices laws, and property marking laws.

Prior to his affiliation with LSAA, Posner had been chief economist for the National Recovery Administration's Department of Compliance. He had graduated magna cum laude in economics at Amherst College, earned a master's degree in money and banking at the University of Chicago, and took his law degree magna cum laude at Harvard. He served as a Research Fellow of the Brookings Institution, a professor of law at American University in Washington, and as founder-head of the Friends of U.S. of Latin America. For his philanthropic and educational activities in Latin America he was officially honored by the governments of Costa Rica, Nicaragua, Panama, and Cuba. In World War II and thereafter his law firm was Posner, Berge, Fox and Arent.

In January, 1964 he became counsel emeritus to LSAA. On March 29, 1965 at age fifty-five he suffered a fatal heart attack.

When Stanley I. Posner became counsel emeritus for LSAA he was succeeded as General Counsel by Donald M. Counihan of the Washington law firm of Counihan, Casey and Loomis. He served LSAA with distinction until his death at fifty-two on Feb. 12, 1969 of congestive heart failure. His law partner, E. Riley Casey, succeeded him as the Association's General Counsel.

A nationally known authority on trade association law, Counihan lectured at many universities on this subject and served as counsel for the American Society of Association Executives as well as other trade groups. A graduate of the University of Michigan and the Marquette Law School, he did postgraduate work at Cambridge University in England.

He entered the practice of law in Milwaukee in 1947 and a year later became administrative assistant to Congressman Charles J. Kersten of Wisconsin. He engaged in private practice from 1949 to 1953, and then for two years served as assistant to the Secretary of Health, Education, and Welfare as that department's first legislative liaison officer.

At the time of his death he was national president of the Alumni Association of the University of Michigan.

Following the presidency of Roy J. Friedman in the years 1944-1947, the heads of the association each served a two-year term. Their names and cities are as follows:

Richard T. Moore	Boston	1947-1949
Moe Struminger	Pittsburgh	1949-1951
John Isaacs	Detroit	1951-1953
Arthur R. Chambers	Long Beach, Cal.	1953-1955
Jack A. Quigley	Chicago	1955-1957
Lawrence C. Kline	Philadelphia	1957-1959
Joseph A. Robertson	Lawrence, Mass.	1959-1961
Herman Gitlow	Philadelphia	1961-1963

G. Walker Morgan	Chicago	1963-1965
M. Maschke Jr.	Cleveland	1965-1967
Arnold R. Knapp	Salt Lake City	1967-1969
Alvin S. Gross	Ft. Lauderdale	1969-1971

The assignment of special services to staff members is depicted in the following 1969 staff assignment list:

Administration—*John J. Reinecke, Samuel B. Shapiro*

Advertising Counsel—*Robert A. Dahne*

Business Management—*John J. Contney*

Convention—*Thomas P. Rowland*

Cost Accounting—*Frank Cooke*

Customer Contract Service—*Samuel B. Shapiro*

Data Processing—*Frank Cooke*

Delivery—*Robert Knaggs*

Executive Development Institute—*Thomas P. Rowland*

Exhibit—*Thomas P. Rowland*

Industrial Engineering—*Frank Cooke, Robert Knaggs*

Insurance—*John J. Reinecke*

Laundering Problems and Test Assembly Service—*Robert Knaggs*

Legislative Matters—*Samuel B. Shapiro*

Linen Conservation and Security—*Robert Knaggs*

Linen Supply News Administration & Advertising—*Donald T. Smith*
Editorial—*Charlotte E. Caffrey*

Management Problems—*Samuel B. Shapiro, Frank Cooke*

Marketing—*John J. Contney*

Motion Pictures & Slide Films—*Robert A. Dahne*

National Affairs—*Samuel B. Shapiro*

Operations—*Franke Cooke, Robert Knaggs*

Personnel—*Thomas P. Rowland*

Public Relations—*Robert A. Dahne*

Research:
Apparel/Styling/Fabrics—*Howard Rosenfeld*
Chemical—*Anthony B. Marmo*
Delivery—*Anthony B. Marmo*
Finishing System—*Howard Rosenfeld*
Machinery—*Anthony B. Marmo*
Roster-Buyers' Guide:
Advertising & Production—*Donald T. Smith*
Listings—*John J. Reinecke*
Safety—*John J. Reinecke*
Sales Promotion and Training—*Thomas P. Rowland*
Speech Preparation for Members—*Robert A. Dahne*
Textile Control—*Robert Knaggs*

The Association is highly self-critical of its activities, and members frequently appraise its work through mail surveys, evaluations of meetings just before the sessions conclude, and other methods. For example, at the suggestion of then LSAA director John R. Blanchard, president of Banner Laundering Company, Detroit, all current and past officers and directors meet regularly at the annual convention to criticize on-going programs.

The Association can do tremendously effective work for its members because of their recognition that through the pooled efforts of their key people working with thousands of similar executives in linen supply, impressive results can be achieved.

CHAPTER 8

NEW GIANTS
EMERGE

**WITH GROWTH
COME EVER-CHANGING
RESPONSIBILITIES OF MANAGEMENT**

New faces, new problems, expansion and change—these were elements in the pattern that characterized the immediate years after World War I for smaller linen supply firms and the large ones alike. Dynamic forces exerted their impact on the entire industry, impelled by entrepreneurs from other industries as well as those within, and motivated by new concepts of doing business.

The year 1923 marked the end of a group of five leading linen suppliers in New York that had been compelled by the Government, in 1917, to join together. The government had acted for one reason: to save on trucks and tires, gasoline, and other supplies during the war. Consolidation of competitive suppliers was one means employed to cut down the use of supplies.

Two firms led these top five suppliers. One was New York Linen, formed in 1909 by three men, Leopold Tropp, Morris Turitz, and Solomon Liss, as New York Barber Supply. They started New York Towel in a basement at 32 Cooper Square and soon were swamped with so much towel business that they opened their own laundry in 1910.

The company flourished. Daily, the three men went out on their routes, sold new customers, delivered towels, built routes for new employees. In 1913, from out of the blue, came business that catapulted New York Linen to new heights. Solomon Liss, delivering towels in the Wall Street section, walked into a barber shop. There a man who was getting a haircut watched him exchange the clean towels for the dirty ones.

"How's business?" said the man to Liss.

"No complaints."

"Do you have many customers?"

"Sure," said Liss, "we have many satisfied barbers, downtown and all over."

"You serve just barbers?"

"Yes, that's our specialty."

"Say, do you think you might be able to supply napkins, too?"

"Of course, certainly. We'd gladly supply napkins."

"Well, then, meet me at my office tomorrow. We'll discuss terms."

The man handed Liss his card. He was president of Exchange Buffet, then one of the largest, if not the largest, chain restaurants in New York City.

The next day, Liss made certain he was at the office promptly.

"We want to rent napkins for all our restaurants. Tell me about your service, your prices."

Liss easily concluded the sale. He now had one of the best accounts in the city, an account that was to become enormous as Liss in later years began to supply it with other items that the cafeteria-style restaurants needed.

The second major firm was Cascade, owned by Louis Bonoff, which had started by serving butcher shops from a push cart in the late 1890s. By 1917 it was a major linen supply force, with branches in many parts of the city, each specializing in either garments or towels.

After World War I, Cascade and New York Linen—plus three other firms who made up the Big Five—were still united. While there were certain advantages in working together, the disadvantages outweighed them. Each owner had been accustomed to running his own shop his own way and with five firms operating jointly, disputes were inevitable.

In 1921, a capable attorney, O. N. Thurman, was brought in to be president in the hope of settling these differences. Two other companies joined the "Big Five," but harmony seemed impossible.

In 1923 the firms agreed to disband. Cascade left the organization, which then consisted of New York Linen and two smaller firms.

Even at the time of the reorganization, many people prophesied continuing stress and strain. Comptroller Joseph Weiss suggested that the stock of the organization be placed on the market. When the owners agreed, he conferred with brokerage houses, only to find that they wanted too much money. When the decision therefore went against placing the stock on public sale, a breakup appeared imminent.

But Leopold Tropp of New York Linen came up with an idea. Meeting with a friend, Maurice Reinitz, who was a member of a prominent investment house which had bought some wet-wash laundries in Brooklyn, he explored the resources of several companies. The other principals agreed and eventually a new company, Consolidated Laundries, emerged. One of the new breed of "giants," it has held its position ever since.

In a brief passage from its 1965 Annual Report, commemorating "40 Years of Evolution," the company speaks for itself:

> 1925 was a year of great optimism. An exuberant American cheered Amundsen on his flight to the North Pole. Henry Ford introduced the first airplane freight service between Detroit and Chicago. President Coolidge was inaugurated for a second term. Red Grange was everybody's hero, and, in this era of sports popularity, the gala opening of New York's Madison Square Garden took place. The wide-spread popularity of the "Charleston" symbolized this energetic age.
>
> At the end of that eventful year, on December 8th, 1925, Consolidated Laundries Corporation came into being and was incorporated under the laws of the State of Maryland. Beginning actual operations in Jan-

uary, 1926, the company at that time was an amalgam of 18 separate companies, predominantly family laundry operations. During these early formative years, we served a limited marketing area consisting of greater New York City and the area in New Jersey immediately across the Hudson.

Forming the original Consolidated Laundries Corporation were Household Laundry Corp., Avon Steam Laundry, Inc., Unit System Laundry Corp., Select Laundry Co., Inc., Volunteer Laundry, Inc., West End Laundry, Inc., Spotless Laundry, Inc., Coney Island Laundry, Inc., Pride of the Kitchen Co., Clenital Laundry Service Corp., K & K Laundry Co., Inc. and New System Laundry. All of these companies (except Household Laundry) were in later years either sold or the business moved into another Consolidated plant and the corporations dissolved. Also in the original 18 were the Pride Laundry Corp., and Autostop Towel Cabinet Co., Inc. which were legally dissolved during the course of the years that followed.

Headquarters for the new corporation were at 1440 Broadway in New York City. The first president was Charles B. Kilby. Leopold Tropp and William Berkowitz were vice presidents. Joseph Weiss, who had been in linen supply since 1913, was treasurer; Oscar Friedlander served as secretary; and G. V. S. Williams was chairman of the board.

A new management team headed by Thomas H. Blodgett and A. S. Jenkins took over in 1928. Jenkins, an executive from American Chicle, was accustomed as one associate phrased it, "to knocking heads together, making people cooperate, putting an organization on its feet." With him he brought a young executive, W. B. Dean, a salesman not too long out of Knox College, Jenkins' old alma mater, who later became long-time secretary of Consolidated.

One of the first objectives the new management team tackled was the development of a corporate image. The 300 trucks used by Consolidated salvaged from earlier, individual plants, were of different makes and different colors, and still had lettered on their sides the individual plant names. Similarly, some of the route salesmen wore uniforms, while others did not.

Another project was to coordinate purchasing. Tons of coal and thousands of gallons of oil were being sold to the various plants of Consolidated, but since each plant was purchasing separately, they were paying higher prices. Central purchasing remedied this, and an immediate saving of $40,000 a year was achieved. Overall, the new men applied modern business methods to the outdated, separate operations. Out of the near chaos emerged a much more efficient and unified company with a new corporate image.

Subsequent executive heads of Consolidated, Murray Cohen and

Jacob Landau, helped materially to keep Consolidated in the forefront. In 1968 the company, now a division of Sears Industries Inc., with its board chairman and president Charles Clore and its executive vice-president Max H. Stettner, reported annual dollar sales of $53 million-plus. This included $36½ million for Consolidated.

Office procedures in the old linen supply plants were a far cry from what they are today, as recollected by a veteran of the early Twenties, Ben Schmones. When he first joined the old Lackawanna Laundry & Linen Supply, in Newark, New Jersey, which two years later became part of the newly formed Consolidated Laundries, he called for an audit of the petty cash box.

Lackawanna then had a one-room office equipped with huge ledgers and stools typical of the day. Sometimes, in the evenings, the girls took the books home to work on them so that they would not have to come in on hot days. There was other widespread inefficiency, which young Schmones set about to correct. The office staff petitioned management to remove the newcomer, but to no avail.

Schmones recalled:

> It was not unusual for me to double and triple in brass in those days. During one period, I was office manager, sales manager, and assistant plant manager. This ended when I found myself writing memoranda to myself.
>
> I can remember also receiving blue memoranda from the General Office pertaining to the decrease in the number of bags of manure (which was sold as fertilizer). That was a serious topic in those days of buggy whip manufacturing.

Small firms floundered and failed largely because, while the owner worked long and hard, others did as little as possible. Consolidation, and the formation of larger, more efficient, companies, was one solution during the up-and-down years of the Twenties.

Another practice of the day was frequently unsettling to efficient business procedures. An opportunist would move into the linen supply business in a territory where there was a larger, established firm. The tactic then was to offer cut-rate prices, thereby taking away so many customers from the original firm that the latter would finally buy out the new business—at a handsome profit to the fly-by-night operator. The practice died out, with occasional flare-ups through the next decade, when the older firms saw the light. They simply would resist the "holdup price" and sit tight until the new business strangled itself by consistently selling below cost.

The established companies were now on a solid enough footing to weather business fluctuations. Physically, as well as financially, they were becoming substantial parts of the American economy. Some of the plants were imposing buildings, five and six stories high. One trade editor wrote, in the late Twenties, after a visit to a linen supply plant:

> One enters a large, well lighted and beautifully furnished public reception room. This leads into a huge business office where more than a score of girls in bright colored aprons are found at work. . . .
>
> The plant now has four large locker and shower rooms where the workers are given an opportunity to help keep up the company policy of cleanliness by improving their own personal appearance. Besides this, the company has installed a large and completely equipped dining room where the employees can secure the best quality home-cooked foods at cost. . . . On the outside of the building, the company has provided a park of about a quarter of an acre which is filled with flowers and shade trees and shrubs.
>
> A new loading department was added which allows the drivers to work under cover and drive their trucks into such positions that they can work with ease and dispatch. A fine new drivers' room was also added.

Another plant, built in 1927, was considered one of the leading examples of efficiency. With approximately 70,000 square feet on five floors, built at a cost of about half a million dollars, it had many features. On the roof were the typical landmark signs of a big laundry: two water tanks (each with 35,000 gallon capacity, one for hot water, the other for cold) and a soap house where the products the plant needed were made in what was considered one of the most modern soap manufacturing plants in the country.

When the route salesman returned with his soil to the laundry, he placed it on a factory truck which then went onto an elevator and was carried to the counting room, where the contents of each bundle were listed. From the lists, a duplicate bundle was made up of clean linen so that the route salesman could load up without delay.

Soiled linen was then sorted, the washer loads were weighed, and each load had to be laundered cleaned with a special wash formula. The continuous towels were laid out by a machine in a series of 4-foot lengths and tied in the middle so they would not tangle.

The washroom on the fourth floor had forty-two wash wheels, mostly 42 by 48 inches, sixteen extractors, and six dryers. Pressing, mending and manufacturing were done on the third floor where there were sixty presses. The floor was ventilated by twelve large fans. The first floor included the loading dock, sorting room, the route salesmen's delivery room, and the offices.

The first national convention of laundrymen in the U.S.A. was held
at the Hotel Florence, Chicago, Ill., October 1–3, 1883.

An early linen supply plant operation, probably 1900–1910.

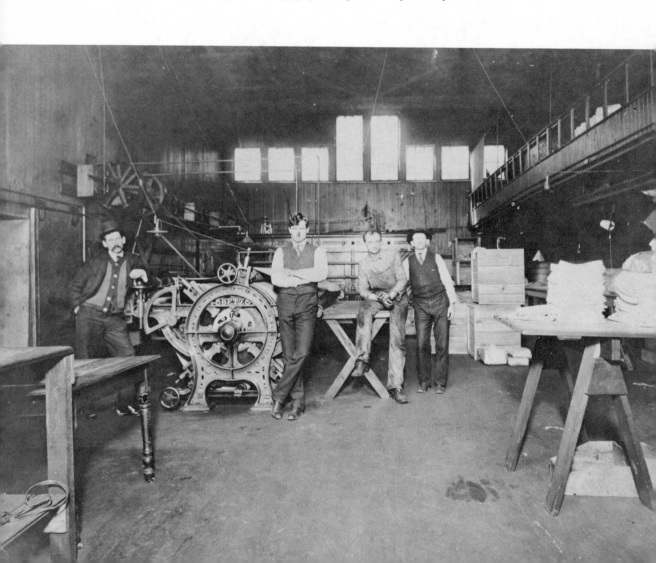

"Push-cart No. 1" was first used by American Linen Supply at Salt Lake City, Utah, March 1, 1895.

Horse drawn vehicle operated by Reliable Linen Service, Detroit, Mich. about 1910–1915.

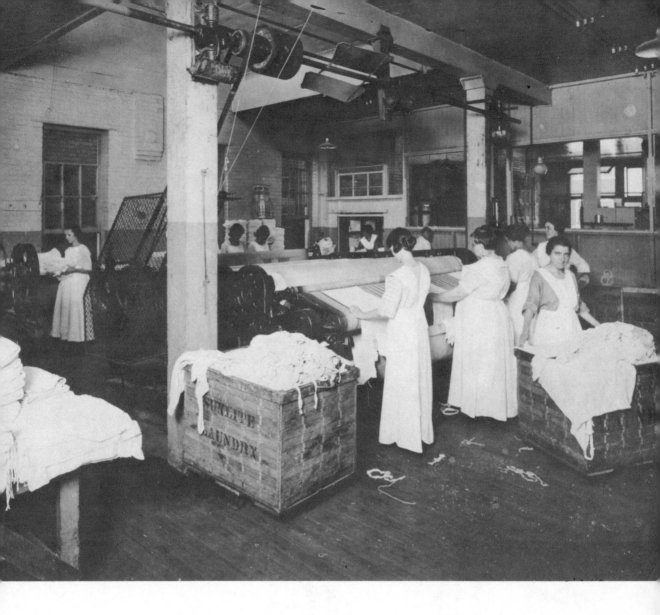

Pressing room, circa 1920. Photo courtesy Atlas Linen and Towel Service,
St. Louis, Mo.

Meeting of linen supply company employees during the early 1900's.

At the turn of the century, washers and extractors were constructed basically of wood and powered by a communal overhead drive belt. Plant was operated by Chicago Towel Company. F. W. Means & Co., Chicago, Ill.

Sorting soiled linens circa 1920. Photo courtesy of Atlas Linen and Towel Service, St. Louis, Mo.

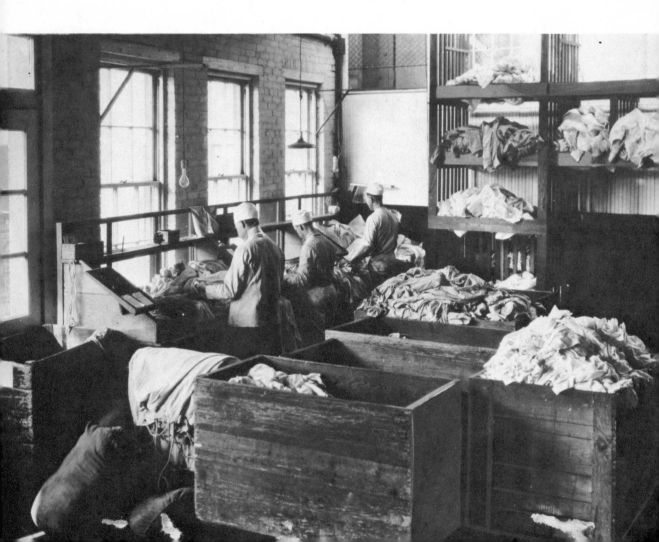

Lineup of delivery vehicles and drivers ranging from horse-drawn wagons to automotive trucks. Plant building of American Linen Supply Co., Minneapolis.

Plaza Hotel, Cincinnati, Ohio, was site for meeting of the Interstate Linen Supply Association in 1913.

Rutter's Linen Service, Inc., Lawrence, Mass. Poster on wall features U.S. Presidents Lincoln, Washington and Woodrow Wilson. Wilson was inaugurated in 1913.

The fourth annual convention of the Interstate Linen Supply Association was held at the Claypool Hotel, Indianapolis, Ind., March 16–17, 1916.

Folding, wrapping and tying linens in bundles and stacks, circa 1920. Photo courtesy
Atlas Linen And Towel Service, St. Louis, Mo.

Linen supply men wore white suits and their ladies donned "H
Hoover was held on the White House Lawn on May 22, 1929, durin

1 ANNUAL CONVENTION, LINEN SUPPLY ASSOCIATION.
HINGTON, D.C. MAY, 22, 1929.

as" in honor of the occasion. Reception with President Herbert
annual convention of the Linen Supply Association of America.

Woman's uniform at the turn-of-the-century.

The "Harvey Girl" Uniform

Office scene about 1920. Photo courtesy of Atlas Linen and Towel Service, St. Louis, Mo.

Pressing and folding linens in Finland, 1969.
Photograph courtesy of Laina Tekstiili oy, Hämeenlinna.

Original site of National Linen Service Co., on Walker Street, Atlanta, Georgia,
in 1919.

Main office building for National Service Corp., Atlanta, Ga., 1970.

Linen supply delivery vehicle operated in 1969 by Laina Tekstiili oy, in Finland.

Plant at Lexington, Ky., 1969.

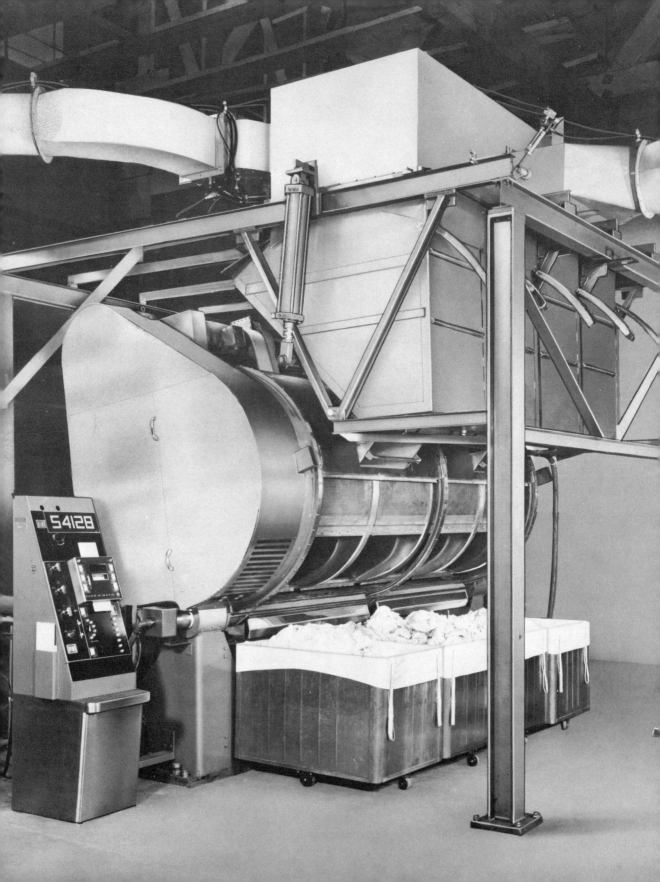

Header-type, Belt Driven Washers—1910

High Capacity Unloading Washer and Wet Loading Hoppers.

Today's Modern Combination Washer-Extractors for Blends

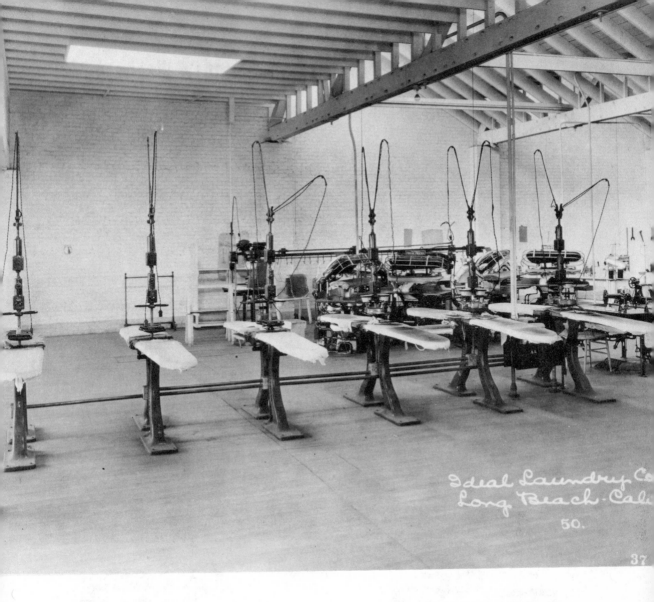

Wearing Apparel Pressing Department—1910

★ 112 Years of Progress in Laundry Washers ★

1840 Hand operated, paddle-action washer.

1860 Power-driven washer with wringer.

1870 Wood washer with cylindrical shaped tub.

1905 Wood washer with gears enclosed.

1915 Motor driven metal washer with brass cylinder and tub.

1925 Metal washer with horizontal partitions in cylinder.

1940 Push-button operated Monel metal washer.

1952 Automatically unloaded washer with Full-Automatic Washing Control.

Illustration courtesy of American Laundry Machinery Co., Cincinnati, Ohio.

Flatwork Ironer—1912

Modern, High Production Flatwork Ironing System
With High-Speed Ironer and Automatic Folders.

In Chicago about this time another resourceful man with great leadership ability, T. M. Quigley, was on his way up. He was brought to Chicago by F. W. Means, to become general manager of the F. W. Means Company whose branches, then numbering fewer than two dozen, were known as Clean Towel Service.

A former laundry routeman, Quigley had many years earlier met a representative of the F. W. Means Company.

"Any time you need work, let me know," the man had assured this bright young Irishman.

Quigley contacted the F. W. Means representative, who offered him a job as manager of the Racine branch. Quigley seized the opportunity and did so well that he soon won a promotion and became a leading representative for F. W. Means. He traveled through nine Midwestern states, opening linen supply branches. Always on the move from one town to another, he would review the situation, hire a branch manager, find a laundry to do the wash, train the manager, sell accounts for all kinds of linen service and help the business get on its feet. Then off to another city to repeat the process.

Business developed by Quigley in one city would expand until it served the entire area, almost touching the marketing limits of another city. Then Quigley would go to that neighboring city and set up another branch. Always, though, the branches were without laundries. Not until 1944 did Means build its first laundry outside of Chicago.

In Zion, Illinois, the local church was a potentially tremendous account. The church owned a department store, lace factory, printing company, bakery, and butcher's shop. Quigley went to Zion to sell the account. At 9:00 A.M., he strode down the street, thinking of how to make the sale. The church bells rang the hour. Quigley kept on walking unaware that at nine in Zion, religious custom required that everyone stop wherever he was. He was asked to leave the town immediately which he did, but only to return to Zion later the same day. And he made the sale.

Change was in the wind in the mid-twenties. The continuous towel was a new business phenomenon. Some people thought of it as a competitor to the individual office towel since if one long continuous towel were placed in a washroom, an office might stop delivery on individual towels. But Quigley was certain that both kinds of towels had their place, and one of his first management decisions was to build a continuous towel business. His future with the company was at stake, and he proved to be right.

A decision was also made to expand Chicago Towel from primarily an office towel company to a full-line linen supply company. In February, 1928, the co-partnership operating as Chicago Towel, and the Clean

Towel Service was incorporated. The new company made industry history when it became the first publicly owned linen supply company to be listed on a stock exchange.

Its name, Chicago Towel Company, was changed in 1960 to F. W. Means & Company. By 1967, the company headed by Jack A. Quigley had reported $60 million in annual sales.

Another interesting element in the pattern of the industry is typified by the business established by Eric Di Stanislao who founded Exchange Linen Service of Oakland and Santa Rosa, California. His wife, a daughter of linen supplier Augustus Bruni, who had her own linen supply company in New York. The sale of that business provided the capital for the Bruni and Di Stanislao families to move West.

Eric Di Stanislao went to work for Bruni in 1919, delivering coats to barber shops from a horse-drawn wagon. He received $22 for a six-day week, and nothing for overtime on Sunday.

Eventually Di Stanislao bcame a partner in the business, so that when it was sold he had enough capital to get a modest start in San Jose in 1936. It was not easy convincing barbers, restaurant owners and other prospective customers that they should rent aprons and jackets, for they were long accustomed to owning their own linens and sending them out to be laundered. His son Philip went to work for him while still in school, at the age of sixteen. He liked the business, and soon was running his own operation.

Augustus Bruni, founder of the original firm, lived to be ninety-four and was active in the business to the age of seventy-five. His son Nicholas became active in the business—the International Barber Towel Supply Company, on First Avenue in New York City—at the age of nine. The horses were an important part of the business. They were so accustomed to the routes that a new salesman could take over almost without prior knowledge of the stops required. A route salesman had to hustle to get on his wagon because the horses were so anxious to be off they would start prancing immediately.

During 1936 and 1937, Nicholas Bruni followed his brother to the West Coast where at about the same time the Marinis and the Di Stanislaos were gaining a foothold by buying smaller linen supply companies. Each was quite small, but put together they became a sizeable firm. Some companies indeed, were so tiny that they were purchased for $300 to $400. By the end of 1937, Nicholas Bruni employed fifteen people and grossed $5,000 to $7,000 weekly. By 1950, when California General Linen Supply Company was grossing $35,000 to $40,000 a week, his son came into the business.

An interesting account of the history of the West Coast operations is given by Dan Marini:

Nick Bruni, who was part owner of the Belmont Coat & Apron Company in New York City and who was my brother-in-law, interested me in the coat & apron business. I started as a driver in this concern and acquired a small interest which the Bruni family and I ran for many years.

In 1933 the opportunity presented itself to buy a small company in Los Angeles, which Frank Bruni ran for several years. This in addition was of great physical benefit to him as he suffered from a severe sinus condition and because of the wonderful climate in Los Angeles got us all interested in coming to California.

Nick Bruni, Victor Bruni, Augustus Bruni, Eric Di Stanislao and I bought the California Linen Company in San Francisco. In 1936 we started that company and called it California-General Linen. Several years later Eric Di Stanislao started in San Jose and Oakland.

In 1950 California-General Linen, which was also connected with Exchange of Oakland and San Jose, split, Nick Bruni acquiring the California General Linen Supply Co. Eric Di Stanislao, Victor Bruni, and Augustus Bruni, the father of the Brunis and I kept Exchange linen of Oakland & San Jose. My son, Mike Marini, was discharged from the Air Force in 1946 and came to work at the California General first as a routeman, and then as a salesman and in production.

A new company was formed in San Francisco, "Peninsula Linen Exchange" and Mike was put in charge of operating this plant along with me.

In 1951 we started the Exchange linen of Santa Rosa which was then operated by Eric Di Stanislao and his son Phil.

In 1954 we started the Contra Costa Linen Exchange in Antioch, California, operated by Victor Bruni and his son, Arnold.

In 1963 we moved Peninsula Linen into our present modern plant which we are very proud of. Mike is now general manager & vice president. We would welcome any linen supplier who visits us any time he is in San Francisco.

This story about the growth and spread of linen supply keeps repeating itself, substituting only new names.

Thus, Jack Landale, Sr., in 1921, the year before he graduated from the University of Nebraska, went to work for his uncle, Fred Whyte, of Southern Service Company, Pomona, California (now headed by G. G. Whyte, son of Gordon Whyte). Landale left in 1945 to start his own company in San Diego. By 1969 his firm had 13 plants in six cities in Arizona, California, and New Mexico, engaged in industrial laundering, linen supply, dry cleaning, and family work. Second generation Jack Landale, Jr., had by that time taken over the direction of the company.

But the industry is becoming more complex. Increasing numbers of specialists have come into it to cope with challenges relating to research, engineering, marketing, personnel relations, and delivery. In the past these all-important matters were handled by top executives of linen supply as part of their regular work, a situation which is no longer possible in an age of diversification and technological specialization.

CHAPTER **9**

THE PROBLEMS OF
MULTIPLE CHOICE

**RISING DEMANDS FOR
DIFFERENT TYPES AND COLORS
BUILD BUSINESS BUT
CREATE COMPLICATIONS**

"We must drop the idea that change comes slowly . . ." wrote Donald M. Nelson, World War II administrator:

> Today changes must come fast; and we must adjust our mental habits, so that we can accept comfortably the idea of stopping one thing and beginning another overnight. We must discard the idea that past routine, past ways of doing things, are probably the best ways. . . . We must stop assuming that a thing which has never been done before probably cannot be done at all.

With every step forward in the long process of growth of linen supply came the necessity for adapting to change, sometimes slowly, but more often with swiftness and decisiveness. By the 1920s the typical large linen supplier had become a fairly complex company, a fact which in itself attested to the industry's willingness to accept new concepts and procedures. Companies furnished many products besides hand towels and the traditional offerings, some of which have long since receded into the history of fashion and culture, while others have come into increasingly widespread use.

A booklet published by the Morgan Service Company in 1927 illustrated sixty different items that the company then rented, one of which was the waiters' apron—a wide, wrap-around cloth fitting a man's waist loosely and falling almost to his shoe tops. Those who saw the young Eddie Cantor playing the part of a waiter in an oldtime movie, will remember him wrapped in this long apron, typical of the times. Similar aprons are still used in old-fashioned kitchens of restaurants around the world.

Almost non-existent now are the white chair covers which slipped over the backs of wooden or metal chairs, giving soda fountains and ice cream parlors a touch of luxury. In those days, leather and plastic chairs were hardly known in the average average restaurant. One popular item then—and today—was a tea apron. As the Morgan booklet said, "Owners of tea shops have found that they effect savings in their laundry and linen bills by renting these attractively designed aprons from us."

The apron had deep V-necks, with wide bands going back over the shoulder, and a pointed bottom front edge which reached almost to the knees. The photographer's model pictured with it also wore a headband, useful in keeping the very long hair then in style out of the customer's food.

Another common item of the twenties was the Hoover gown. It was a dress-length garment, falling just below the knees, and had a stylish 3-inch belt wraparound, a collar, and short cuffed sleeves. "These aprons are quite as attractive in appearance as many wash frocks and may be procured in all sizes," the Morgan booklet announced. Also supplied was a bungalow apron with a square cut neck line, and short sleeves which came with or without a blue border.

For barbers, there were coats and trousers (in those days barbers were often dressed entirely in white, in the tradition of the old tonsorial parlor). Also supplied were knee length, wrap-around barber gowns. Of course, the barber also needed absorbent towels, special soft massage towels, and the same hair cloth that barbers drape over customers to this day. Since barbers gave more shaves than now, the list included shaving cloths which were shorter versions of the hair cloths.

Although the beauty shops of the twenties were not as popular and widespread as now, linen suppliers furnished them with manicurists' towels, massage towels, turkish towels (then used to dry a woman's hair), and hair cloths, similar to those supplied to the barber shops. Beauticians, later called cosmetologists, also could rent wrap-around gowns to make them look neater, as well as protect their clothes from ointments and lotions.

For bartenders there were all-white sleeve vests, mop towels and glass towels.

Other products available for rental were similar to those supplied today: wiping cloths, sold in bags of 5, 10, 25 and 50 pounds each; printers' aprons; bootblacks' aprons; coveralls, called "unionalls"; butchers' frocks and bib aprons; grocers' bib aprons; doctors' gowns; dental towels; individual and continuous roll towels as well as towels on grommets or chains; pillow slips; sheets; napkins and tablecloths; ladies' shirt aprons; and dish towels.

If suppliers were willing to accept the changing concepts of products, not all were agreed on color. Most items were white. Few garments, towels, napkins, or tablecloths came in colors, and linen suppliers dreaded the thought of having to stock a variety. Colors would create major washing problems, since dyes then were not fast, and processing colored items would be difficult and costly. Most important, any increase in the number of colors would create a significant inventory problem.

The typical challenge to a linen supplier was as complicated as determining how many men's suits—of what color and what fabric and what size—should be stocked in a large men's clothing store. The linen supplier had to do much more than maintain a stock of many items. He also had to carry in inventory, besides flatwork, many garments in enough sizes to supply all customers, no matter how tall or short, how thin or fat their employees.

As for color, linen suppliers were apprehensive that if they bought colored garments or table linens for one customer, they would be unable to rent them elsewhere should the customer change his mind.

At a 1928 meeting of LSAA, for example, Austin Torney of Chicago pointed out:

> We tried to ignore the colored garments, but in the trend of events they become a necessary evil. The public demands them. First, color-trimmed garments appeared, and now they are extremely popular, especially with the tea rooms and higher grade eating places. Chicago has a lot of them now, both in Hoover gowns and coats. We have a differential in price from 5 to 10 cents higher on each garment. While we all prefer the white, the demand for color cannot be stifled. We prefer to supply color-trimmed garments rather than full colors because in many cases the trimming can be removed and the garments used over again.

Clarence Roskoph of Cleveland agreed:

> We carry a large stock of colored garments and colored table linen because there is a demand for it. Our competitors do it, and we must face competition as well as public demand. We get 25 per cent more per garment for colors, although we admit there is not as much turnover as on white—which we would prefer to supply.

Walter Allowell, a linen supplier from Massachusetts, said, "In Boston, we try to stay away from colors wherever possible, and there is very little of it in our town."

A New York City supplier, Clarence Hughes, commented:

> This is an age of specialization, and we must face the fact that the demand for colored goods came about through the demands on the part of the customer. Everybody wants to be distinctive from his neighbor. We in New York have been able to put the customer under contract where he agrees to buy garments at 75% of their cost price if he decides to discontinue using them.

Harold C. Bonoff, in Brooklyn, came to the defense of color in an article he wrote for *Linen Supply News* in July 1929:

> I was very much against the introduction of colored garments, for the reason that it was very hard to get a fast color. The second reason why I was against colored garments and which was overcome by my father was that it costs so much more for colored garments than for white. But today our percentage of cost compared to our collections is about the same as on white garments. So we called our salesmen together and told them: "When anyone wants a colored garment, you make every effort that you possibly can to sell these colors or color combinations that we have."

These colored garments have opened up a very, very large field for the linen supply dealer, a field we never dreamed of in the past years, I'm sure. Today in New York we are supplying places that we never supplied before. We are supplying clerks in law offices, and clerks down in the financial district. We are supplying clerks in the United States Cigar stores. There is no factory, there is no office, in which we haven't some service that we can give today. Shoe stores represent another field now opening in our city. This colored garment fad has come to stay in our business, and it is up to us to handle it carefully and intelligently.

About the same time another trend was forming. Until the 1930s few linen suppliers uniformed their salesmen in cotton although some used woolens. In fact, uniformed route salesmen were seldom seen in any business. Then foresighted suppliers got the idea that their route salesmen would make a far better appearance if they wore neat cotton uniforms. These in turn would help to promote uniform rentals. One such supplier was Frank Selmier of Indianapolis, one of the pioneers of LSAA. While visiting a friend he noticed one of his own route salesmen dressed in an unkempt rain-soaked suit, and Selmier's friend commented in highly uncomplimentary terms on the man's appearance.

When Selmier returned to his office he observed that his brother, who was getting out some dusty records, had protected his clothing by wearing a white coat. Selmier thought "Why not make my own men look clean and neat the same way?" From then on his route salesmen wore a white sports coat. Writing in the October 1923 issue of *Linen Supply News*, Selmier said:

You have the proper uniform for a towel and linen supply salesman right in your own business. If you use it you will gain business for several reasons. First, you show your patrons and the public a sanitary clean appearance. Second, you are keeping up with modern ideas of sanitation and cleanliness. Third, the public comes to know the fallacy of woolen uniforms. And fourth, you will set an example for bakeries, creameries, milk delivery and others that is sure to net you increased business.

About the same time, the U. S. Department of Commerce reported in the *Commercial Standards Monthly:*

Increasing interest is being evidenced by employer and worker alike in the many advantages inherent in the use of uniform dress for certain industrial and occupational work for women, according to information received from the Women's Bureau of the U. S. Department of Labor. While the need for uniforms varies with the kind of work per-

formed in many industries, a special work dress may be essential for
any of a number of reasons—sanitation, comfort, safety, the protection
of the clothing, the identification of the worker in the group where the
public is also present, and the creation of a desirable work morale among
employees.

In the years that followed, uniformed route salesmen were seen not
only in linen supply but in many other industries as well. In a 1937
Forbes Magazine there appeared an article describing the advantages
of uniforming route salesmen.

Since that year the use of rented uniforms has become universal.
Today, many union contracts have this provision. Almost every company provides uniforms for its route salesmen. Uniforms build the
company's image, protect the wearer's clothing, and improve the
morale of employees.

In 1934, Ralph A. Presher, then general manager of the Arrow Towel
& Laundry Company of Oakland, started to rent linens to homes.
Presher said, "We look forward to the time when the housewife will
rent by far the major portion of the linens used in her home, owning
very few articles herself."

Presher offered every kind of linen used in the home: tablecloths
and napkins, bath towels, tea towels, face towels, sheets, pillowcases,
maids' uniforms, men's dress shirts. "In no other instance," stated *Linen
Supply News,*"has the service been complete, or has any concerted
effort been made before to develop this branch of the business in
this general way. Mr. Presher's efforts have been distinctly of a pioneering nature."

This bold entry into a new field was not followed by many linen
suppliers, although a few companies still rent table and bed linens
and towels to households as well as dress shirts. By 1967 the total
sales volume in the U. S. for this type of service did not exceed $7
million. The major reasons for the lack of growth in household service
are the difficulties in making delivery because "no-one is home,"
inadequate size of the order which makes delivery uneconomic, and
the feeling of the housewife that she can do the work herself for less.

The efforts of the linen supply industry have been reflected in
changing patterns of cleanliness. Before World War II, a person could
drive for hours without finding a rest room with sanitary facilities
and clean towels. Only after World War II did oil companies insist
that their franchise-holders have clean sanitary facilities. Restaurants
followed this example and many more customers began to rent continuous cotton cloth towels.

Not only were public restrooms lacking in the cleanliness to which
we are now accustomed, but so too were school washrooms. The

Children's Fund of Michigan found in 1932 that there was "no washing equipment of any kind" in some schools in Michigan. The committee making the study found that even where washroom facilities existed, there was often neither soap nor towels, and individual cloth towels were seldom seen.

Of 1,000 schools surveyed, only 365 had handwashing facilities. A later study of 1,511 schools showed that only 799 had such facilities. To improve cleanliness in the Michigan schools, reports of the survey were distributed to teachers throughout the state which pointed out that sanitary methods of handwashing would help prevent the spread of contagious disease, and that better equipment would enable children to develop habits of cleanliness.

Towels, the first items supplied by the industry pioneers, have been oddly enough a continuing source of competition. In the early years of towel rental, individual and roller towels gained wide acceptance. When the roller towel was deemed unsanitary, the continuous towel cabinet was devised as a more hygienic way to dispense towels. This equipment was perfected just at the time when paper distributors entered into direct competition with the linen suppliers.

Linen Supply News editorialized in this vein:

> It was presumed, by manufacturers of linen towels and men identified with towel service companies, that the people were satisfied with linen towels and that there would come nothing to take their place . . . We did not accept the opportunity when we had it of instilling into the minds of the people the advantages and comforts of the uses of linen towels. We were awakened, suddenly, to the fact that an outsider had stepped in, and by showing an aggressiveness that was commendable and well worth our efforts to excel, began a campaign of propaganda to interest the public in the idea of the paper substitute for linen . . . This campaign was written, prepared, financed and placed before the public by the manufacturers themselves. Almost before the linen supply men were aware of what was happening to the trade, the war came along. It is not necessary to remind anybody what happened to the linen industry and consequently to the trade and the linen supply during the war when there was a severe shortage of fabric.
>
> Through all this era of depression in the trade, the paper towel sailed along serenely. The men behind the propaganda, sure of their supply and with a knowledge that the linen industry was crippled, made the most of their time and opportunity. Now, we find that the linen supply trade, still suffering from war's effects has seen huge inroads made into its business by the paper towel.

To counteract this invasion, Jake Smith suggested a national educational program which unfortunately never got off the ground. Linen suppliers were still faced by a shortage of fabric, and prices were high. Mills operated at about 60% of capacity. The cotton industry was depressed. Linen suppliers turned therefore to the continuous towel cabinet. Smith stated:

> Some very interesting tests have been made in the past few years, which have proved conclusively that a slight saving can be effected with a 75-foot continuous towel over paper towels. We have yet to find anyone who prefers a paper towel to cloth towels if the cost is the same.

By 1923 the tide had begun to turn in favor of the linen supplier, pushing him toward new records of towel service volume. Practically all of the towel supply people who in the past had lost business to paper now reported that they were gradually getting it back again.

Nevertheless, as linen suppliers regained towel business, the paper towel business also expanded. What was happening was that total towel usage in public places was increasing. The consumption of paper towels and paper napkins jumped from 11,500 tons in 1921 to 70,000 tons in 1927. Although statistics do not indicate the breakdown between private and public use, the difference is significant. "Their expansion must of necessity inhibit ours," Al Gresser of the newly formed Consolidated Laundry Company said, in exhorting fellow suppliers to promote cotton towels intensively, "Their growth must stunt ours."

Paper towels were often ordered only for specific purposes. Thus, "The use of paper towels by our company is restricted to certain places in the manufacturing department," wrote an executive of Proctor & Gamble, "when the use of linen towels would not only be illogical but prohibitive. They are not used as part of the washroom equipment, but as a means of removing stains, greases, and chemicals from the hands of the workmen."

Even in 1932, during the depth of the depression, about 1,000 continuous towel cabinets were placed into service each month.

Many linen suppliers decided that if the customer wanted paper they would become paper towel distributors too. By 1939 about 135 linen suppliers distributed paper towels with an estimated annual volume of $1 million, about 1% of linen supply sales.

The paper industry had also made inroads in other areas of linen supply. By 1962, according to *Linen Supply News*:

> The paper people have moved against our cloth napkin business. We have done very little to improve the quality or reduce the cost of our napkins, and, as things stand today, the paper people have taken most

of it away from us. They now produce approximately 600 million pounds of paper napkin stock a year, and their growth and quality is constantly improving. They are now making other heavy inroads on our industry with paper doctor towels, paper dental towels, and paper barber and beauty towels. Not so long ago, most windshields were washed and cleaned with cloth—today paper towels with special wet strength and glass polishing ingredients do the job. The paper towel people, over the past ten years, have come into the market with paper fender covers and paper wipers. Paper wipers are the newest and fastest growing paper product. In these ten years the output has increased by 333 percent to approximately 2 million cases per year.

The National Paper Trade Association, in a letter telling its members about this increase in 1962, reported that about 4,200 establishments making cosmetics and pharmaceutical products in the United States were excellent prospects for paper wipers. They urged their members to switch these concerns from cotton to paper.

"$20,000,000 YEARLY ON PAPER RESEARCH" said a trade news headline in 1963, reporting that fifty paper companies doing a business of $3 billion a year, employed some 1,000 scientists plus auxiliary personnel in their research departments. To match these potent competitors, the linen supply industry would have spent $3½ million a year for research. The actual figure was closer to $350,000 for expenditures on all research and development by the Association and its members.

CHAPTER **10**

WORLDS NEW AND OLD

THE DEVELOPMENT AND GROWTH OF LINEN SUPPLY IN OTHER COUNTRIES

While in the main, linen supply grew much the same way around the world, there are differences. Returning from a 1928 trip to Europe, Walter Mayer of Theodore Mayer Company, manufacturers of linens and towels, reported: "Office towels are pure linen . . . On the average they use heavier and more expensive goods than we do here. Even dish towels are of a high quality; table linens are of medium grade but heavy."

In Denmark, Mayer found the most linen supply-conscious country outside the United States. In the land of Elsinore and Tivoli Gardens, linen supply had achieved a greater penetration of certain markets than anywhere else. In Copenhagen, he reported, all hotels and restaurants rented all their linens. In the provinces more than 95% of the hotels and restaurants used linen supply.

This acceptance of linen supply began in Denmark about the same time that it did in the United States, largely through the pioneering efforts of Ludwig Simonson. He had come to linen supply by a roundabout route, first having started another service business, polishing windows and draining slop pails for customers. After establishing that business, he realized he could easily develop another related service. As long as he visited customers anyway, he reasoned, he might just as well provide them with clean towels and pick up the soiled.

Other Danes also took up the idea in the years that followed, but linen supply did not gain a substantial foothold until a twenty-eight-year-old Copenhagen waiter, Robert R. Friberg, decided that he could make more money by renting out clean towels and uniforms to waiters than he could by serving customers. A man-about-town, Friberg gained many customers for his firm, which he named FIX.

Four major linen suppliers operate today in Copenhagen. FIX specializes in serving restaurants and in the rental of dust-control equipment and towels to offices and shops. Thor serves the large hotels and other large businesses. Geismar serves barbers and hairdressers. N. L. Dehn specializes in renting smockfrocks, blouses, and working clothes. So advanced is linen supply in Denmark that it was here that LSAA's Garment Finishing System (described in a later chapter) was first installed in Europe. In April, 1965 the system was shown at N. L. Dehn's plant to the several hundred registrants of the World Linen Supply Congress held in Elsinore and three of the first five European installations were made in Scandinavia.

As well accepted and essential as linen supply is for Denmark's business establishments, suppliers have had to contend with a public attitude, predominant in Scandinavia and in other parts of Europe, that generally precluded the acceptance of rental of linens for in-home family use. Even so, there are signs of change and the growing acceptance of linen supply that promises soon to open new marketing areas.

In recent years, 5,000 families in Copenhagen have become renters of family linens.

While the linen supply business was gaining a foothold in Denmark, the men to the north, in Sweden, took little notice of it until after World War II. In 1946 S. J. Robertson, now managing director of AB Forenade Tvatt of Stockholm, one of the three largest linen suppliers in the country, traveled to the United States to learn more about American dry cleaning and laundry methods. He had no interest then in linen supply; he did not even know what it was. Yet wherever he went in the United States, he saw continuous towel cabinets. Intrigued by the possibility of spreading their use in Sweden, he contacted the Steiner Company.

"I'd like to be your sole agent for all of Sweden," he told Steiner executives. They agreed, but because Swedish law prohibited imports, he could not bring the cabinets to Sweden until 1952 when the law was repealed. Five years later his firm introduced still another service: uniform and overall rentals.

Linen supply is still young in Sweden, but it is growing fast. Though linen supply services are provided to Swedish industry, offices and hotels, general acceptance has been slow in coming. The largest segment of AB Forenade Tvatt's business, for example, is in towel cabinets—about 40% of its gross linen supply business. Next largest is linen supply to hotels and restaurants—about 25 % of the total. The remainder is made up of coverall services and dust control, a service growing rapidly there.

Other companies which have become important in Sweden today are A. B. Textiltjanst, under the direction of Lennart Hellstedt; Tvattbolaget I Malmo AB, under Magne Malmstron; Konsumtionsforeningen Orebro, under Ake Ekstrand; and A. B. Tvattman.

In the British Isles significant strides have been made in the development of linen supply. In 1968 it was conservatively estimated that the annual dollar volume was about $60 million for the major companies. Many family-type laundries share in the remainder of the linen supply market. In 1964 London's *Financial Times* estimated the annual volume at nearly $50 million.

The largest of the linen supply firms, Initial Services, Ltd. supplies the country from fifty-five branches and forty plants. Its customers generally are the small trader and hotelier. The second largest company, Advance Linen Services, Ltd., does a substantial part of its business in towels and towel cabinets, mostly with small businessmen. Kenneth E. Garcke, who practiced law for a few years after his graduation from Cambridge, was chairman at his death in 1969, of both Advance and Initial through his affiliation with the parent organization, the British Electric Traction Co., Ltd., a giant organization founded by his grandfather. He saw, before others, that the future of domestic laundering was not too bright, but that the opportunities for developing linen supply, especially continuous towels, and commercial laundering were great. He also served as president of the Association of British Launderers and Cleaners.

As powerful a position as the large firms have in the market, they are meeting increasing competition from a number of companies which have been growing rapidly. In response to competition from office-cleaning firms, the major linen suppliers have also entered into office cleaning.

One of the companies now in linen supply in England was in the laundering business in 1868 when James Hayes established a laundry at Rushey Green in Kent. Power laundering was then in its infancy, and most commercial establishments that needed laundering of any kind simply hired people to do the chores by hand. Hayes was one of the first to sense a need for a service that would provide his type of power laundering away from the premises. Under the name of "The Royal," his company began pioneering in contract services of this type. One early customer was the London Stock Exchange, today Hayes' oldest customer.

By 1900 Hayes' Laundry (the name, "The Royal" had largely been dropped) was growing more rapidly than ever. In 1926 the firm was acquired by J. Lyons and Company, which had built a great name in the catering business. One of the major functions of Hayes now was to supply laundering service for the hotels, restaurants and other establishments operated by the parent company.

It was not until well after World War II, however, that Hayes—which had become the largest laundry in the world—ventured into linen supply ("linen hire" in British terminology). "Linen hire was now seen to be the fastest-growing service in the laundering complex," reported a brief company history published in 1968:

> So the Hayes management, in which Jack Pennell (now managing director of the present company, James Hayes & Sons Limited) was now starting to play a leading part, set about building up this class of trade. The service, designated Haylin, began in earnest in 1962. Its expansion has been so rapid that today it constitutes about 50% of all Hayes' business.

Linen supply was apparently started in England in 1902 by a Canadian businessman, Arthur Bigelow, and his wife, who brought the linen supply idea from Canada. In its early years, their firm, known as Initial Service, because it supplied towels and dusters with the customer's initials, grew rapidly, purchasing competitive firms as well as building its own sales. For years it was the only linen supply firm in the British Isles. Even as late as 1927 there were few other supply firms in Great Britain (Hayes, of course, not yet having entered that phase of business). That year two automobile mechanics, finishing work and taking off their grimy overalls, jibed at each other.

One of them, Dick Geary, joked: "I'll bet I can make more by cleaning them than by dirtying them."

"You might have something there," replied his buddy, Jim Stevenson.

Pursuing this idea, Geary and Stevenson leased a 400 square foot tin shed, installed a used household washing machine with a washing capacity of six overalls, borrowed an old car, and began to sell the first uniform rental service in England. In 1933, they built their first plant. Six years later they built a second story onto the plant, and today it is the leading firm in uniform rentals.

For many of these intervening years, Initial Services continued almost alone in the towel business in London. In 1933, however, when Madame Prunier opened her London restaurant, she approached another company, Advance, which was then a large commercial and contract laundry, and asked the principals to supply her with linens. They agreed, and still have the account today, though it is now the only restaurant account they serve.

In the mid-thirties, F. R. Oliver arrived in England, having fled the Nazis in Germany where he had once founded a linen supply business. In London he found a territory almost as untilled for linen service. Oliver immediately began to apply his skills and knowledge. Gradually, he too built a major company in the London scene, the London Linen Supply Company.

About the same time another laundry firm, the New Era Laundry, made its entry into linen supply. Thus by 1939 the stage for greater linen supply growth in England had been set. A number of able and aggressive firms had entered the field, and were ready to meet the growing demand for linen service.

But World War II intervened. Growth of linen supply was checked until the end of the war when the linen supply industry in the British Isles really began to expand. Executives of commercial and contract laundries who visited the United States returned to Britain impressed with the possibilities of linen supply service in their own country. One such firm was Spring Grove, which, as a small laundry, entered the linen supply business in 1948. By 1965 it had become a major force in linen supply with twelve plants in the Isles.

The growth of linen supply was further stimulated when Advance introduced the continuous roll towel, which it is estimated now accounts for about one third of all linen supply rentals in the British Isles. During these postwar years, linen suppliers also became suppliers of other items, such as soap, soap dispensers, paper towels, and even vending machines. As tourism grew in England during the 1960's, even more impetus was given to growth. Hotels and restaurants, flourishing in this growing trade, needed more services of linen suppliers. And as the market grew, many small laundries entered the field for the first time to try to gain their share of the business. More than 100 laundries are in linen supply in some small way in the British Isles.

In France, as in England, the advantages of linen supply were not readily apparent in the early part of the century. Consequently, until World War I little linen supply existed. Small laundries catered to individual store owners and employees who bought their own towels and aprons. But between World War I and World War II, linen supply was first introduced in the slaughtering industry, then found a market in a few hospitals, nursing homes, dentists' offices, and restaurants.

The linen supply industry had a very slow start in France, according to P. L. Carpolleto, executive manager of the Blanchisserie du Bois de Boulogne, one of the leading Paris firms located in an industrial suburb near the Seine River. Prior to, and during, World War II, there was little linen supply. But after the War the French markedly increased the use of linen service, particularly in urban regions. Factories, department stores, service stations, and laboratories represented areas of quick growth. New industries, and especially the government-controlled firms that make up 30% of French industry, began to change old habits and to rent linens and uniforms.

For a long time the problem was that Frenchmen preferred to own rather than to loan. To rent "strange" linen is still alien to many, especially in the smaller towns. The large urban centers, such as Paris, Bordeaux, Lyon, Marseilles, Lille, and Strasbourg have attracted most of the business.

In the case of the Blanchisserie du Bois de Boulogne, one component of a group of companies founded some eighty years ago in Pantin, another industrial suburb of Paris, the tiny laundry started a special service to the butchers massed in the neighborhood. Located near the slaughterhouses made famous by French writers during the late eighties, Maurice Leduc, grandfather of the present owner, catered mainly to individuals as a starter.

This linen supply service grew rapidly in the early days since so many butchers were involved—and still are—in the daily slaughter of animals. Strict hygiene laws require a daily change of the large traditional apron worn like a Roman toga by the butchers.

Restaurants are a major market in France since there are many of them, even though they are small. The more leisurely patterns of French dining lend themselves to linen supply.

Major companies in linen supply in France are Blanchisserie de

Grenelle, Seine, headed by Serge Demeny, one of the founders of the World Linen Supply Congress, and a strong exponent of electronic data processing: Group Elis headed by J. Marot; Blanchisserie et Teinturerie de Boulogne under Jacques Decroix; Pierrette Blanchisseuse under Andre Humbert; Blanchisserie de Pantin under Maurice Leduc; Teintureries et Blanchisseries Associees under Robert Marx.

In the Netherlands the linen supply industry began about the end of World War I, when the N. V. Linmij Company, which now has about 250 employees, entered the business. It did not begin, however, with towels, or coats and aprons but rented rags to industry. Before World War II, it had already started renting towels and white and grey coats for office workers which are now fully identified with the name of the wearer, the day of collection, and the route number.

In the intervening years, other firms entered the supply business, too, but not until 1957 did another major firm accidentally discover that there was a potentially big market for a linen supplier in The Netherlands. That firm was Ter Weeme, T. V., a cotton goods manufacturer, that had been making 45-yard lengths of toweling and shipping them to the United States without realizing that they were being used for continuous towels. That year, though, one of the directors of Ter Weeme traveled to the United States, in part to find out for what purpose the toweling was being used. While visiting one of the companies that had been buying the toweling, he asked, "What do you do with those long pieces of toweling?" he asked.

"They're for continuous cabinets," it was explained to him.

Recognizing that there was a tremendous potential for a business supplying this toweling to institutions, hotels, and other businesses in his own country, he immediately obtained a license to export U. S. cabinets to The Netherlands. There, his company, Ter Weeme, set up another company to provide linen service. Named Hokatex, this company gradually began to show Dutch businessmen what the advantages of continuous towels were. Today, 80% of Holland's towel cabinets are in industrial and office washrooms.

Having found initial success with the toweling, Hokatex branched out. It added tablecloths, napkins, bed sheets, and uniforms for hotel, restaurant, and industry employees. As Hokatex's volume expanded, it acquired a laundry plant which then, and now, does the laundering for the Palace in the Hague, though the Palace uses its own heirloom linens.

In recent years, Hokatex began a new service of renting blue towels. It also branched out into sanitary napkin dispensers, toilet water dispensers (which men use more than women), and incinerators.

Though towel use grew rapidly, most of the bigger hotels and restaurants in the country maintained their own laundry plants and used linens embroidered with their own names. As these plants become obsolete, linen supply in The Netherlands will gain a greater share of this market.

The Dutch linen supply industry faces the same basic problems that challenge all Dutch industry, a shortage of qualified labor. Yet the plants cannot offer higher wages to attract more personnel because wages are set in government-supervised industry-wide negotiations which also determines significant working conditions. As a result, all plants try to find other ways to cater to their employees.

Because of the shortage of labor, as well as other factors, labor costs increased 15% in 1964 and 15% again in 1965. Wages in The Netherlands have been reportedly rising twice as fast as in the rest of Europe. In Russia there is no linen supply industry.

In Mexico the linen supply industry has had substantial growth, led particularly by one firm which was founded in 1936 by Dr. Fritz G. Burkart, a German lawyer who had fled the Nazis. Today his four plants in Mexico City and one in Acapulco are known as Lavamex, Lavita, Servisan, and Batas and provide services to hotels, hospitals, restaurants, and industrial accounts. His son, Federico, is now actively associated with him.

Another major linen supply firm is Lavanderia la Europea in Mexico City which has grown rapidly under the direction of Antonio Jacques whose father started the enterprise.

In Canada linen supply growth has been dynamic. In the decades from 1951 to 1961 the Canadian government census reported an increase from $9 million to $29 million. The number of linen supply firms went from fifty-one to eighty-one of whom thirty-five had their own plants. Most of this growth occurred in the populous provinces, particularly Quebec and Ontario. By the end of 1961, sixty-nine linen supply firms in these two provinces grossed $23 million and employed almost 3,000 people. Fifteen of these companies were in Montreal, twenty-five in Toronto.

Since that time the use of linen supply services has expanded rapidly with an estimated $65 million for 1969—on the conservative side. There is usually a tendency to compare Canada with the United States, but Canada's population is only about 20 million. Much of this population is non-urban, and linen supply services are more feasible in metropolitan areas.

The major difference between Canada and the U. S. is probably that Canadian firms are faced with higher textile costs and higher machinery costs.

One of the big areas of growth in Canada has been in the continuous towel field which several years ago was described as "astronomical."

In Japan the linen supply industry got off to a late start. During the tense years of the Korean war, Roy Horoshige had a laundry close to the Tokyo airport where he served customers on American military bases and civilian employees who lived near or in Tokyo.

Hiroshige's volume fast outpaced his plant's capacity to wash. Yet investing in new plant expansion did not make sense because if the Americans left the area he would have a plant with great overcapacity. On the other hand, if he didn't invest in a new plant, he might miss a major opportunity for expansion. To solve this dilemma, Hiroshige decided to introduce linen supply. At first, there was no acceptance. But Hiroshige persisted. Finally, he found an opening in the market. Chinese restaurant owners, then arriving in Tokyo from war-ruined Yokohama, agreed to try linen supply.

In the years that followed, Hiroshige found more need for his services—so much so that he started to devote all his time to linen supply.

Linen supply is growing rapidly now in Japan. A number of companies specialize in hospital laundering and rental on a large scale. Others furnish the osiburi, a small towel—hot or cold—to clean hands and face before eating. (It is served also on airlines that fly the Far Eastern routes.) Probably well over a hundred firms engage in linen supply in conjunction with their laundry and dry cleaning services.

Linen supply in Australia traces its beginnings to Harvey C. Wheeler (an American mentioned in chapter 4). By 1925 he had expanded into Europe. As he looked around with his wide-angle vision he noted that Australia did not have linen rental services. He sent Canadian John Herman Barratt, and later George Henry Lokes, and formed the Associated Australian Linen Supply. Using the Wheeler system of franchises, Barratt opened branches in Sydney, Newcastle, Brisbane, Melbourne, Adelaide, and Perth. Nine years later, Alan B. Hazard was appointed general manager of the company. It was sold subsequently to Steiner-American Corp. and its name was changed to ALSCO Linen Service with branches in seven capital cities.

As the Wheeler organization grew in the early days, competitors entered the field. Alan Hazard recalls that in 1928 his firm bought a linen supply business in Adelaide from an elderly woman who had about 100 customers, mostly for hand towels. Growth after the 1920s was slow, until the end of World War II. Since then linen supply volume has increased rapidly.

Participating in this growth are at least 16 linen supply companies, including the largest linen supplier, Ensign Holdings, Ltd., a progressive public company under the direction of A. J. Chessel, who keeps his organization up to date by sending his key executives regularly to visit major linen supply companies around the world.

As the linen supply industry flourished in countries around the world, a desire for understanding and cooperation among linen suppliers from all continents became evident. In turn, this desire led to concrete action: linen suppliers from many countries joined the Linen Supply Association of America. By 1969, there were ten members from Australia, six from New Zealand, two from Brazil, seven from South Africa, seven from Japan, forty-eight from Canada, and one each from Venezuela, Mexico, Bahamas, Barbados, Panama and Guam.

In Europe, too, an ever-increasing number of companies have shown their desire to gain understanding by international cooperation, to learn from the activities of other linen suppliers. The Linen Supply Association of America now has as members: 6 Danish, 3 Belgian, 15 English, 6 French, 1 German, 1 Scottish, 2 Dutch, 1 Irish, 1 Israeli, 2 Italian, 7 Swedish, 2 Norwegian and 4 Finnish firms. In turn the Linen Supply Association of America is a member of the British Laundering Research Association.

International cooperation among linen supply companies is illustrated by the World Linen Supply Congress, first started by the LSAA with a conference in Paris in 1959. Since then, three more have been held—the second in Brighton, England in 1962, the third in Copenhagen in 1965, and the fourth in Miami Beach in 1968.

In each Congress, panels give the experiences of linen suppliers from various countries. In each Congress the delegates tour plants in the host country and elsewhere, too, to observe current linen service processing and other techniques. Thus, in June and July 1965, linen suppliers from the United States, Mexico, and Canada, after meeting in Denmark with their fellow suppliers from many other countries, visited plants in England, Sweden, Italy, Switzerland, and France.

CHAPTER 11

RESEARCH AND DEVELOPMENT

**THE NAME OF
THE GAME**

"Research" has glamorous implications as LSAA's Sam Shapiro observed in one of his articles:

> It conjures up the genie and his miracles. More staidly, we see the white-coated scientist staring intently through his microscope discovering the secrets of cancer, or the mathematician poring over his equations to find suddenly $E = MC^2$. We envisage the team of researchers breathlessly crashing through frontiers to give us The Bomb, synthetic rubber, antibiotics, ever-newer communication devices. Part of this is myth (most of it in all probability), for research is compounded of much perspiration and painstaking tenacious work. But it also has its share of urgency and exhilarating insights as indicated by Nobel prize winner James D. Watson in his book *The Double Helix*. The results are frequently exciting, and in applied research they are tomorrow's consumer goods and services, and industry's profits.

Any industry withers eventually if its member companies do not engage in adequate research, or if their association fails to do so, or if they do not use the research results obtained elsewhere. The linen supply industry did not undertake technical research until the 1950s. Yet interestingly enough, it is one of the few service industries that has taken a bold and imaginative approach to its research needs. It has thought in terms of large systems as well as pieces of equipment and isolated methods and textiles.

"This year American industry will spend close to $9 billion on various forms of research and development," reported *Forbes* magazine on November 15, 1968. "This is less, to be sure, than it spent last year to advertise its wares ($18 billion) or on new plant and equipment to produce them ($64 billion). But in many ways, R&D spending presents far tougher problems."

As the article pointed out, "The payoff from R&D may not come for years. It may never come at all."

The big question American industry asks today is this: "*Is* business getting its $9 billion worth? Top businessmen are by no means certain that they know the answer."

"To walk up and down the aisles here with the looms before you, snapping deafeningly, their shuttles darting and shooting backwards and forwards across the warp, busily weaving so many patterns and colors is enough to dazzle one's eyes," Roy Turnbull wrote in August 1921. He was reporting to the industry on a trip the Board of Directors of the young LSAA had taken to visit mills owned by the Marshall Field organization in the Carolinas:

From these mills we were taken to the bleachery, where the muslins, sheetings, tubings, long cloth, nainsook, dimity bedspreads, and pillowcases are bleached by vast machinery through caldrons and tubs as large as a swimming pool. The manner of conveyance of these miles and miles of yardgoods is through porcelain tubes placed at various points through which the goods are drawn from all over the factory into the solutions of washing and rinsing of perfect bleach. For a moment it appears as if you are in a laundry of giants.

Even in 1921, members evidenced a keen awareness that they had much to learn, that their future rested on gaining knowledge and pooling their efforts to disseminate that knowledge. A field trip such as the one Turnbull reported on was of little value if only those who participated received the benefits of better understanding. The findings must somehow be communicated to other industry members unable to attend.

There was much to be learned about processing, delivery, sales, costing, administration. LSAA members realized that often they would have to find their answers together. But "R&D" was then relatively unknown. Few private businesses spent much money on applied research and development. LSAA was still groping for direction and finances did not permit them to do much more than keep members informed at periodic meetings.

Despite these handicaps, in the ensuing years sporadic efforts were made to develop information that would enable members to run their business better. Qualified people spoke at conventions and articles written by specialists were printed in trade publications. Men like Max Neuberger of Neuberger & Company, accountants, wrote on profits. W. H. Bryan of the Salesmanagers Bureau of St. Louis spoke on training solicitors. Leland Strader, who had been credit manager at United Linen in Los Angeles, spoke on improving collections from delinquent accounts. J. B. Crowe talked on low-cost stain removal. Guidelines to costs were attempted. A sales manual was published for route salesmen.

Meantime, since the roller towel had been banned, efforts were made by linen suppliers to invent better ways of serving towels. The grommet device used by many permitted the user to take a clean towel from a shelf, slide it down a chain or rod, wipe his hands or face, then drop the towel into a bin. A variation enabled 100 small towels to be locked together with a small padlock. Many experiments were conducted with a continuous towel cabinet but for a long while difficulty in loading made them uneconomic. Eventually the cabinet was improved so that it won out over other devices. According to George

Steiner, the name "continuous towel" was first used by Charles G. Parks, branch manager of the Chicago plant owned by the Steiners.

Except for work in the cabinet towel field, few linen suppliers engaged in technical research. Companies in other industries were improving laundry machinery, chemicals, and vehicles. But their efforts were directed to all laundry owners, fleet buyers, and other business-men, with benefits to linen suppliers deriving indirectly from their being part of these broad groups.

Although in 1923 real technical research was still years away, the idea of research was not completely new to the industry. In March of that year a "research report" was released to the trade press by a member of the linen supply industry. By actual test, a continuous towel had passed through a Burroughs Cabinet 86,400 times and yet it was "not half worn out." Elementary as this test may seem today, it nevertheless indicated that a linen supplier was concerned enough about service to run tests.

In 1950, LSAA launched a program to help members monitor their laundering formulas in cooperation with Dr. Pauline Beery Mack, then at Pennsylvania State College and subsequently at Texas Women's College. Companies that subscribed to this service received a test assembly every three months. After being processed through the wash-wheel a certain number of times, linens were returned to the laboratory for checking. The laboratory then sent a report to the subscriber which informed him of the effectiveness of his washing process in terms of soil removal, whiteness retention, and textile strength loss. The over-all results were periodically published by the Association. This service has continued until the present. It has been replaced by a newer service made possible by the research of a joint committee of the Association and the Institute of Industrial Launderers.

LSAA's first Research Committee was appointed in 1953, with Frank G. Steiner its first and Louis Zipperman, its second chairman. With a grant of $25,000 from M. C. Goldberg, then president of the Keystone Manufacturing Company, the committee allocated the funds to several projects, including a study of textile mildew. Because of limited funds, and because the need for intensive applied research had not yet be-come apparent, after the several projects were completed, this effort was discontinued.

Meanwhile, LSAA engaged actively in advertising, by itself and also in conjunction with the National Cotton Council, M. Snower and Company, Wellington Sears, and Angelica Uniform Company. In one year the concerted expenditure for advertising exceeded $200,000. Training films and booklets were prepared, management engineering was started with appropriate staff people employed, books were pub-lished on laundering chemistry, linen conservation, costing, and the like.

At their October 9, 1956 meeting in New York City the LSAA Board of Directors considered the possibility of establishing a budget of $50,000 for applied research for 1957. This was to be done by revising the dues schedule to relate dues to annual dollar sales rather than vehicles operated. Representative members expressed opposition to such a revision, although not to the need for research. The Board therefore decided not to change the dues schedule and stated that the research program though needed could not be initiated via dues.

On December 4-5, 1956, Jack A. Quigley, then LSAA President, called a meeting in Chicago of members who reportedly had an annual sales volume of more than $2 million dollars. Eleven members attended. Chairman Quigley announced that he had called the meeting to determine how the industry could more effectively meet the growing competition of paper, synthetics, and other substitutes, and how it could cope better with rising labor costs and a thinning labor market. The group decided that major improvements were needed in machinery, textiles, laundering processes, and office and delivery systems. They also concurred that no individual company in the industry, regardless of size, could do the job alone.

The group agreed that the research work should be done through LSAA, and not a private agency, and in behalf of the entire industry regardless of the number of members who financed the plan. They concurred that the funds should come initially from a small group of larger member companies who would pledge their financial backing for a five-year span. Despite these statements the meeting ended on a note of uncertainty.

Quigley called a second meeting for February 26-27, 1957, at Bal Harbor, Florida. Fourteen companies were represented. Prior to the meeting a memo had been distributed which stated that the industry had not kept pace in machinery, textiles, laundering, and other improvements; that too much labor was being used; that vast improvements were imperative to meet and beat competition of paper and other products and services.

The group unanimously agreed to finance a research and development program, and committed themselves for five years for a sum equal to three times their 1957 dues, to be paid annually or semi-annually. An annual budget of $100,000 was decided on, and the sponsors elected Quigley chairman of the group, with the LSAA Board to have veto powers. A committee of eight was selected to develop the programs.

The committee at its 1957 meetings agreed that their basic objectives were to cut production costs, to reduce office, delivery, and textile replacement costs, to investigate new concepts of service, to increase and maintain customers through market research, to improve working conditions for employees, and to maintain consistent quality. In addition, they would encourage associate companies to develop inventions that would speed the processing and distribution of linen.

Arthur D. Little, Inc., was retained to help explore research possibilities for the industry, develop new products, and long-range objectives. A research staff was employed.

In 1963 when the research sponsors had grown from the original sixteen to one hundred and forty companies, the membership expressed its approval of the entire program by incorporating the cost of research into dues, and by providing for a standing research committee to direct the work. Twelve members serve on this committee with staggered four-year terms. Chairmen of the committee since its inception, following Quigley, have been Herman Gitlow, Lawrence C. Kline, John A. Morgan, Frank G. Steiner, and Robert L. Viner.

Associate members who have made direct financial grants to the research program include American Laundry Machinery Industries; Angelica Uniform Company; duPont; Eastman Chemical Products, Inc.; H. Kohnstamm & Co., Inc.; Klopman Mills, Koratron Co., Inc.; Shane Uniform Company; M. Snower & Company; Tall Industries, Inc.; Troy Laundry Machinery Co. Other associate companies contributed substantial manpower to LSAA research efforts, including American Uniform Company; Coats & Clark; duPont; Eastman Chemical Products; Koratron Co., Inc.; Klopman Mills, and Wyandotte Chemicals Corp.

Since 1958 nearly fifty LSAA research projects have been undertaken. Some have resulted in direct and immediate benefit to members. Others have encouraged and stimulated associate companies to develop much needed products and machines for the linen supply industry. A brief description follows of a number of LSAA's research projects:

Research Possibilities for Linen Supply (1958)—This study by Arthur D. Little, Inc., outlined a general research program for the industry and detailed specific projects that could be explored first.

New Products for Linen Supply (1958-1959)—A study by the W. J. J. Gordon group of Arthur D. Little, Inc; developed more than a score of possibilities for new linen services. Included were drapes, rugs, venetian blinds, continuous hair cloths for barber chairs, wall ceiling light shades, chaise lounge covers, continuous counter-mats. Subsequent market studies showed little promise for most of these products.

Long Range Objectives (1958)—This included an evaluation by Arthur D. Little, Inc., of the capabilities and limitations of a continuous washer being developed by the American Linen Supply Company, a comparison of the costs of continuous versus conventional washing, and an analysis of garment finishing methods. The study showed that the newer methods for washing and finishing were feasible but would require further development of machinery and fabrics.

Automatic Continuous Towel Winder (1958-1965)—A feasibility study was made by Arthur D. Little, Inc. Several models were designed and built, but they did not give reliable performance. The project was terminated in 1956 because manufacturers, now aware of the need, had begun their own development programs. Several improved towel winders are available as a result.

Automatic Inspection Machine (1960 to present)—The Research Committee saw the need for a device to detect automatically stains, holes, and tears in linens. They contracted with Armour Research Foundation and Atronic Products Corporation to develop separate concepts for such a machine. They decided against the ARF approach and directed Atronics to continue its development and build a prototype. The resulting optical-electronic device looked promising, and orders were taken in 1964 for machines that would be built by Stewart Warner Electronics. At that time it was determined that the design specifications were marginal, and that the device would not perform adequate inspection without major modification.

The project was held in abeyance until 1967 when American Electronic Laboratories proposed a new concept, using a modified television camera as a scanning device. In 1969 specifications were established by AEL and the Research Committee, and orders were placed by members for fifty units. The prototype is now being tested in the laboratory.

Sling Study (1960-1964)—This indicated that considerable savings could be realized with a material handling system that used slings to transport soiled and washed linens.

Textile Improvement Feasibility (1958)—This study by Arthur D. Little, Inc., indicated various ways for improving textile products. It covered blending cotton with synthetics, fabric treatments for stain resistance, wrinkle resistance, or greater life, and possibilities for non-woven fabrics.

Mildew Control (1958-1960)—This work by Arthur D. Little, Inc. evaluated the effectiveness of numerous chemical products for inhibiting mold growth in solid damp linen. The most practical were shown to be sodium pentachlorophenate and P.M.A.—phenyl mercuric acetate salts.

Stain Removal and Suppression (1958)—A number of phosphate salts were evaluated by Arthur D. Little, Inc. to see if they imparted stain resistance to fabrics. None of the treatments was lasting enough to be useful for linen supply.

Resin Treatment for Garment Finishing (1958)—This was an evaluation of an early resin finish by Arthur D. Little, Inc. The finish was not practical because it weakened the fabric severely.

Rust Prevention (1960)—A reduction in rust stains can be achieved by treating linens with sodium nitrite, but the cost could not be justified for a rust-inhibiting treatment for all linens unless there is a high incidence of rust stains. The study was done by Arthur D. Little, Inc.

Stain Investigation (1961-1960)—As a result of the rust prevention study and the work done in mildew control, LSAA investigated the incidence of various stains not removed in the normal wash process. The majority of the stains and holes were caused by mildew. Few rust stains were reported.

Non-Woven Fabrics (1960-1961, 1962, 1968-1969)—The feasibility of non-woven fabrics for linen supply use has been evaluated periodically. The cost of processing a continuous towel conventionally is compared to the cost of manufacturing a clean non-woven towel by reconstituting soiled non-woven towels. Resins and fibers are reclaimed to the fullest extent.

The first evaluation done by Arthur D. Little, Inc., indicated that non-woven costs were in excess of conventional costs. A study by Charles T. Main, Inc., in 1962 verified this. Further review by Arthur D. Little, Inc., in 1968-1969 indicated that non-woven processing costs for the continuous towel were still greatly in excess of conventional processing.

Fabric Treatment Machine (1960-1964)—A device for spraying mildicide on flatwork items as they passed through the ironer was developed by then staff member Peter Pano working with Arthur D. Little, Inc. Further development was discontinued despite satisfactory field trials because of the possibility that fumes from the toxic chemicals sprayed on the fabric might be a health hazard.

Dress Finishing Machine (1961)—The Research Committee gave support to Colmac for the development of a steam-air finishing machine for synthetic garments. The well-known "Connie" resulted from this effort.

High Styled Garments (1961-1963)—LSAA sponsored a "We Wash—You Wear" program to provide more attractive garments for linen supply customers and prospects. Customers were apparently willing to pay more for these garments but at the time the quality required could not be provided consistently. The project encouraged further developments in higher quality apparel for linen supply.

Continuous Washer Tests (1961–1963)—LSAA conducted a series of evaluations on several continuous washer concepts: Steiner American, Jet-Stream, and Riggs & Lombard. The tests showed that the machines were capable of adequate washing, but that further development was needed to produce reliable and economical devices.

Garment Finishing System (1961-1969)—Working jointly with American Uniform Co., Coats & Clark, duPont, Klopman Mills, and Proctor & Schwartz, LSAA developed a polyester-cotton garment and a processing method that materially reduced finishing costs, increased garment life, and improved appearance. Heart of the system which is described in greater detail in Chapter 15 is the LSAA Hot Box, an invention of staff member Howard Rosenfeld. It applies controlled moisture, heat, and agitation to laundered garments passing through the box on hangers. George E. Mathiasen of Denmark and Hydraxtor of the United States have been licensed to manufacture and distribute the Hotbox. The LSAA garment finishing system is now extensively used in Europe and the United States.

Orientation (1962-Present)—The Research Committee has a continuing interest in developing a machine for picking, flattening, and orienting linen items so that they can be fed to an ironer or a folder. The technical problems associated with handling a limp fabric item have made slow progress. In 1962, Stanford Research Institute investigated a variety of ways to pick up and spread linen items. A prototype was built which consisted of a series of belts that would capture the corners of small items and carry them through a number of maneuvers until the items emerged flat and square. Too many of the items had to be rejected and recycled.

In 1967, American Electronic Laboratories proposed a method for flattening linen items by capturing them in an area of single thickness and applying air pressure. AEL was given two contracts, one to evaluate the capabilities of the flattening concept, and the other to perform a limited study of fabric dynamics. The first study showed that small items could be flattened at the rate of 1,200 pieces an hour. The second resulted in a chute which orients and centers any rectangular item as it slides down the chute. AEL also developed a rotating vacuum picker that takes single items from a tumbled pile. Prototypes of all of these devices have been built. Work is now under way to combine them into an economical and reliable small piece handling device.

Delivery Study (1963-1966)—In conjunction with a Research Sub-Committee, A. T. Kearney & Co. Inc., developed guides for the industry which made it possible to schedule each route salesman for a fair day's work. Other techniques were developed for determining the best delivery frequency and the best delivery system. Workshops are held periodically to advise members how to use the delivery guides to reroute for maximum efficiency and to improve their overall operation. Significant reductions in delivery costs have been made through use of the guides.

Press Covers (1963-1965)—An LSAA research study of a variety of newer fabrics indicated that Nomex nylon had from three to seven times longer life than conventional press cover fabrics. Associate companies were encouraged to make this fabric available to linen suppliers. Nomex is now used extensively.

Electronic Data Processing (1964)—A textile rental merchandise glossary and code manual was developed by LSAA and IBM. It contains a short code (four digits) and a long code (seven digits) which can be used to describe fully all textile rental items.

Soil Handling (1962-1969)—In 1963 Stanford Research Institute did preliminary work on automatic pickup of soiled items but discontinued this effort in favor of clean linen orientation methods. In 1965 a research subcommittee was formed to pursue new developments in automatic soil counting and recording, and sorting into wash classifications. A film was produced which described the best manual and automatic methods. Work is being continued to find improved soil handling methods.

Water Re-Use (1962-1964, 1968-present)—A system for reclaiming laundry effluent developed by Mineral Industries Corporation of America was tested in 1963. As results were not promising the work was discontinued. In 1968 at the request of LSAA Rex Chainbelt developed another concept for water reclamation. Their system and others are being considered by LSAA, the Institute of Industrial Launderers, and other interested textile maintenance organizations.

Systems Analysis (1966-1968)—A Research Subcommittee worked with Dunlap & Associates to develop a mathematical model of the linen supply industry to provide insights into industry needs. A Material Flow/Cost/Cash Flow model of a linen supply plant was prepared. Further work was deferred indefinitely, pending review and appraisal of the model by interested linen suppliers.

Sanitation (1967-Present)—Long-time high temperature washing processes used by linen suppliers were shown to produce practically sterile linen in tests conducted years ago. Recently, the hotel and motel industry has promoted short-time low-temperature laundering of no-iron linens. Tests conducted in 1968 at the Applied Biological Sciences Laboratory showed that this procedure would not kill harmful bacteria. LSAA is working with the National Sanitation Foundation and the American Public Health Association to establish standards for laundering and handling of linens for public use.

Computer Assisted Route Development (CARD) (1966-present)—Successful manual application of the LSAA Delivery Guides indicated to the Research Subcommittee and A. T. Kearney & Co. Inc., that a more widespread use of these modern techniques would be achieved if a computer could be enlisted to perform the routine but highly complex chores. Kearney developed a powerful set of computer programs that now have that capacity, and LSAA staff member Anthony Marmo has the assignment to implement this project. A ROAD program produces a computer presentation of the network of roads, streets, and expressways in a metropolitan area; a PLOT program locates the plant and its customer locations in the road network; an ANALYZE program determines the efficiency of the present delivery operation, and what can be saved by reducing delivery frequency; a ROUTE program develops the best routes to serve the customers of the plant. Pittsburgh is the first city to start the CARD program (1969). Application of CARD should reduce delivery costs sharply.

Processing of Garments on Hangers (1968-present)—This is an extension of the LSAA Finishing System. It envisions complete on-hanger processing from the time the garments enter the plant until they leave. A research subcommittee directs this activity. Tests performed at Wyandotte Chemicals Corporation indicate that garments can be cleaned on hangers by soaking, spraying, and brushing. The concept will be presented to interested machinery manufacturers.

Flatgoods Orientation (1968-present)—A concept for orienting large flatwork items is under investigation. It requires the development of a memory fabric and appropriate machinery to dry and transport this fabric under such conditions that it will flatten and orient. American Laundry Machinery Industries, Burlington Industries, and Celanese have expressed an interest in this project.

Fabric Research and Development (1968-present)—Through this project mills are encouraged to make fabrics compatible with linen supply processing systems. Fabrics under study are tricots or knits of man-made fibers, plied yarn construction for polyester/cotton blends, and all types of polyester/cotton durable press finish.

Market Research—Until 1969 when the work was turned over to LSAA's Marketing Committees, market research had been directed by the Research Committee. Studies had been conducted by Leo Shapiro & Associates on the future needs and wants of customers, washroom services, potentials for home linen supply, and the use of a continuous countermat for restaurants. The same organization prepared detailed guides to the supermarket and restaurant fields. Arthur D. Little, Inc., engaged in project at Jordan Marsh Department Stores in the Boston area to develop a model for member use in renting front-of-the-store apparel to retail establishments. An aid to decision-making in marketing was prepared by the Management Analysis Center of Cambridge. Other marketing studies were done in the hospital and nursing home fields, in disposables, executive shirt rentals, colleges and universities, as well as in the preparation of a series of design guides for architects.

Research By Associate Companies—While LSAA has made immense strides in applied research for linen supply, many associate companies have invested much money, time, and effort in modernizing and improving their products. Improvements and new products have greatly widened the choices of linen suppliers and reduced their operating costs. Included in addition to newer machines are new methods of mending torn fabric through the use of special heat patches, emblems in color for customer identification, improved towel cabinets, floor mats, new locker systems to permit each employee in a plant to keep his workclothes in a private locked compartment for which only he and the route salesman have the key, major innovations in cloth and fabric with the principal change being the development of polyester/cotton blends, improved materials handling systems—to mention but a few of many useful changes.

The linen supply industry has come a long way from the 1920s when running a towel continuously through a single cabinet to test its durability was considered a research milestone. It still has a distance to go until it achieves its goals of maximum mechanization, but the industry knows the direction to take and is confident that within a few years a sharp reduction in processing costs will be achieved and that many of its other objectives will be attained.

CHAPTER **12**

EDUCATION:
A TURNING POINT

**HOW A YOUNG INDUSTRY
BEGAN TEACHING ITSELF
FROM SCRATCH**

One of the important developments in education is the concept of learning as a continuing progress. It has always been that; yet the traditional outlook saw education as stopping at a certain point. The college diploma does not mean as once it did that the recipient was finished with education and could get on to the business of a career. Now it signifies that a milestone has been passed. Today's college graduate is usually aware that he has many more educational milestones ahead. Paraphrasing a college president in his speech to the graduating class, "He who graduates today and quits learning tomorrow is uneducated the day after."

In his book *The Autocrat of the Breakfast Table,* Oliver Wendell Holmes wrote, "Everybody likes and respects self-made men. It is a great deal better to be made in that way than not to be made at all." The linen supply industry members many persons who could be described as "self-made men." Even in the contemporary technological world, hundreds of linen suppliers began their careers in business without specialized training. Sometimes with no formal education whatsoever, they made extraordinary names for themselves in the linen supply industry.

The "self-made man" is the person who is constantly in the process of re-making himself. This is education, requiring a sense of strong purpose to achieve the highest possible goals. Also needed is the ability to discriminate between education as a nourishing process and information-gathering, simply gorging one's head with data.

A British author, writing in the 1870s on the subject of riding, cautioned his readers against plunging too zealously into the learning process with the advice, "Education should be as gradual as the moonrise, perceptible not in progress but in result."

Today, when many products are labelled "instant," some people believe that everything has to be done at breakneck speed to be effective. "Mini-courses" are popular for quick self-improvement and supposedly lasting success. In business many a harried executive has hurried off to a brief high-impact seminar under the delusion that when he returns he will be miraculously transformed. The results have often been disappointing. The ideas seemingly crystallized at the one or two-days' session have dissolved like sugar in hot water when exposed to the heat of everyday work.

The industry almost has to teach itself as it goes along, having only limited precedent as a guide. Since it is constantly exploring areas where the quantities and qualities are unknown, it cannot easily succumb to the tactical error of trying to establish "courses" that will transmit "instant knowledge."

The Linen Supply Association of America has embarked on a broad and continuing program of education and reflective study in an effort to achieve permanent rather than superficial results.

The initial university program of the linen supply industry was LSAA's First Executive Management Institute, held at East Lansing, Michigan, for a week in January, 1958. Sponsored in collaboration with the College of Business and Public Service of Michigan State University, the Institute was attended by executives from both large and small linen supply firms. This program, the objective of which was "to broaden executive interest in an understanding of general administrative problems," covered a wide range of subjects from corporate organization to employee relations, finance, and labor and was condensed on a high level. Among those giving lectures and leading discussions were professors from Michigan State, Notre Dame, and the University of Chicago, as well as a top-ranking management consultant from New York City.

The first Institute established a broad pattern for subsequent ones to follow. Themes under discussion, for example, included "Creativity in Modern Business," "Psychology and Business;" "Human Relations."

Although this first formal program did not take place until 1958, the industry had been involved for more than a decade in many LSAA regional and local clinics on Sales, Production, Delivery, Human Relations, administration and the like. These sessions were specialized and much shorter than the Institutes that would follow.

A second Executive Management Institute was held in 1959 at Michigan State University, followed by a third in 1960 at the Harvard Business School. As in the case of their predecessor, these were designed for higher-echelon executives of member companies of LSAA. The Harvard curriculum covered Communication, Administrative Practices, Problems in Labor Relations, and Business and the American Society, with emphasis on case studies.

The nature of the Institutes was pinpointed by LSAA President Lawrence C. Kline who stated, "The Institutes give industry members a rare opportunity to learn what is new and basic in management. This is the kind of education that is a must for forward-looking businessmen." Referring to his attendance at an LSAA Institute, one member said "It was the most exciting intellectual experience of my life."

In 1962, an LSAA Executive Development Institute was held in Houston, in collaboration with faculty members from the University of Houston's Management Development Center. Topics selected were characteristic—Effective Leadership, the Management Process, Fundamentals of Human Relations, Administration. In the same year another Institute was held at the University of Colorado. In succeeding years Institutes were also held on the West Coast in cooperation with UCLA.

Through 1968 six of the Institutes have been held at Harvard. Participating professors at Harvard have included among many others, Robert W. Austin, Stephen H. Fuller, Ralph M. Hower, Thomas Kennedy,

Theodore H. Levitt, F. Warren McFarlan, Martin V. Marshall, Benjamin M. Selekman, John R. Yeager, Professor Hower has served as LSAA Harvard Institute Director from the inception.

Even only a week together of classroom discussions with top-drawer professors and small bull sessions with soul-searching exchanges results in a different perspective for the participants. Such exchanges breed a greater willingness to tolerate ambiguities and a better understanding of the axiom that there are often many roads to truth. Industry members who have attended the Association's one-week institutes at Harvard, UCLA, and other universities have felt sufficient kinship to form an Institutes Alumni Club which meets annually at the convention to hear a short address by a distinguished educator. During the year they also receive reprints of relevant articles from *Harvard Business Review, California Management Review,* and similar publications. They have their own officers; C. H. Rohman served as the first president, and for the 1967-1969 period the president was Hilda Folkman, who also composed the club's own alumni song.

Numerous other educational programs were launched by LSAA. Hundreds of sessions lasting from one to three days have been held on all phases of linen supply with industry leaders and other participating as speakers, workshop chairmen, and resource persons.

With fourteen Executive Development Institutes already held at major universities, and with many specialized meetings an integral part of its educational work, LSAA plans to accelerate its programs in education. From the first technical sessions which remain as necessary as ever to the solution of common problems, the industry has reached the point where its members are delving into even more sophisticated subjects.

Together, linen supply executives explore the behavioral sciences, ethics in business and the broad implications of economic change. In 1967 LSAA developed a "Management Training Game," which through simulation and the use of computers, provided practical exercise in management functions. The Association emphasizes the importance of data processing—both manual and automatic—and has a comprehensive program devoted to management information and data systems.

The industry recognizes that technology is changing so rapidly that much more than annual training sessions are needed. Education must be a continuing process at all levels. The Association stresses both specialized and broad training so that the executive and other employees may set their sights on higher objectives.

CHAPTER **13**

THE REASONS
FOR GROWTH

HOW AN INDUSTRY
DEVELOPED THROUGH
SERVICE

"In the business of life," wrote V. C. Kitchen, "Man is the only product. And there is only one direction in which man can possibly develop if he is to make a better living or yield a bigger dividend to himself, to his race, to nature or to God. He must grow in knowledge, wisdom, kindliness and understanding."

The linen supply industry has experienced a growth more meaningful than simply an increase in customers and dollar volume. Its growth also includes the intangibles of service. As a result, linen supply has increased itself almost tenfold in the last three decades. While it is true that a substantial percentage of the increase is related to the general increase in the U. S. gross national product, much of it is due to new and more effective ways of doing business, the development of improved processes and equipment, and increasingly better public and customer relations.

On September 27, 1965 the linen supply industry reached another milestone. On that date, a major article in *Barron's National Business and Financial Weekly* headlined "No Washday Blues," portrayed the industry's bright financial picture.

"Things are heating up throughout the unique business," wrote *Barron's* reporter, Norris Willatt. "Part of the reason, surely, is the general trend toward leasing rather than purchasing goods of all kinds. At the same time, the linen suppliers are growing through diversification—of both products and services—as well as by expansion into new markets."

As the article explained, mergers had transformed many small firms into a few big ones, "although at least 1,600 still compete coast-to-coast. . . . Modernization of plant and equipment, with the accent on automation, is helping to keep profits as snappy as a hot towel."

When the Linen Supply Association of America was founded in 1917, the industry was still extremely small. No one dreamed then that in less than fifty years more than 200 linen supply firms would each have annual receipts of well over half a million dollars, some of them many times that figure. In fact, there were barely 200 firms at the time, although the industry was at least thirty years old. Most were small operations with limited routes. Linen supply was such an infinitesimal fraction of the gross national product—then about $80 billion—that it was not mentioned in economic and financial reports.

At that time most of the industry was centered in the populous Midwestern states, and on the Eastern seaboard. Towns, let alone smaller cities, did not even know about the existence of such a service as the supply of towels and linens. It was remarkable that Brace Helfrich found competition in a city the size of Wichita. More typical was the case of Meyer Stettner who moved to Allentown, Pennsylvania, where he found no evidence whatsoever of linen service.

In those days, there was relatively little urban population for until almost 1920, the majority of Americans lived on farms or in towns of fewer than 2,500 people. The 1910 census reported 49 million people living in places with a population of less than 2,500 and 41 million in bigger towns and cities. By 1920 the movement toward bigger cities had gained momentum. That year, there were 54 million people in towns of more than 2,500 and 51 million in smaller places. Few men would have been willing to try to build a linen supply business in areas where there were at most 2,500 people, of whom only a small percentage could have used their services.

Other factors hindered growth, particularly in smaller towns not too far from big metropolises. Roads were poor and travel by horse was slow. Few suppliers had large enough businesses to afford cars. Since there was no way they could bring towels and linens to the small towns on an economic basis, these towns did without linen supply.

Even in the large cities, manufacturing and processing firms were much smaller and there were fewer restaurants and hotels. There was less prosperity and people did with fewer of the "good things" of life. There was also much less awareness of the necessity for cleanliness. By the twenties, however, many new trends were under way, each of which contributed to, and accelerated the growth of, the linen supply industry and the use of its services in more areas of the country. Roads improved and small towns adjacent to larger ones were serviced by new, faster vehicles. Industrial and processing firms expanded; restaurants and hotels did more business. To those already in the linen supply industry, these trends presaged a bright future.

Linen supply expanded comfortably until 1929.

With the Depression, linen supply volume decreased, yet, at the same time, the number of firms increased because many domestic launderers seeking to stay in business had entered linen supply.

Describing the Association in 1933, Albert Gitlow, then president, observed that "the membership of the national association is about 400 firms, which do about 75% of the linen supply business in the country. Practically all of the members of the national Association also belong to local associations." The industry, he said, could be divided in general into five main divisions, although quite a number of companies furnished a range of linen supply services.

First, the office towel division: Firms providing this service generally furnished cabinets, brushes, combs and soap for use with their towels.

Second, the table and bed linen division: These firms rented table linen to hotels, restaurants and clubs, and bed linens to hotels and rooming houses.

Third, the barber towel division which rented face and massage towels and hair cloths.

Fourth, the professional towel division: supplying doctors and dentists.

Fifth, the coat and apron division, which rented to stores, factories, and restaurants.

By 1940, the total dollar sales volume had reached about $106 million. There was a slow pace in the thirties, basically a reflection of the times, for the country's overall industrial output had also decreased and was making slow recovery. The U. S. gross national product which was $104 billion in 1929, had shrunk to $56 billion by 1933.

After World War II, survival became a problem for many linen supply firms. Those that did survive followed different paths than the companies that came into existence in earlier years. For example, consider City Linen Service of Dallas, Texas, a linen supply company that started in 1940. It is now one of the larger linen supply companies in Dallas. It was founded by C. R. Leatherwood, who terms himself a "country boy" who entered Texas Technological College in 1931 but dropped out because of the Depression. Later, he attended the University of Houston.

In 1952 City Linen went into linen supply, servicing all types of customers, with the exception of motels and hospitals which were added in 1958. "Because of the desire for better-looking garments," said Leatherwood, "we have lost a lot of cottons in recent years. Now that we are putting in the 65-35 blend apparel, we hope to increase our wearing apparel services."

The trend toward replacing linens with paper products has not yet affected the Dallas area much, he said.

> Some customers have gone to paper in napkins and washroom towels. We have added paper napkins to our supplies. Because napkins can be an unprofitable item, we would rather sell the paper napkins than furnish the linen ones. So far we don't sell a lot, because some accounts object to them. For others, there is no objection at all.

City linen's development and growth are somewhat similar to what happened to many other firms in earlier years. To attain the size which City Linen felt was necessary, in the fall of 1968 it finalized plans for a merger with a publicly owned corporation, Gulf Continental, Inc., with a diversified group of companies.

Resurgence of linen supply after the Depression took place after World War II. From that time until the present the growth of the industry has been substantial.

In 1948, according to the U. S. Census, there were 1,176 linen supply establishments in the United States, and in 1963 according to the census there were 1,591. During the same period there was a trend toward mergers.

"Perhaps the most compelling reason," wrote one linen supplier, Louis Zipperman of Community Linen Rental Service, Sacramento, California, "is the fact that as the years go by the linen rental industry has increasingly outstripped its horse and buggy days."

> Then all it took to go into business was a supply of white dresses and coats, some towels and aprons, all of which you got on long-term credit, perhaps a second-hand truck, a laundry that wanted to help fill its volume gap, a strong pair of legs to make lots of calls and the ability physically to work some ten to fifteen hours a day six days a week and many times seven.
>
> Then, as the owners found their businesses growing larger, they found a small laundry plant for themselves.
>
> Contrast that situation to today, furnishing items that were not considered part of the rental industry ten years ago. White shirt rentals, a complete line of linens for hospitals, lint-free, static-free dust control surfaces. Our research group has talked about such things as linen covers for walls and floors. We have seen a launderable cotton venetian blind. We have discussed the possibilities for a machine which will be fed soiled items and automatically wash, extract, iron, reject for stains and holes, stack and tie the clean textiles into bundles.

Present-day demands require a large capital investment and more managerial talents than normally available to a smaller company.

Why do some firms grow while others stand still?

As in any industry, some firms are better managed than others. The executives of the firm that grows know how to develop systems and procedures for an ever-enlarging organization, and how to price their service properly so that they have additional capital available for expansion. These abilities, though, only lead to expansion when there is the desire to expand. Some fairly large firms, with four or five or more plants often reach plateaus.

One linen supplier, who had expanded and acquired three other plants, was even looking at another plant. "But," he said, "look, I'm too old to build more. We have enough problems running our present organization. New, younger management won't be ready to take over for a while."

Said another, "We've been trying to attract more young management executives to the industry and to our firm, but it isn't easy."

A third told of an executive they had hired who had become company treasurer, but who decided to accept another position in another industry for less money:

> It was a glamour industry. The linen supply industry is not a space-age industry. Its challenges are those of any other business, and good execu-

tives have an excellent future here. But some would rather work for less money in an industry that does something more exciting, whose accomplishments are headlined in the press or talked about in speeches or written up in popular magazine articles.

Yet linen supply is exciting to the discerning who see in its people, technology and problems a tremendous challenge. As Professor Robert Tannenbaum of the Graduate School of Business Administration, University of California, expressed it to an LSAA audience:

> Rather than being concerned with "I'm Boss, and I have the authority and the right to tell you what to do," the manager of the future is increasingly going to see that his job is to create the right atmosphere and environment for his people. He will create a setting in which his employees are able to say, "This is a good, exciting and stimulating place to work . . ." You, as people looking toward the frontier, need to consider what it will take on your part to become the managers who create this atmosphere.

Part of the "atmosphere" will be developed through the use of more sophisticated equipment, as was the case with Mission Linen. In June, 1962 Mission Linen Supply, headquartered in Santa Barbara, California, and headed by G. B. Page, realized the necessity of computerizing to control more effectively their services. A pilot program using NCR equipment was put into effect in Hawthorne, California. In January, 1963, two programmers were hired and a contract was signed for the first Mission Linen Supply computer. By June of 1964 the computer was found inadequate and another was installed. All of Mission Linen's twenty-three plants were put on the machine. Mission has realized a marked reduction in its linen replacement and office costs and also has improved its cash flow.

In mid-1966 the data center was turned into a full-scale service bureau known as the SANTA BARBARA DATA CENTER, serving other companies as well as Mission. Sixty linen plants are now serviced by the system. Another Mission Data Center has been opened in Kansas City, Missouri.

The growth of linen supply has paralleled the growth of the nation's economy for the most part. The industry's volume is about one-tenth of 1% of the gross national product. From 1940 when linen supply sales were estimated at $106 million, the industry has grown to about $930 million in 1969. (Detailed figures are given in the appendix.)

Per capita expenditures in the United States on linen supply for non-agricultural employees was $4.69 in 1948, $9.05 in 1963, and $10.41 in 1967, according to the U. S. Census. (A chart for census years is included in the appendix.)

In 1958 the average linen supply company with payroll had an annual dollar volume of $292,953. In 1963 it was $388,126, and in 1967 it was $511,410.

Yet, as *Barron's* reported:

> All this expansion is barely keeping up with the demand of a growth market that seems to be boundless. Spurred by rising population and living standards, the market is broadening, too—as more industries, institutions, and private individuals are won over each year to the idea of renting instead of owning the towels, bedsheets, aprons, and other linens they keep in constant use.

Among the factors contributing to growth is the increasing effectiveness of marketing programs. For many years, the term marketing was considered almost a synonym for selling. But as has been pointed out again and again by men like Samuel B. Shapiro, "An essential distinction must be made between selling and marketing. In selling you are concerned primarily with satisfying your own needs, whereas in marketing you are largely concerned with satisfying the needs of the consumer or prospective customer."

Professor Theodore Levitt of the Harvard Business School, one of the nation's authorities on marketing, pointed out recently that an executive has to examine carefully what he is doing, because he may not really be in the business he thinks he is in. If you head a railroad, you severely cripple yourself by thinking you are in the "railroad" business when in reality you are in the "transportation" business.

Speaking of marketing and the growth of an industry, he says, "There is no such thing as a growth industry. There are only companies organized and operated to create and capitalize on growth opportunities."

In recent years, the LSAA, as part of its marketing work, has made studies and produced "Guides" to enable linen supply firms to meet changing customer needs. In early 1967, for example, four leading U. S. architectural firms were selected to prepare "Design Guides" in each of four areas where there is much linen service potential: hospitals, nursing homes, hotels and motels, and colleges. The industry has also engaged in a promotional campaign to make architects more aware of the space-and-money-saving possibilities with linen rental instead of in-plant laundries.

In a July 1966 survey, the LSAA reported on the information returned by some 20 per cent of 1,500 architects questioned. The response indicated that architects are influential in recommending the source of linens for a wide variety of clients. They can influence these clients to consider linen rental rather than in-plant projects. The report also showed that architects tend to favor outside linen supply because that gives them an advantage in using space more effectively and working within budgets. The study covered many types of buildings that would be occupied by users of linen supply.

Presenting the proper information to architects can be of considerable significance, because they may otherwise take action that helps substitutes for linen service. When architects plan buildings, for example, they may specify dispensers for paper towels, thus effectively blocking out washroom linen supply. A spokesman for F. W. Means in Chicago says that one effective method is to sell architects on the idea that they should provide tenants with a choice of either linen supply or paper. But linen suppliers, who otherwise might develop business through architectural channels, often make the mistake of not acting soon enough.

The trend toward market research in linen supply is relatively recent. John A. Morgan, president of Morgan Service, Inc., Chicago, had this to say:

> There was practically no coordination of market research and technological development until about 1920, when the industry began to develop specifics regarding manufacturer requirements. More notably, the coordination remained at a minimum industry in 1946 . . . Perhaps the most important step in my 36 years of experience has been the industry's pooling of knowledge, producing the expertise developed because of the coordinating effect of the national association.

Marketing research, technological development and growth are words and phrases all too easily bandied about. The healthy growth of any industry comes from many and complex sources: the correct diagnosis of consumer needs, providing the right products and services at reasonable prices, a satisfactory return on capital investment, a challenge to enterprising people who become interested in participating, excellent management teams, and reliable personnel.

Market research precedes new products and services and the innovative machines necessary to produce both new products and old at lower costs. Technological research has to be planned and put into action to develop new machines and other equipment. Linen supply's growth has been healthy largely because LSAA and associate companies have been research-oriented.

CHAPTER **14**

INDUSTRIAL LAUNDERING

A RELATED
SERVICE
INDUSTRY

NOW THEY'RE PACKAGING PEOPLE!

This startling headline, appearing in *Newsday* in the summer of 1968, announced an event that "was bound to come," but as the article it introduced queried, "who expected it before 1984?"

"They've done it to everything," *Newsday* continued "fruit and vegetables, frozen food, clothes, hardware, sports equipment and now—brace yourself—they're doing it to people."

While this is hardly news to people in linen supply, few can fully appreciate the extent of the trend, or its implications for the future. Using the Work Wear Corporation, "largest of the industrial uniform makers and renters," as a case in point, the magazine discussed the future of this unique service and its benefits to customers. Industrial laundering is so closely related to linen supply that frequently the two overlap.

And just how does linen supply relate to industrial laundering? An interview with Joseph B. Kirshbaum, an officer of Work Wear Corporation, and a former president of the Institute of Industrial Launderers as well as a former director of LSAA, sheds some light on the relationship.

Mr. Kirshbaum, reported the writer who interviewed him for this book, "is a big man, about 6 feet 2 inches, pleasant, very knowledgeable about the business and very excited about its future."

He has four children, including two sons who will probably come into the business. Joe went into industrial laundering in 1946 when he got out of service after World War II. He first went to work in Chicago with Kovocar Company, a firm established by his father, Harry L. Kirshbaum, in the mid-thirties. Harry and Joe's uncle, Irving Kirshbaum, had been in the dry cleaning business before then. Kovacar rented fender covers to garages and serviced customers through agents in key locations. These agents shipped the soiled covers to Chicago where they were laundered and then returned to the customer via the agent. Irving Kirshbaum is now Chairman of the Board of SERVISCO, a public company in the industrial laundering field and related industries with an annual income from services and sales in excess of 41 million dollars for 1969.

In 1947, Joseph Kirshbaum moved to Los Angeles, where he has resided ever since. His brother Ira, who works with him, is in charge of engineering and production. The two men had considerable experience in linen supply as well as industrial laundering, having bought Commercial Linen Supply, Oakland, California. "This was done," reported the interviewer, "because they both feel that industrial laundering and linen supply are naturally related. Many of their customers are clients of several of the companies in Work Wear, although salesmen specialize in their own particular field."

The Kirshbaums have been active in both LSAA and the Institute of Industrial Launderers. They believe that the contacts and functions of both associations have been extremely valuable to them.

Initially, the differences between industrial laundering and linen supply could be summed up in these words: dirty and not-so-dirty. Industrial laundering dealt largely with the rental of wiping cloths, mechanics' overalls, protective covers for automotive vehicles being serviced, gloves, and the like—all essentially greasy, petroleum soiled items. On the other hand, linen supply was associated with towels and toweling, table and bed linens, doctors' jackets, waiters' apparel, barbers' smocks, and similar products used to improve sanitation and, in the main, not of a heavy greasy kind. Thus, in a presentation made May 7, 1948, for LSAA and the Institute of Industrial Launderers before a subcommittee of the U. S. Senate Committee on Labor and Public Welfare, Stanley I. Posner made the following distinction between the two allied fields:

I am general counsel for the Institute of Institute of Industrial Launderers, a national organization whose members are engaged in the rental and laundering of overalls, coveralls, work shirts, work pants, such as are used by workers in steel plants, shipyards, railroad roundhouses,

and gasoline stations throughout the country. I am also general counsel
for the Linen Supply Association of America, a national organization
comprising approximately 800 members engaged in the rental and laundering of washable service apparel, restaurant table linens, barber and
beauty shop towels, office towels and similar articles.

Another contrast was made on Feb. 20, 1967, by Clarence T. Lund-
quist, administrator, Wage-Hour Division, U. S. Department of Labor,
in connection with the Service Contract Act:

> The department will include, within the definition of linen supply
> items, dresses, uniforms, bibs, aprons and other wearing apparel of the
> type used by barbers, doctors, waitresses, nurses, food workers, beau-
> ticians, etc. However, uniforms worn by mechanics and production
> workers in heavy industry, machine shops, garages, service stations and
> the like, where the garments are likely to be heavily soiled or greasy
> by the nature of their use, will not be considered as linen supply items.

As both industries moved into newer markets, definitions became
more complex. Both industries, however, involve textile maintenance,
other than diapers, on a rental basis.

In recent years the two types of service have edged closer together.
Industrial launderers, like linen suppliers, are involved in furnishing
rental textiles for clean room facilities and dust control. Both types
of services have found new business in the white collar markets, where
once the industrial launderer was considered to be limited to blue
collar applications with a grease-soil implication. In many cases the
industrial launderer is also a linen supplier. Both groups constantly
engage in research to perfect fabrics and garments and to develop
more effective systems of cleaning them and reducing wear and tear.

Is there much difference in their plants, equipment, employees,
related matters? The once marked differences have become far less
noticeable, although an industrial launderer is still less likely to have
flat work ironers unless the company is also engaged in linen supply,
and the industrial launderer uses more dry cleaning equipment, though
dry cleaning techniques are also being increasingly employed by linen
suppliers.

A tour through the plant of a modern industrial launderer is proof
that the industry, like linen supply, is becoming more complex. Specialized equipment manned by trained employees removes the heaviest
of work soils from wiping towels, chemically treated mops, shirts and
slacks. Large inventories of garments and dust control devices fill
storage areas. Frequently a computer in the office handles a wide range
of needs in billing, inventory, quality control, and scheduling. At the

dock the delivery vehicles manned by route salesmen are unloaded as the men exchange soiled textiles for clean supplies.

Industrial laundering is big business. According to the U. S. Census of Business for 1967 there were 918 industrial launderers with payroll in the U. S. with an annual dollar sales volume of $561,459,000. This compares to 1963's figures when there were 868 industrial launderers with an annual dollar sales volume of $372,431,000. Of these in 1963, there were 768 industrial launderers with payroll with annual dollar sales of $371,735,000.

A major contribution by industrial launderers to healthy business operations is the concept of flat-rating plus minimum delivery charges. These salutary practices are increasingly being adopted by linen suppliers.

In the early part of this century, worker recognition of the importance of clean clothing was demonstrated by the advent of industrial laundering. The industrial launderer met the worker as he left the plant, collected his soiled garments in exchange for clean, and took home the dirty apparel for laundering. Utilizing primitive washing equipment—wooden cylinder wash wheels and hand-fed coal boilers—he removed the heavy soil as best as he could.

Eventually plant management began to recognize the value of clean garments for the health and safety of employees and started to rent them. The industrial launderer, like the linen supplier, became not only a buyer and processor of garments, but also became involved in design. He contracted with plant management to have the necessary supply of uniforms at all times and in the proper sizes to fit individual employees. He assumed the responsibility for keeping garments in good repair, in addition to the cost of replacing apparel that was no longer adequate. The plant executive was free to concentrate on manufacturing those products which could achieve a profit for his company. And such matters as textile purchasing, processing, equipment investment, operation, maintenance, and inventory control became the problems of the industrial launderer.

Rental uniforms help to reduce labor turnover and to boost employee morale. Garments kept clean and neat at no expense to the employee contribute substantially to his pride in his work.

Rental of wiping cloths is an important part of industrial laundering services. Before these scientifically produced standardized towels were available, plant workers and mechanics had to wipe down machinery with assorted rags. These were bought in large quantities and had to be stored, thus taking up valuable space. A further problem was the disposal of the greasy rags. As machines became more complex and costly managers realized that assorted rags of varying fabrics had many drawbacks. They often had buttons or snaps which scratched equipment, and the time spent by the employee hunting the right kind of rag was costly.

Wiping cloths currently available from an industrial launderer are of uniform quality, highly absorbent, and leave no lint or foreign particles. It is therefore not surprising that millions of such cloths are in daily use.

The industrial laundering industry has been greatly strengthened by the excellent work of the Institute of Industrial Launderers which provides basic services in research, standardization, promotion, and education.

CHAPTER 15

BREAKTHROUGH!

CHALLENGE: THE FORCE
THAT TEMPERS
AN INDUSTRY

Not so many years ago, any author audacious enough to write about a fabric with a "memory" would have been promptly labelled a science-fiction writer. Although "memory" still seems perhaps too human an attribute to apply to a piece of inanimate fabric, it is as explicit a word as one can use to describe a remarkable phenomenon. "Memory garments" have, after all, attained an important place in linen service.

To focus more graphically on this dramatic area of linen supply research and development, we must go back several years to an event which took place, prosaically enough, in Brooklyn. The setting was a linen supply plant in which a small section had been set aside for experimental purposes. On the particular day with which we are concerned, the atmosphere was tense. Everyone in the room sensed that something unique, perhaps momentous, was in the offing. The occasion, nevertheless, combined both serious and humorous elements. The actors in the little drama were, in the main, sober-faced and quiet, although some of the plant employees glanced toward one corner of the room and joked about that "funny big box," a contraption 10 feet long, 8 feet high, and 6 feet wide.

Four men glued their eyes on the weird object, alien to anything else in the otherwise conventional enough linen supply plant. One of the four, a man in his late forties, dressed in a business suit, busily pushed two long rods in and out of the box. His face expressing extreme anxiety, he slapped one rod with his palm, stepped back and said, "Let's hope that does it and that what we see is as it should be." He emitted a short, unconvincing laugh, and moved forward to open the compartment door.

The man was Howard Rosenfeld, manager of Textile Products Research and Development for LSAA, and he was testing a revolutionary concept in garment finishing. If the device succeeded, linen suppliers would be able to finish difficult-to-iron but better looking and more expensive cotton-synthetic blend garments economically. New markets would open for the industry. Customers would look better, feel better and better appreciate their rented garments.

Success would also mean a major advance for linen supply research programs. Here would be the most conclusive proof yet that research does yield results and answers the difficult problems that linen suppliers face.

Rosenfeld opened the door of the big box, and extracted from it some synthetic cotton garments draped over hangers.

The garments were totally and unbelievably wrinkled.

"Pretty sad," said one of the other men, Arthur Maslow, as he looked at them. Maslow, as one of the heads of Standard Coat, Apron and Linen Service, had allowed the box to be tested in his plant at Rosen-

feld's request. Robert Maslow, his brother, was with him, as was Peter
V. Pano of the LSAA staff.

"Some hot box, some system," Rosenfeld scoffed, trying to act light-
hearted, yet evidently depressed by the dismal failure.

Something unexpectedly and unaccountably had gone wrong.

Looking at the results, Rosenfeld felt his shoulders slump. Scarcely
a wrinkle should have appeared on any of the garments. What might
have proved the first successful new concept in laundry finishing in
years had turned into a bust. Instead of making garments wrinkle-free
without pressing, the process had make them look worse than if they
had come out of a drier.

The three other men tried to soothe Rosenfeld's feelings.

"Maybe there's an answer still in the box," offered Arthur Maslow,
but without much conviction.

"Think a little. Maybe you'll come up with the answer," added Bob
Maslow encouragingly.

Rosenfeld thanked them, picked up his notes and walked to his car.
The theory was right, of that he was certain. Why did it break down
in practice?

Over and over in his mind, he recreated the development of the
theory, the creation of the big box. The idea had been conceived by
him not long after he had come to LSAA in 1961 as consultant on
man-made fibers. Garments made of these new fibers were beginning
to grow in popularity. They looked better, felt better, but they cost
more than cotton and had to be finished by a laundry the same way
as cotton by time-consuming and costly pressing. The high cost of
a synthetic blend garment, added to the high cost of pressing it, meant
that linen suppliers had to charge more money than customers were
willing to pay for rentals. As linen suppliers contemplated using the
new fabrics, they were understandably skeptical. Would they hurt
business? Or was there some way they could be used to advantage?
For possible answers, suppliers turned, through the Association, to
Rosenfeld, a Harvard graduate whose expertise on man-made fabrics
was widely known and respected.

In his quest for a new finishing method, Rosenfeld concentrated
on a single approach. There must be come way that a synthetic could
have a "memory". If the new garments could be "taught" to recall
the shape they had when they were first manufactured, then there
would be no need for ironing or pressing, nor for expensive, time-consuming labor. The concept was by no means a blue-sky idea. At that
time fabrics that would hold permanent pleats had already been perfected, using new types of fibers. Although there were as yet no practical "durable-press" fabrics, the theory of "fiber memory" was common knowledge. The question was how to apply theory to practice.

As Rosenfeld was to state later, "a high-performance fiber, obviously, is basic to the achievement of an improved garment product." What he foresaw was a fabric which had such strong characteristics for returning to its original smoothness that the wrinkles could literally be blown out through a hot-air system, thus eliminating the old pressing operation.

At the time of the Brooklyn experiments it was felt that there might be some parallel in the way the fabric was manufactured and the way the garment made from that fabric should be finished.

As synthetic compounds, the new fibers were heat-set in textile mills at 385 degrees fahrenheit, at which temperature the synthetic actually became a fiber. Possibly, to refinish a garment in a laundry, something should be done to reheat the fiber, maybe not to 385 degrees but perhaps to a temperature ranging from 190 degrees to 385 degrees in order for the fiber to return to its original shape.

Driving home in the car, Rosenfeld recalled his first crude experiment which had taken place in the basement of his apartment in Riverdale, New York. One morning, he went down to the washer and drier room in the basement carrying a few shirts made of synthetic fibers.

There he ran tests, one after another, each confirming his initial theory. A garment could be washed, put in a drier, run full course, and end up totally wrinkled. But, if he stopped the drier's cycle midway, he could pull out an unwrinkled garment which, if hung on a hanger, "remembered" its shape, and did not have to be pressed. Success obviously depended on the right balance of temperature and humidity.

That was where the idea for the more ambitious experiments had originated. Looking at the dry and unironed yet reasonably neat shirts, Rosenfeld reasoned that the same results would take place if he could put a multitude of laundered garments on hangers and expose them, under the right conditions, to the proper combination of heat and humidity. With one further element in the process, something to agitate the garments, the fabrics would recall their original shape. Then, when they cooled, they would have a pressed, yet fluffy look.

The first problem was that nothing like the enclosure he envisioned existed anywhere. Who could design and manufacture such a box? A few days later, Rosenfeld struck upon what seemed a partial answer in the then-new permanent creases in all-wool trousers. These creases were made durable through a process that involved spraying the fabric with a solution and then "curing" it in an oven. Checking further, he located a manufacturer of this kind of equipment, Automatic Steam Iron Company. But the hitch was that the temperature in these curing ovens was only 160 degrees. Since heat needed to re-set fabrics was

300 degrees, obviously, a new type of equipment would have to be designed and constructed.

The cost to build a new box was $3,000. The LSAA Research Committee said "go ahead" and the box was built, the very one that had turned into such a dismal failure in the demonstration in Brooklyn.

As he drove home, Rosenfeld went over the steps, one by one. Preliminary experiments in the basement of an apartment house had worked. The theory was right but what could be wrong with its practical application?

He had done something that he had not thought would create any different results. When he had arrived at the Standard plant to make the experiment, the nearest available washwheel had been one for processing 400 pounds of laundry. Using that big a unit for only the twelve garments he wanted to experiment with did not make sense, so he instead placed them in a net to separate them from the rest of the wash. Then they were placed in the box.

The garments in the net had been kept in a fixed position in the wash wheel. They had been that way for 60 minutes. Perhaps they had been in that position too long. Could the wrong combination of heat and time actually reset fibers? Maybe temperatures lower than 385° over too long a time removed the fiber's memory.

Rosenfeld turned the car around. With growing excitement, he drove back to the Standard plant. It was almost deserted, except for maintenance men. If fabric memory were a combination of heat and time, rather than just heat, he could easily prove it. He walked rapidly to a steam iron which heated to 330 degrees, and began to press out the wrinkles on one of the synthetic garments. Instead of pressing for the normal amount of time, he held the iron down longer. When he finished, the synthetic shirt had no wrinkles. Fabric memory was indeed a combination of heat and time.

He next located a 50 pound washer. He put in the twelve garments and waited till they were rewashed. Then back to the box. With the garments in it he agitated the rods, moving them back and forth methodically. At last, the time was up. When he opened the door, he pulled out wrinkle-free garments that looked as if they had been pressed by an iron. Success! True, the seams were puckered, but the experiment substantiated the theory. A revolution in garment finishing had begun!

But, many other problems remained to be solved. First, how do you eliminate puckered seams? Second, since synthetic garments last longer, more stains would accumulate which would have to be washed out without damaging the more expensive fabric. Third, no bleach would efficiently whiten synthetics. Fourth, what was the correct ratio of synthetic fiber to cotton? Fifth, what was the exact temperature, precise amount of steam, proper duration for garments in the box, needed agitation, correct distance between garments and right length for the box? And finally, Mark I, Rosenfeld's name for the box, was still a crude prototype and had to be re-designed as a materials-handling system.

Only recently had Rosenfeld come to realize the need for making the box part of a system. The concept of systems was spreading at this time. When he began to experiment at the Standard plant which had a considerable number of conveyors in operation, he was concerned by the amount of manual handling still necessary. He resolved that the LSAA box would incorporate a materials handling system.

The problems ahead were many. One man could not handle them all and Rosenfeld did not have the technical knowledge, time, or budget. He pondered how to go about bringing the box to fruition. There was not enough money to hire all the specialists needed, to set up laboratories, to make tests under working conditions. Yet, among the associate industries were men who could be of immense help. Why not draw on their resources?

Several firms were approached—a fiber company, a fabric mill, a chemical company, a thread company, a sewing machine company, a fabric manufacturer, a garment manufacturer, a linen supply company, a washing machine manufacturer and a hardware manufacturer. Each had the talent needed. The thread manufacturer, Coats & Clark, would try to develop a shrink-resistant sewing thread, thus stopping the seam from puckering so it would lay flat and smooth. The chemical company and synthetic fiber manufacturer, E. I. duPont, de Nemours & Co., would try to determine the best fiber blend. The fabric manufacturer, Klopman Mills Inc., would make a fabric with the blends for testing in the field. To see how the new fabric blend would wash best, Ciba Chemical and Dye Company and duPont would work on new wash and bleach formulas. To enable the committee to make actual experiments in the field, at first M. Snower & Company and then American Uniform Company, would make uniforms or garments with the new fabrics. To test-wash the new garments, the Ludell Manufacturing Company would modify washers. To try the garments in practical application, Standard Coat, Apron & Linen Service would deliver them to a customer, where they would be put through daily use. Then Standard would wash them with new formulas to see if correct whiteness would be attained and stain accumulation minimized. Singer Company would make tests to determine whether better sewing techniques would stop the puckering of the seams.

The basic plan was to get the most out of this great supply of talent in each company. Yet for every experiment, changes would have to be made in the fiber blend, for example, and in everything else—the sewing threads, and sewing methods, for example. The wearability would have to be retested. Backtracking would often be necessary. Should the final tests—the actual use and wash tests—not work satisfactorily, the whole process might have to begin anew.

Moreover, all this work had to be coordinated. Men from each company met with Rosenfeld frequently. He and scientists at duPont saw or phoned each other almost daily. Meetings were held at whatever place seemed most practical—in Ohio, Tennessee, Wisconsin, New York, Delaware, Florida, "Let's get together," someone would say, "to hash things out, find out where we are, plan the next steps."

At the meetings the experts discussed problems, analyzed progress. What was happening with the tests at duPont, for example? A researcher there spent almost a year testing different synthetic fibers, blending each with cotton to develop the most suitable synthetic cloth. He checked all the variables, studied blends of 65% dacron and 35% cotton, others of 70 and 30, 80 and 20, 90 and 10, any combination of any dacron fiber (there are many kinds) and cotton that might conceivably do the job. First he would run laboratory tests on one blend. A satisfactory blend would then be made into a fabric at Klopman Mills. Then that fabric had to be wash tested and box-tested. Did it wash efficiently? If not, why not? Once washed, what were the right conditions in the hot box?

To reduce puckering of seams, Coats & Clark searched for a thread that was both shrink- and stretch-resistant, which could withstand shrinking in up to 190 degrees in the wash wheel and over 300 degrees in the finishing tunnel, and which would not shrink more than 1%. It also had to be strong enough so that it would not break during sewing. It had to be durable, to last as long as the garment, and it had to withstand the new wash and bleach solutions popularly in use.

Coats & Clark's research facilities showed that seams lay flatter and look better when the sewing machine operator uses a finer thread, a smaller needle, and less sewing tension. Thread was developed that would not break, despite its slender construction.

Laboratory technicians working with rubber gloves and dustfree uniforms finally developed thread that was durable; that retains even tension during sewing; that does not creep, pucker, or shrink; and that resists stretch under temperatures varying from 170-190 degrees wet while washing to 300 degrees while drying.

As new threads were being developed, so was a new system of sewing. First, American Uniform Company had to test for the best stitch for the new synthetic threads. Should it be a chain stitch, or perhaps some other? Should the sewing be done on the bias? How many stitches per inch should there be for greatest strength of garments? How big should the needle be? Which way should button holes and hems be sewn? How fast should sewing machines go with the new thread?

The tests led to the development of a number of improvements in sewing techniques. A new lock-stitch in place of the conventional chain stitch was developed to prevent unraveling during laundering. To reduce puckering, it was determined that a maximum of ten stitches an inch should be used, that machine speed should be slowed down to 3,000 stitches a minute, and that machines should employ a smaller needle. Researchers also found that button holes should be lock-stitched to prevent unraveling and that there should be a new way to sew hems so that they lay flatter and smoother.

The problems were just as complicated for determining the correct washing formula and washing procedures. Were there maximum loads in each kind of washer on the market? Ludell Manufacturing Company had to analyze the washer wheel requirements of each new fabric. Needed were formulas (how much and which type of soap? water level in the wash wheel? water temperature? how long to wash? etc.) for proper laundering. Finally, a new wash wheel was developed to provide maximum efficiency, though Ludell found that most existing wash wheels were satisfactory, provided controls were maintained.

In addition researchers had to check temperatures, time of garments in washing, sudsing, bleaching, and rinsing. Were there some washing supplies commonly marketed that did not help the cycle? Were there bleaches on the market that did not do a satisfactory job? Ciba Chemical & Dye Company finally had to develop a special agent, an optical brightener, and test it to be sure it did not damage the fabric.

There were just as many questions to be answered about the box itself. What would be the right temperature, the right humidity, the right amount of agitation? What was the correct amount of air flow? What would be the best way of transporting the garments through the box?

Now, "Hot Box" became the generally used term for the box, and later more officially the "LSAA Garment Finishing System."

A second and much larger Hot Box was made. Manufactured by Proctor & Schwartz, Inc., it incorporated LSAA's ideas for materials handling. Here was not only a new system for drying and finishing garments, but also a method for drastically reducing the cost of materials handling. Garments did not have to be handled and rehandled. Instead, garments coming out of the wash were placed on hangers, suspended from a continuously moving conveyor. As they moved through the Hot Box, the garments fluff dry, iron smooth, crisp and clean for the next customer, did not require re-handling, achieving substantial labor savings. No one had to take them off the conveyor until they were sorted for routes.

This Hot Box was commercially successful with a conveyor that made it a production system. Thirty-five basic linen supply and industrial garment styles were created for the new fabric, in white plus twelve colors. The service life of the garments would be about twice that of a cotton garment.

The story of the creation and development of the LSAA Garment Finishing System and the "memory garment" is a continuing story. Research and development will never cease as long as there are creative people around whose daring will be greenbacked by imaginative businessmen.

CHAPTER 16

"FUTURE" IS A PLURAL WORD

AS THE INDUSTRY GROWS MORE COMPLEX, NEW OPPORTUNITIES MUSHROOM

"Lend me the stone strength of the past," wrote poet Robinson Jeffers, "and I will lend you the wings of the future. . . ."

The linen supply industry is assuredly one that has been built on "stones," the many individual businesses which accumulated over the decades to become a recognized part of the American industrial scene. It has grown from what one commentator termed "a handful of push-carts," whose owners knew practically nothing about laundering techniques, to an industry composed of well organized, smoothly operating companies. Or, as M. Maschke, Jr., President of LSAA, expressed it, "The industry has come a long way from the scattered instances of the push cart and the horse and buggy to the several pages of the *Congressional Record* (10748–10757) of May 24, 1966, in which it was favorably covered."

The dynamic character of an industry or company is indicated in part by the willingness of the next generation to enter the business and then to take over when their seniors wish to withdraw. In linen supply, while more and more non-family professionals are becoming associated with the industry, two-generation companies are legion.

Among the families with two generations or more in linen supply (this is only a partial listing) are Bishop and Smith of Alabama; Chisum, Drachman, Haskell of Arizona; Applebaum, Bruni, DiStanislao, Drachman, Gordon, Haskell, Landale, MacAulay, Marini, Miller, Presher, Sloan, Wilkinson of California; Sandler of Colorado; Willard of Connecticut; Clarke, Klinefelter, Viner of District of Columbia; Goldstein, Gross, Herskowitz, Vamvaks of Florida; Weinstein of Georgia; Killam and Magoon of Hawaii; Buik, DeNormandie, Lello, Morgan, Quigley, Stavrakas of Illinois, Hertz and Leve of Indiana; Helfrich, Johnston, Sights, Spalding of Kentucky; Ballard and Kean of Louisiana; Bonnano, Chonin, Churchill, Connors, Cummings, Falvey, Fitzgibbons, Fishman, Frawley, Gilman, Lewis, Linn, McDonough, Richardson, Robertson, Shapiro, Spilios, of Massachusetts; Auslander, Baxter, Genematas, Robertson, Rosen, Sandler, Schumer, Shulevitz, Singer, Zinger of Michigan; Fink, Gross, Steiner of Minnesota; Carlson, Heilman, Kartsonis, Pepper, Schuh, Spanos, Spence, Wayne of Missouri; Berger, Dudley, Rohman of Nebraska; Gladstone of New Jersey; Abelove, Alpert, Ames, Anderson, Band, Foley, Frey, Ginsberg, Gordon, Kradjian, Maslow, Potack, Ross, Schneider, Settel, Troy, Walmsley of New York; Edelstein, Fraser, Gross, Lane, Miller, Roskoph, Ruwe, Spero of Ohio; Georges, Lawrence, Rawlinson of Oregon; Black, Gitlow, Kline, Landy, Maslow, Moses, Mosler, Stark of Pennsylvania; Pear of Tennessee; Leatherwood, Lohmann, Shepherd, Wright of Texas; Knapp, Pollock, Steiner of Utah; Struminger of Virginia; Keeler, Maryatt, and Tomlinson of Washington; Wilson of West Virginia; Christopher, Drolet, Hector, Jolicoeur, Pitsiladis, Rill, Yaffe of Canada.

Among the three generation families in linen supply are the Hertzes of Muncie, Indiana—Maurice, Ben and Jack; Morgans of Chicago—Kenrick Ebenezer, his sons John, Kendrick and George Walker, and the sons of Kendrick—Charles and Scott, and of George Walker—George; the Gordons of New York City—Louis, Murray and Robert; the Maslows of Philadelphia—Joe, Lawrence and Steven; the Klines of Philadelphia—Jack, Lawrence and Stuart; the Landys of Reading, Pa.—George, Lewis, and Charles; the Steiners of Minneapolis—Frank M., his twin sons George R. and Lawrence M., and Lawrence and Robin, sons of George R.; the Pollocks of Salt Lake City —William R. Pollock, Sr., his sons William R., Jr., Richard S., Robert D., and William R. Pollock III, son of William R., Jr., and Robert D., Jr., son of Robert D.; the Jolicoeurs of Montreal—Nephtali, his son, John Paul, and his son Andre Robert; and the Laverdures of Montreal—Georges, his sons Roger and Bernard, and Roger's son, John Pierre.

A fourth generation family in linen supply are the DeNormandies of Chicago—Joseph B., his sons John, Grant, Theodore and Roland, their sons John B., H. Grant, Robert T., and Roland T., and their sons Jack, Allan, Grant H., Robert T., Jr.

As suggested before, increasingly, professionally educated managers from outside the industry are making their careers in linen supply. At the same time entire families of the newer generations, also professionally trained, are involved in linen supply. Thus, the four sons-in-law of Sam Spatt of Central Coat of New York City are heads of the company's various operations. The three sons of Roy L. Maryatt, Jr., on the West Coast direct the company's business in Seattle, San Francisco, Los Angeles, and elsewhere. Seven Maslows of the second and third generations are engaged in linen supply. Nine of the DeNormandies are still active in the company.

From the days of the one-item business, linen supply has expanded into a complex of many garments, many products, many fabrics. From the days of erratic methods and processes, with each little firm fending for itself, the industry has matured to the point where its members together turn mutual know-how into substantial progress. From the days of the crudely equipped washing room, the industry has advanced technologically to the point where total automation is not too far away.

As linen suppliers look ahead, they know with certainty that the future holds change in store for them. Change is what they have experienced in their lives and businesses especially in the last two decades, and they expect more: in processing, in record keeping and information retrieval, in management concepts, in marketing. They look forward to increased mechanization and perhaps some day even automation. There will be problems, many of them, yet each problem also brings new challenges and opportunities.

They anticipate garments made of newer miracle fabrics. They foresee markets hardly dreamed of in the 1960's and markets that are barely tapped now. They expect changes in the structure of the industry. As industry members continue to fight a cost/price squeeze, that is, as the cost of labor textiles, chemicals and other supplies increases faster than the prices charged for their services, more companies seek greater efficiency. Plants are enlarged with greater capacity for efficient operation and routing, and possibly running two or three shifts.

By 1980 the linen supply plant will be a far cry from the most mechanized linen supplier of today. Automation means basically two things: automatic handling of materials and automatic controls. To date, soiled linens cannot be put through the plant automatically, that is, without anyone touching them. But the industry is edging closer to this point.

Work is continuing on procedures that can automate the plant of tomorrow. In one of the Chicago plants of F. W. Means & Co., a continuous towel washing machine handles towels from the soil room to automatic rolling. The LSAA Garment Finishing System should eventually provide for similar no-hands processing again from the soil room to route-makeup; and other continuous processing is under development.

Looking toward this eventuality, S. A. Laurie-Walker of J. Stone & Co., Ltd., in London, wrote in August 1965:

> In the process industries, in the drive for increasing production and lower costs, the trend is always toward continuity. Paper, for example, is produced in continuously high speed machines. Concrete for highways is now being laid as a continuous process, and even the brewer is trying to brew beer continuously rather than batchwise. The oil refinery is probably an example of the most highly developed process in existence today . . . The washing processes and the subsequent elimination of moisture from the articles have already been mechanized considerably. Washing and hydro-ing are done in the same machine; and fully automatic machines which receive and disgorge their contents automatically are already in service. The finishing process has also been mechanized, and long ago the hand iron was replaced by calender irons.

These ran at speeds up to 50 feet a minute. They were replaced by six to twelve roll flatwork ironers which run at speeds up to 200 feet a minute, impossible a few years ago.

Laurie-Walker points out that the transfer of articles from washing to finishing has always required manual handling. The Stone Company has developed a continuous washing machine, currently being tested, with automatic transfer to a flatwork ironer.

At Gordon Davis Linen Supply Company in Philadelphia an electric eye counts each item of soiled linen while a punch-card operator keys in information describing the item. The total count is automatically transferred to the punch card. Eventually, it is hoped, equipment will be developed that not only counts the items but also reads a code number that tells which customers rent the garments, and that also determines the washing process to which the garment should be automatically conveyed.

Equipment is now in use that automatically mixes the correct solution for each washer load. The water is tested automatically and the equipment dispenses chemicals as required.

As we peer into the future we can foresee the time when soiled linens will be removed from delivery vehicles by mechanical equipment. The soiled textiles will then be placed on conveyors where they will be counted and sorted automatically and at the same time produce information for production and billing.

Although for years the linen supply industry used textiles made of cotton, in the late 1950s it started to supply polyester/cotton garments. In the 1960s such garments were increasingly provided. Just as suppliers discovered in the previous decade that many electronic and other manufacturers needed synthetic fabric garments to avoid lint, so too in the future unforeseen industrial developments will probably create a need for garments made of new fibers.

More and more of the garments rented by linen suppliers are being drycleaned. Companies in the industry are therefore installing dry cleaning equipment, and research can be expected for newer and better methods of dry cleaning by linen suppliers.

Many linen supply firms have moved into the rental of dust mops, mats, and cloths for building maintenance. These items are chemically treated to be electro-static and bacterio-static both of which this permit more efficient control of dust. The linen supplier picks up the used items, launders and then chemically re-impregnates them before they are returned to the customer.

Like the automotive and aerospace industries, linen suppliers look forward to an increased demand for their services because there will be more people to use them. As the standard of living rises, more services will be required. New markets will open, and older markets may well expand beyond normal population growth.

For example, in the early 1900s there were only 268,000 college students in the United States. Not until after World War II were these students thought of as a market for linen supply. By 1967, there were more than three million college students, many of whom receive weekly clean bed linens and towels, and sometimes blankets, from linen suppliers. The potential is still very big.

Summer camps also present a large potential market. Millions of youngsters go to camp every summer, many of them bringing their linens from home and paying to have them laundered. In recent years, camp directors, parents, and linen suppliers have recognized that the camper can use linen rental services just as the student does in school. (The same applies to the renting of gymnasium apparel to students.) As more campers use rental services, linen suppliers, who rent to schools and colleges, will find year-around markets for their products.

Other markets where linen suppliers expect tremendous growth are nursing homes, hospitals, and motels and hotels. With the advent of Medicare, nursing homes particularly became a marketing target for the linen supplier.

Medicare will increase substantially the population of our nation's hospitals and newer convalescent homes, and, therefore, linen service. More hospital administrators now realize that their own laundry plants are not as efficient as linen supply plants.

Gaining a foothold in the ever-growing hospital market involves problems—and therefore challenges. Inventory requirements in a hospital mean an investment of up to $250 a bed. The linen supplier may have to provide service seven days a week. Also, hospital administrators are often not provided with information for correctly assessing their in-plant laundering costs. Losses of sheets and pillowcases in hospitals are high. The processing of hospital linens requires extraordinary care because otherwise staph aureus and other germs may spread disease. Consequently, many suppliers have developed special facilities for handling hospital linens.

As the public becomes more mobile, more hotels and motels are built which in turn produces a greater potential for linen rental services. This potential is threatened by the use of on-premise laundering facilities. The linen supplier contends that such equipment is often uneconomic for motel and hotel management, and that frequently it does not produce linens that are as hygienic as those that come from such commercial processing plants as linen supply. It will be one of the fringe benefits the unions will negotiate. You will see every plant across the country providing apparel furnished by a linen supplier." Progressive plant managers increasingly provide such rental apparel to their employees to save wear and tear on their own clothing and to improve morale.

The newcomer to linen supply must be fortified not only by adequate management talents, but also by substantial capital. Modern linen supply must be buttressed by up-to-date machinery and an inventory in depth of textiles.

In an article that appeared in *American Laundry Digest*, May 15, 1958, Percy Brower, Jr., president of Clean Linen Service, Birmingham, Alabama, after five years of linen supply experience that followed years in family laundering, wrote:

> The linen supply business requires plenty of capital . . . If a plant runs about $40,000 per month in family laundry, and wants to get that same volume in linen supply, it would need approximately a quarter of a million dollars in linens, eleven to twelve trucks, two flatwork ironers, three or four large automatic washers, eight press units, boiler and building. It can add up quickly to half a million dollars! . . . It is not possible to talk about the linen supply business as a sideline to the family laundry business. It is an entirely separate and different kind of business. It is as different as running a restaurant or manufacturing shoes.

A spokesman for the American Institute of Laundering said in 1963:

> Linen supply is a big business that should not be entered into without thorough investigation. Linen supply embraces practically all of the processes of the laundry in addition to being much more complicated to operate successfully. The laundry owner who plans to go into linen supply should prepare himself to be in a thoroughly unfamiliar field . . . Few economies are possible in a combination organization. Laundering costs, if they are charged fairly against a linen and towel subsidiary, offer no economy.

A consideration that linen suppliers face is the possibility that some linen supply needs will be served by disposable garments and other linens. Here, for example, is a report from an independent business writer in Cleveland, Ohio:

> In this area, much concern and no little confusion is evident as to the industry's future. Tradition causes virtually everyone involved to hope for a continuation of the status quo. Everyone seems to agree, that this probably is not likely in the long run. Most of the companies in the Cleveland area are now supplying paper towels in cases where it is do that or lose the business. Most of them are not blind to the various paper and synthetic substitutes that are constantly entering the market. They are listening to the sales pitches and proceeding with product evaluations. An exception to this is Penn-Ohio which reportedly has gone all-out for an all-service operation with substantial success.
>
> The consensus in Cleveland is that there will always be a place for the linen supplier, but the business never again will be as straight-line, uncomplicated and profitable as it was during the past. Also those who eventually forego their sentimental attachment to the "good old days" and go *all-service* will undoubtedly fare much better economically than those who do not.

Some technological developments strengthen the linen supplier's position. "Soil release," for example, overcomes many of the acute staining problems that developed when durable press garments were rented. It aids appreciably in avoiding the tenacious retention of stains. In some instances mills apply "soil release" along with the permanent press resins. "Soil release" makes it possible to lift easily spots that are made by foods, grease, ink, and soot, by altering the surface of the blend fabrics. The complex chemicals and their careful application increase the basic cost, but this is likely to decline steadily as more of the product is sold and improvements are made in its manufacture.

Meantime, other trends are developing. Linen suppliers have tried diversifying into janitorial and window cleaning services, the furnishing of deodorizers, selling burglar alarm systems, etc.—and not always with success.

How far will diversification go? Will linen suppliers become multi-faceted firms, providing all kinds of services? Diversification in rental services will be aided by the growing shift to rentals in the American economy and in other countries as well. In 1955 few firms rented automobiles. Now, hundreds of thousands of automotive vehicles are rented. In 1955 few firms rented business furniture. Today it is a widespread phenomenon, as is the rental of tools, garden equipment, and hundreds of other items. As more products become everyday rentals, the linen supplier, a professional in supplying and servicing rented textiles, will be ready to meet the new demands.

Such demands will not be slight. In a 1966 convention address to the LSAA, Richard R. Salzmann, then director of public services of the Research Institute of America, said:

> More will happen in the next ten years, more change will occur, more growth will take place, more inventions needed, more distance covered, more needs satisfied, more goods made, shipped, sold, junked than in the entire civilization called Rome, or that period of Europe's most creative years called the Renaissance . . . We are just beginning a transformation of American society which will make of the next years an era radically different from what we have become familiar with since the mid-30s. The possibilities are there—but what will be the structure of this new time which lies ahead?

Whatever that structure, the linen supply industry now alert to the changing needs of its market, and motivated by the imperative of service, will have an increasingly significant part in the world of tomorrow.

APPENDIX TABLE OF CONTENTS

THE GROWTH OF LINEN SUPPLY SALES
1940-1969

The figures for 1948, 1954, 1958, 1963 and 1967 shown on the chart below are the actual dollar sales for linen suppliers reported by the U. S. Department of Commerce Census. For 1968 and 1969, linen supply sales volume has been estimated on the basis of LSAA's Business Growth survey.

Year	Linen Supply Industry Sales Volume (Million Dollars)	% Increase From Previous Period	Gross National Product (Billion Dollars)	% Increase From Previous Period
1940	106	—	101	—
1948	238	124.5%	259	156.4%
1954	326	37.0	363	40.2
1958	433	32.8	445	22.6
1963	571	31.9	589	32.4
1967	734	28.5	794	34.8
1968	808	10.1	866	9.1
1969	864	6.9	930	7.4

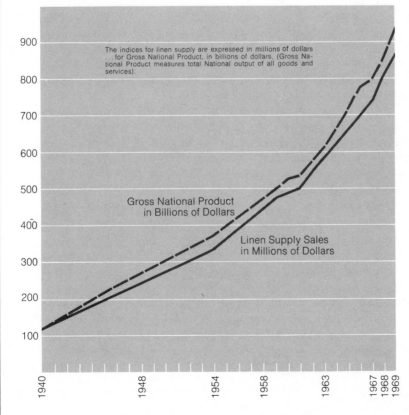

The indices for linen supply are expressed in millions of dollars ... for Gross National Product, in billions of dollars. (Gross National Product measures total National output of all goods and services).

Gross National Product in Billions of Dollars

Linen Supply Sales in Millions of Dollars

U.S. CENSUS OF BUSINESS—LINEN SUPPLY ESTABLISHMENTS WITH PAYROLL AND THEIR RECEIPTS, * 1948, 1958, 1967

STATE	ESTABLISHMENTS (NUMBER)				RECEIPTS ($1,000)		
	1967	1958	1948*	1967	1958	1948*
Alabama	20	7	8	$ 11,171	$ 4,509	(D)
Alaska	1	N/A	N/A	(D)	N/A	N/A
Arizona	21	14	6	10,976	5,347	1,337
Arkansas	13	7	6	4,199	2,082	974
California	142	117	89	83,489	46,002	25,112
Colorado	23	15	12	8,833	2,906	1,240
Connecticut	20	22	16	11,204	7,083	2,837
Delaware	3	4	2	(D)	(D)	(D)
District of Columbia	9	10	10	5,516	3,538	(D)
Florida	51	42	23	32,366	15,443	5,769
Georgia	17	16	9	16,888	6,959	2,914
Hawaii	6	N/A	N/A	3,773	N/A	N/A
Idaho	4	2	1	(D)	(D)	(D)
Illinois	103	121	132	46,198	29,736	22,472
Indiana	31	49	35	11,467	8,312	4,775
Iowa	20	32	22	(D)	(D)	2,088
Kansas	15	13	9	3,896	1,627	546
Kentucky	17	12	11	7,280	(D)	2,133
Louisiana	27	17	4	11,633	5,025	(D)
Maine	7	8	7	1,497	(D)	(D)
Maryland	19	16	10	7,122	2,976	2,581
Massachusetts	57	83	62	21,136	13,637	7,411
Michigan	56	70	65	33,373	23,327	13,995
Minnesota	20	15	12	13,518	6,968	3,678
Mississippi	5	3	2	(D)	(D)	(D)

Missouri	37	42	38	17,571	11,260	6,854
Montana	6	3	2	1,575	415	(D)
Nebraska	12	10	9	5,431	2,228	909
Nevada	8	6	2	7,489	3,375	(D)
New Hampshire	6	6	6	1,723	898	(D)
New Jersey	57	63	43	25,406	16,559	7,970
New Mexico	10	4	2	3,318	(D)	(D)
New York	196	258	226	98,650	76,292	50,023
North Carolina	18	11	9	14,687	6,090	3,019
North Dakota	1	1	1	(D)	(D)	(D)
Ohio	59	74	55	35,313	26,565	17,595
Oklahoma	12	12	12	4,278	3,128	(D)
Oregon	17	8	2	11,881	2,514	(D)
Pennsylvania	67	76	74	33,343	23,623	13,578
Rhode Island	9	15	11	3,381	2,435	1,093
South Carolina	6	7	5	(D)	(D)	(D)
South Dakota	5	6	1	1,571	(D)	(D)
Tennessee	19	16	13	13,602	7,196	4,304
Texas	74	73	50	40,231	21,076	8,265
Utah	4	6	6	(D)	(D)	2,358
Vermont	4	4	1	1,135	674	(D)
Virginia	15	15	8	12,760	7,215	3,203
Washington	18	8	5	15,379	4,881	2,740
West Virginia	10	10	10	2,619	2,364	(D)
Wisconsin	44	43	31	11,093	6,937	3,968
Wyoming	3	2	1	(D)	(D)	(D)
TOTAL WITH PAYROLL	1,435	1,474	N/A	$733,874	$431,812	N/A
ALL ESTABLISHMENTS	N/A	1,588	1,176	N/A	$433,022	$238,203

* 1948 Data includes all reporting establishments

(D) — Withheld to avoid disclosure
N/A— Not available at time of Publication

SALES TRENDS

Significant changes have taken place in the types of customers served by the linen supply industry in the past 15 years.

Since 1953, the industry has added five new major types of customers. These new customers, which now represent over 15% of the industry volume, include colleges and universities, nursing homes, hospitals, executive shirt rental customers and grade and high schools.

All except three of the principal types of customers served in 1953 have shown a decline in their percentage of total industry volume. The three types of customers that have increased in percentage of sales are restaurants, hotels and motels and food processors.

Customer types that have declined in their percentage of rental volume include food stores, industrial accounts, medical offices, taverns and bars, barber and beauty shops, miscellaneous retail stores, buildings and office accounts and drug stores.

The most significant increase in volume from traditional customers served since 1953 came from the hotel and motel customer group. This customer category increased from 8.2% of total sales in 1953 to 11.6% of sales in 1968, an increase of 3.4%. Second in percentage of increase were restaurants — up 3.2% from 1953's 22.7% of overall sales volume to 1968's 25.9%.

The two accounts showing the sharpest decline were the food stores and buildings, offices and miscellaneous towel account customer groups. Food stores now represent 8% of total industry rentals compared to 14.6% in 1953. Buildings and office towel rentals now account for only four-tenths of 1% of total volume compared to 5.8% reported in 1953.

The 1968 data is the result of an industry wide LSAA survey. There were 71 responses. The 1954 survey was based on 58 completed questionnaires.

Sales Trends
1953-1968

Customer Category	Percent of Annual Dollar Volume		Net Change
	1953*	1968**	
Restaurants (Includes Country Clubs)	22.7	25.9	+3.2
Food stores, (Grocery Stores, Supermarkets)	14.6	8.0	−6.6
Industrial (Other than Food Processors: Includes Gasoline Service Stations and New-Used Car Dealers)	9.2	7.6	−1.6
Hotels and Motels	8.2	11.6	+3.4
Medical (Doctors, Dentists, Clinics)	7.5	4.6	−2.9
Taverns, Bars, Cocktail Lounges	7.2	5.3	−1.9
Barber Shops	6.4	2.8	−3.6
Miscellaneous Retail Stores (Not listed elsewhere)	5.9	4.0	−1.9
Buildings, Offices, Miscellaneous Towel Accounts	5.8	0.4	−5.4
Beauty Shops	6.4	4.2	−2.2
Food Processors (Includes Dairies and Dairy Farms)	4.3	6.1	+1.8
Drug Stores	3.5	1.9	−1.6
Colleges and Universities	n/r	4.5	+4.5
Nursing Homes	n/r	3.8	+3.8
Hospitals	n/r	2.5	+2.5
Executive Shirt Rental Customers	n/r	2.4	+2.4
Grade Schools and High Schools	n/r	2.2	+2.2
All Other Customer Types	4.9	2.2	−2.7

n/r Not Reported in the 1953 Survey.
* Median Percent of dollar volume. Result of a 1953 LSAA Membership Study conducted by Leo J. Shapiro and Associates, Chicago, Illinois.
** Average Percent of Annual Dollar Rental Sales. Results of a 1968 Membership Study conducted by the LSAA Staff.

1966 SALES, PRODUCTION
AND REPLACEMENT ANALYSIS

The accompanying chart lists estimated dollar sales, number of pieces produced for sales, and the number of pieces of linen purchased for replacement for the linen supply industry in the U.S. during 1966.

This is a first attempt to develop a linen supply industry trend reporting program of sales and replacement purchases by general product type.

These estimates are based on reports on the number of items produced for sale during 1965-1966 by 66 parent companies in the U.S. and Canada. LSAA estimates that these companies represent about one-fourth of the total linen supply industry sales.

Actual Figures Used

The percentage of the total pieces produced for sale to the number of pieces produced are actual figures reported in LSAA's Linen Use Ratio Survey. The gross Replacement Ratio is actual percentage of linen replacement reported by the same companies.

Not all companies said that they served all items. For example, more short coats than long coats were served in the Northeast, Middle West, and Northwest U.S.

Total U.S. linen supply sales of $734 million for 1966 have been estimated by LSAA's Business Barometer. A total of 66 companies operating 187 plants reported that 1966 sales increased by 10.59% over 1965.

Dollar sales by general item type, and the percentage of total dollar sales are projections for total U.S. linen supply. This is based on information developed in the LSAA's Linen Use Ratio Survey and Representative Price Survey.

This chart was prepared, based on 1966 estimated sales of $734 million. Census data released for 1967 indicates that linen supply sales for establishments with payroll was $734 million. Thus, although this chart may overestimate sales for 1966, the percentages of dollar sales and items produced for sale remain accurate.

Estimated U. S. Linen Supply Industry Sales, Number of Pieces Produced, Replacement Purchases, 1966

Item	Dollar Sales	Percent of Total Dollar Sales	Number of Pieces Produced For Sale	Percent Total Pieces Produced For Sale	Gross Linen Replacement Ratio	Number of Pieces Purchased For Replacement
Aprons, Bib/Bar	$ 67,674,800	9.22%	466,720,000	5.41	4.047	18,888,000
Coats, Short	18,937,200	2.58	42,270,000	.49	4.521	1,911,000
Coats, Long	30,461,000	4.15	69,230,000	.80	3.519	2,436,000
Dresses	29,929,600	5.44	85,870,000	1.00	3.818	3,278,000
Pants	42,865,600	5.84	96,111,000	1.11	5.316	5,109,000
Shirts	34,644,800	4.72	112,119,000	1.30	5.078	5,693,000
Overalls, Coveralls	9,909,000	1.35	18,148,000	.21	4.417	802,000
Tablecloths	27,011,200	3.68	204,463,000	2.37	2.715	5,551,000
Napkins	34,057,600	4.64	1,892,088,000	21.95	3.017	57,084,000
Towels, Barber	27,378,200	3.73	1,053,008,000	12.22	2.591	27,283,000
Towels, Bath	38,975,400	5.31	519,672,000	6.03	3.050	15,850,000
Towels, Kitchen/Bar	67,307,800	9.17	1,246,441,000	14.46	5.133	63,980,000
Towels, Massage	36,479,800	4.97	911,995,000	10.58	3.352	30,570,000
Towels, Office	38,314,800	5.22	440,400,000	5.11	4.261	18,765,000
Towels, Continuous	79,492,200	10.83	74,993,000	.87	1.623	1,217,000
Hair Cloths	3,156,200	.43	18,566,000	.22	3.066	569,000
Dust Mats	11,597,200	1.58	10,900,000	.13	3.176	346,000
Dust Mops	13,872,600	1.89	23,121,000	.27	3.774	873,000
Wiping Cloths	9,101,600	1.24	364,064,000	4.22	7.083	25,787,000
Sheets	67,014,200	9.13	503,866,000	5.85	1.865	9,397,000
Pillowcases	21,653,000	2.95	318,426,000	3.69	2.329	7,416,000
Miscellaneous	14,166,200	1.93	147,565,000	1.71	3.000	4,427,000
Total	$734,000,000	100.00%	8,620,036,000	100.00%		307,232,000

Customer Coding
for the Linen Supply Industry

Many linen suppliers recognize the importance of customer classifications for use in marketing analysis and forecasting. They have asked LSAA for recommendations for a customer code to be used in conjunction with their data processing systems.

USES OF DATA BY CUSTOMER CODING

An analysis of information developed by customer type can serve many purposes. Among the many uses of customer data are:

- *Sales Analysis*
- *Sales Forecasting*
- *Assignment of Salesmen's Territory*
- *Assignment of Salesmen's Quotas*
- *Assignment of Quotas by Customer Type*
- *Share of Market Analysis*
- *Volume Contribution by Customer Type*

PURPOSE OF THE PROJECT

The purpose of the LSAA Customer Classification and Coding Project is:

1. To determine specific customer types which represent a significant amount of industry volume.

2. To define these customer types so that the definitions will be compatible with published statistical data, and,

3. To assign a workable coding to each customer type. The end result will be customer definitions and codes which will be consistent with the needs of the industry and compatible with published statistical data.

STANDARD INDUSTRIAL CLASSIFICATION (S.I.C.) CODING

Published U.S. Government statistical data are available which supply information for business enterprises. These business enterprises are defined and assigned a S.I.C. Code number. A complete list of definitions and assigned S.I.C. numbers is available in the publication "Standard Industrial Classification Manual, 1967," available from the U.S. Government Printing Office, Washington, D.C.

S.I.C. codes are four digit numbers. If found practical, the assignment of four data processing card positions would be sufficient to use the readily available S.I.C. code numbers. However, the four digit S.I.C. code number may be too cumbersome to be useful to the linen supply industry.

Previous studies among LSAA members have discovered that a large percentage of the linen supply industry volume comes from a limited number of customer types.

A 1953 study conducted for LSAA by Leo J. Shapiro and Associates asked members for the percentage of dollar volume of various customer categories. The results were:

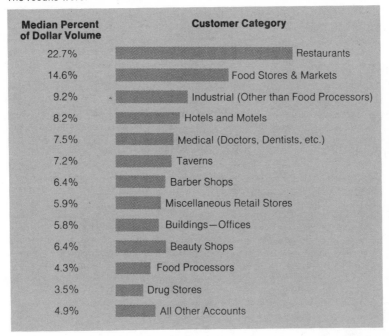

Median Percent of Dollar Volume	Customer Category
22.7%	Restaurants
14.6%	Food Stores & Markets
9.2%	Industrial (Other than Food Processors)
8.2%	Hotels and Motels
7.5%	Medical (Doctors, Dentists, etc.)
7.2%	Taverns
6.4%	Barber Shops
5.9%	Miscellaneous Retail Stores
5.8%	Buildings—Offices
6.4%	Beauty Shops
4.3%	Food Processors
3.5%	Drug Stores
4.9%	All Other Accounts

A 1955 study conducted by Time Magazine asked linen suppliers how their sales volume broke down among groups of customers. Their replies, based on 1954 sales, were:

Median Percent of Dollar Volume	Customer Category
34%	Restaurants, Clubs
15	Retail Stores
13	Barber, Beauty Shops
13	Plants, Factories, Hotels
10	Business Offices, Office Buildings
7	Doctors, Dentists
6	Utilities, Government, Private Homes, etc.
2	Institutions
100%	

An LSAA study conducted in mid-1968 asked members to report on the average percent of rental sales by customer type. The results were:

PERCENT OF ANNUAL RENTAL SALES RECEIVED BY CUSTOMER TYPE, 1968

TYPE OF CUSTOMER	LINEN SUPPLIERS SERVING THIS CUSTOMER TYPE		AVERAGE PERCENT OF ANNUAL RENTAL SALES RECEIVED FROM THIS CUSTOMER TYPE
	Number	Percent	
Restaurants	67	94.4	22.2
Bars, Cocktail Lounges, Taverns	61	85.9	5.3
Food Stores and Supermarkets	59	83.1	8.0
Drug Stores	51	71.8	1.9
Bakeries	49	69.0	0.7
Department Stores	27	38.0	1.0
Variety Stores (5¢ and 10¢ Stores)	20	28.2	0.6
Gasoline Service Stations	44	62.0	2.8
New and Used Car Dealers	31	43.7	2.6
All Other Retail Stores	34	47.9	1.7
Hotels, Motels & Rooming Houses	54	76.1	11.6
Beauty Shops	60	84.5	4.2
Barber Shops	55	77.5	2.8
Country Clubs, Golf Clubs	53	74.6	3.7
Doctor's Offices, Dentist's Offices & Clinics	58	81.7	3.6
Medical Laboratories	19	26.8	0.6
Dental Laboratories	20	28.2	0.4
Hospitals	26	36.6	2.5
Nursing Homes	43	60.6	3.8
Grade and High Schools	42	59.2	2.2
Colleges and Universities	37	52.1	4.5
Dairies and Dairy Farms	30	42.3	1.0
Food Processing & Manufacturing Companies	42	59.2	5.1
Executive Shirt Rental Customers	21	29.6	2.4
Manufacturing & Industrial Customers	10	14.1	2.2
Miscellaneous Towel & Washroom Service Customers	4	5.6	0.4
Automotive Repairs and Parts	3		0.2
Equipment Sales and Service	2		0.2
Airlines	2		0.2
Military Contracts and Bases	2		0.2
Newspaper and Printing	2		0.1
All Other Customer Types Not Identified	9		1.3
		TOTAL	100.0%

Based on 71 completed survey questionnaires

Suggested Linen Supply Industry Customer Listing

The following listing of thirty principal customer types is the recommended linen supply industry customer coding. An additional breakdown of "Restaurants" by principal types is included for those suppliers who want to have a finer control over this customer type.

Following this listing are detailed definitions of these customer groups, based on the S.I.C. definitions. The first column on this list is the common customer term used most often by linen suppliers. The second column is the same customer defined in S.I.C. terms. The third column is the detailed definition of the customer. The fourth column is the four digit S.I.C. code number.

The advantage of this thirty-customer list is that it is short, compact and usable. Although not all inclusive with the complete S.I.C. code listing, the list is adequate for statistical surveys and reporting purposes.

CONCLUSION

Customer classification developed by LSAA defines customers in accordance with the U.S. Government statistical groupings. Use of the classification by linen suppliers opens the door to easy comparison with a tremendous amount of authoritative data generated by the Federal government. We recommend use of these classifications.

The LSAA Management Data and Systems Committee recommends that actual code format be properly left to individual companies. A wide range of coding possibilities is available to suit the diversity of EDP equipment in use. The essential thing is to have the capability of relating occasionally to S.I.C. codes to take advantage of published government data.

Regardless of code format used—two, three or four digits—comparison with government data will be possible if the LSAA classifications are adopted by you.

PRINCIPAL CUSTOMER TYPES

1. Restaurants*
2. Bars, Cocktail Lounges, Taverns
3. Food Stores and Supermarkets
4. Drug Stores
5. Bakeries
6. Department Stores
7. Variety Stories (5¢ & 10¢ Stores)
8. Gas Stations
9. New and Used Car Dealers
10. All Other Retail Stores
11. Hotels and Motels
12. Rooming Houses
13. Beauty Shops
14. Barber Shops
15. Country Clubs, Golf Clubs
16. Doctor's Offices, Medical Clinics
17. Dentist's Offices
18. Medical Laboratories
19. Dental Laboratories
20. Hospitals
21. Nursing Homes
22. Grade and High Schools
23. Junior Colleges
24. Colleges and Universities
25. Dairies, Dairy Farms
26. Food Processing and Manufacturing Companies
27. Executive Shirt Rental Customers
28. Manufacturing and Industrial Companies
29. Miscellaneous Towel and Washroom Service
30. All Other Customers Not Listed Above

Restaurants may be segmented as follows:

*

A. Table or booth service restaurants, with waitress service, retail.

B. Table or booth service restaurants, with no waitress service, retail.

C. Counter restaurants (no tables or booths), retail.

D. Drive-in restaurants — hot foods, retail.

E. Drive-in restaurants — no hot food (dairy bars, frozen custard stands), retail.

F. Carry-out restaurants, retail.

G. Cafeterias, retail.

H. Catering, retail.

I. Industrial food service, such as food service facilities in factories, plants, mills, etc.

J. All other food service not included in the above.

NOTE:

Restaurants are establishments **primarily** engaged in the retail sale of prepared food and beverages. Include other restaurants and food service facilities by the principal business of your customer such as drug stores, department stores, variety stores, hotels, motels, hospitals, nursing homes, colleges and universities, etc.

Principal Customers of Linen Supply

Common Term	S.I.C. Terminology	Description and Types of Business Included In Standard Industrial Classification Category	S.I.C. Code No.
1. RESTAURANTS	EATING PLACES	Establishments primarily engaged in the retail sale of prepared food and drinks for consumption on the premises. Caterers are also included in this industry. Automats (eating places) Beaneries Box lunch stands Buffets (eating places) Cafes Cafeterias Carry-out restaurants— retail Caterers Commissary restaurants Dairy bars—retail Diners (lunch stands) Drive-in restaurants Frozen custard stands Grills (eating places) Hot dog (frankfurter) stands Ice cream stands Lunch bars Lunch counters Lunch rooms Luncheonettes Oyster bars Pizzerias Refreshment stands Restaurants Sandwich bars or shops—retail Soda fountains Soft drink stands—retail Tea rooms	5812
2. BARS	DRINKING PLACES	Establishments primarily engaged in the retail sale of drinks, such as beer, ale, wine, liquor, and other alcoholic beverages for consumption on the premises. The sale of food frequently accounts for a substantial portion of the receipts of these establishments. Bars (drinking places) Beer gardens (drinking places) Bottle clubs (drinking places) Cabarets Discotheques Drinking places Night clubs Saloons (drinking places) Tap rooms (drinking places) Taverns (drinking places)	5813

Common Term	S.I.C. Terminology	Description and Types of Businesses Included In Standard Industrial Classification Category	S.I.C. Code No.
3. FOOD STORES & SUPERMARKETS	GROCERY STORES	Stores, commonly known as supermarkets, food stores, grocery stores and delicatessen stores, primarily engaged in the retail sale of all sorts of canned foods and dry goods, either packages or in bulk, such as tea, coffee, spices, sugar, and flour; fresh fruits and vegetables; and frequently fresh, smoked and prepared meats, fish, and poultry. Delicatessen stores Food & freezer plans—retail Food markets—retail Frozen food plans—retail Frozen food stores—retail Grocery stores, with or without fresh meat —retail	5411
4. DRUG STORES	DRUG STORES AND PROPRIETARY STORES	Establishments engaged in the retail sale of prescription drugs and patent medicines, and which may carry a number of related lines such as cosmetics, toiletries, tobacco, and novelty merchandise. This industry includes drug stores which also operate a soda fountain or lunch counter. Apothecaries Drug stores Proprietary stores	5912
5. BAKERIES	RETAIL BAKERIES— BAKING & SELLING	Establishments primarily engaged in the retail sale of bakery products, such as bread, cakes, and pies, and which produce some or all of the products sold on the premises. Establishments manufacturing bakery products and selling them chiefly through house-to-house routes are classified in manufacturing (industry 2051). Doughnut shops—retail Retail bakeries—baking & Selling	5462

Common Term	S.I.C. Terminology	Description and Types of Business es Included In Standard Industrial Classification Category	S.I.C. No. Code
6. DEPARTMENT STORES	DEPARTMENT STORES	Retail stores carrying a general line of apparel, such as suits, coats, dresses, furnishings, home furnishings, such as furniture, floor coverings, curtains, draperies, linens, major household appliances; and housewares such as table and kitchen appliances, dishes and utensils. These and other merchandise lines are normally arranged in separate sections or departments with the accounting on a departmentalized basis. The departments and functions are integrated under a single management. Establishments included in the industry normally employ 25 or more persons. Department stores—retail	5311
7. VARIETY STORES (5¢ & 10¢ STORES)	VARIETY STORES	Establishments primarily engaged in the retail sale of a variety of merchandise in the low and popular price ranges. These stores frequently are known as "five and ten cent" stores, and "five cents to a dollar" stores, although merchandise is usually sold outside these price ranges. Sales usually are made on a cash and carry basis, with the open selling method of display and customer selection of merchandise. "Five cents to a dollar" stores "Five and ten cent" stores Variety Stores, limited price—retail	5331
8. GAS STATIONS	GASOLINE SERVICE STATIONS	Gasoline service stations primarily engaged in selling gasoline and lubricating oils, and which may sell other merchandise or perform minor repair work. Auto service stations, with or without repair shops or subsidiary lines of merchandise—retail Filling stations, gasoline, with or without repair shops or subsidiary lines of merchandise—retail Gas & Oil—retail Marine service station—retail Service stations, gasoline, with or without repair shops or subsidiary lines of merchandise—retail	5541

Common Term	S.I.C. Terminology	Description and Types of Businesses Included In Standard Industrial Classification Category	S.I.C. No. Code
9. AUTOMOBILE DEALERS	MOTOR VEHICLE DEALERS (NEW AND USED CARS)	Establishments primarily engaged in the retail sale of new automobiles or new and used automobiles. These establishments frequently maintain repair departments and carry stocks of replacement parts, tires, batteries, and automotive accessories. Automobile agency dealers—retail Automobiles, new and used—retail Cars, new and used Motor Vehicle dealers new and used cars—retail	5511
10. ALL OTHER RETAIL STORES		All other retail stores, except restaurants, bars, food stores and supermarkets, drug stores, bakeries, department stores, variety stores, gas stations, new & new and used car dealers.	
11. HOTELS AND MOTELS	HOTELS, TOURIST-COURTS & MOTELS	Commercial establishments known to the public as hotels, motor-hotels, motels, or tourist courts, primarily engaged in providing lodging, or lodging and meals, for the general public. Hotels operated by membership organizations and open to the general public are included. Apartment hotels are classified in industry 6513; rooming and boarding houses in industry 7021, and sporting and recreational camps in industry 7032. Auto courts Cabin camps Cabins & cottages Camps, tourist & cabin Hotel-motels Inns, furnishing food & lodging Motels Seasonal hotels (operating less than 9 months of the year) Summer resort hotels Tourist cabins Tourist courts Winter resort hotels Year round hotels YMCA & YMHA hotels, open to the general public YWCA & YWHA hotels, open to the general public	7011

Common Term	S.I.C. Terminology	Description and Types of Businesses Included in Standard Industrial Classification Category	S.I.C. Code No.
12. ROOMING HOUSES	ROOMING & BOARDING	Establishments renting rooms, with or without board, on a fee basis to permanent or transient guests. Boarding houses, except organization Child care homes, commercially operated Dormitories, commercially operated Homes for retarded children, commercially operated Homes for aged, except organization Homes for unwed mothers, commercially operated Lodging houses, except organization Rental of furnished rooms Rooming houses, except organization Tourist Homes	7021
13. BEAUTY SHOPS	BEAUTY SHOPS	Establishments primarily engaged in furnishing beauty services. This industry also includes combination beauty & barber shops. Beauty & barber shops, combined Beauty culture schools Beauty shops Hairdressers	7231
14. BARBER SHOPS	BARBER SHOPS	Establishments primarily engaged in furnishing barber services. Barber colleges Barber shops	7241
15. COUNTRY CLUBS	GOLF CLUBS & COUNTRY CLUBS	Golf and country clubs, the activities of which are restricted to members and their guests, and which may consist of golf or other sports. Country clubs, membership Golf clubs, membership	7947

Common Term	S.I.C. Terminology	Description and Types of Business Included In Standard Industrial Classification Category	S.I.C. Code
16. DOCTORS' OFFICES, MEDICAL CLINICS	OFFICES OF PHYSICIANS & SURGEONS	Establishments of licensed practitioners having the degree of M.D. and engaged in the practice of general or specialized medicine and surgery. Establishments such as group clinics, in which a group of physicians are associated for the purpose of carrying on their profession, are included in this industry. Clinics, operated by groups of physicians Dispensaries, operated by groups of physicians Gynecologists Neurologists Obstetrics, practice of Oculists Offices of physicians & surgeons (M.D.) Ophthalmologist Pathologist, office of Plastic surgery Psychiatrists Psychoanalysts Radiologist, office of Office of Surgeons	8011
17. DENTISTS' OFFICES	OFFICES OF DENTISTS & DENTAL SURGEONS	Establishments of licensed practitioners engaged in the practice of general or specialized dentistry. Offices of dentists & dental surgeons	8021
18. MEDICAL LABS	MEDICAL LABORATORIES	Medical laboratories providing professional analysis, diagnosis, or treatment services to the medical profession, or to the patient on prescription of the physician. Cancer research laboratories Chemists, biological (not manufacturing) Laboratories: (not manufacturing): bacteriological, biological, medical, X-ray (picture and treatment) Pathological laboratories	8071

Common Term	S.I.C. Terminology	Description and Types of Businesses Included in Standard Industrial Classification Category	S.I.C. Code No.
19. DENTAL LABS	DENTAL LABORATORIES	Establishments primarily engaged in making dentures and artificial teeth to order for the dental profession. The manufacture of artificial teeth other than to order is classified in industry 3843. Dental Laboratories Dentures, made in dental laboratories to order for the dental profession Teeth, artificial—made in dental laboratories to order for the dental profession	8072
20. HOSPITALS	HOSPITALS	Establishments primarily engaged in providing hospital facilities and clinics and dispensaries. Institutions such as sanatoria, rest homes, convalescent homes, and curative baths or spas in which medical or surgical services are not a main function of the institution are classified in industry 8092. Asylums, medical Clinics, operated by hospitals Dispensaries, operated by hospitals Hospitals for people Mental hospitals Nurses' training schools Tuberculosis sanatoria with medical care	8061
21. NURSING HOMES	SANATORIA & CONVALESCENT & REST HOMES	Institutions such as sanatoria, convalescent homes and rest homes, in which medical or surgical services are not a main function of the institution. Convalescent homes Curative baths or spas, operated separately from hospitals Health camps Health resorts Institutions for feeble minded Nursing homes Rest homes Sanatoria, operated separately from hospitals Tuberculosis sanatoria without medical care	8092

Common Term	S.I.C. Terminology	Description and Types of Businesses Included In Standard Industrial Classification Category	S.I.C. Code No.
22. GRADE SCHOOLS & HIGH SCHOOLS	ELEMENTARY & SECONDARY SCHOOLS	Elementary and secondary schools below university grade (ordinarily grades 1 thru 12), including denominational and sectarian. Nursery schools, kindergartens, and military academies are also included. Academies Boarding Schools Day Nurseries Day Schools Finishing Schools High Schools (junior & senior) Kindergartens Military Academies Nursery Schools Preparatory Schools Schools, elementary & secondary Sectarian Schools Schools for feeble minded Seminaries, below university grade Schools & training centers for retarded children, elementary & secondary grades	8211
23. JUNIOR COLLEGES	JUNIOR COLLEGES & TECHNICAL INSTITUTES	Junior colleges and technical institutes requiring for admission at least a high school diploma or equivalent general academic training, and granting associate academic degrees, certificates, or diplomas. Schools having junior college grades in conjunction with secondary grades are classified in industry 8211. Junior colleges Technical Institutes Community colleges (junior)	8222
24. COLLEGES & UNIVERSITIES	COLLEGES, UNIVERSITIES & PROFESSIONAL SCHOOLS	Colleges, universities, and professional schools granting academic degrees and requiring for admission at least a high school diploma or equivalent general academic training. Colleges Professional schools; dental, engineering law, medical, etc. Theological seminaries Universities	8221

Common Term	S.I.C. Terminology	Description and Types of Businesses Included In Standard Industrial Classification Category	S.I.C. Code No.
25. DAIRIES & DAIRY FARMS	DAIRIES	Establishments primarily engaged in the production of cows' milk and other dairy products. Such farms may process and bottle milk on the farm and sell at wholesale or retail. However, the processing and/or distribution of milk from a separate establishment not on the farm is classified in manufacturing or trade. Dairy farms	0132
26. FOOD PROCESSING & MANUFACTURING	FOOD & KINDRED PRODUCTS MANUFACTURING	Includes establishments manufacturing foods and beverages for human consumption, and certain related products, such as manufactured ice, chewing gum, vegetable and animal fats and oils, and prepared feeds for animals and fowls. Meat Products 2010 Dairy Products 2020 Canned & preserved fruits, vegetables & sea foods 2030 Grain Mill Products 2040 Bakery Products 2050 Sugar Products 2060 Confectionery & related products 2070 Beverages 2080 Miscellaneous Food preparation & kindred products 2090	2000
27. EXECUTIVE SHIRT RENTAL		Includes all rental sales for executive shirt rental, service to customers not listed in previous categories.	
28. MANUFACTURING AND INDUSTRIAL COMPANIES		All manufacturing and industrial companies except those engaged in food processing.	
29. MISCELLANEOUS TOWEL AND WASHROOM SERVICE CUSTOMERS NOT LISTED ABOVE		Includes all customers for towel and washroom service, (including flat rate charges) other than those listed in specific categories above, in this group.	
30. ALL OTHER CUSTOMERS		All other customers not listed in the previous 29 categories.	

A Glossary and Cross-Reference of Linen Items as Used in LSAA Reports

Listing and Glossary of Linen Rental Textiles

One of the most common problems in communication between linen suppliers is the varied terminology of linen items. For example, the roller towel to some may be a continuous towel to others. But to still others the roller towel is a short towel sewn on the form of a loop that hangs over a rod usually part of a washroom cabinet.

In many cases the end use of the rental textile determines its name. Yet, the same product may have more than one end use. This is especially true of towels. A doctor towel may be identical in construction to an office towel. Yet one supplier who says he has no office towel business may be renting more "office towels" under the name of doctor towels than he might realize.

The perfect listing would have names of items listed under construction, names of the same items listed under end use, and a cross-reference between the two. But this type of list would be far too difficult to use.

To simplify listings and to improve understanding within the industry, LSAA has developed a short listing of thirty-four separate product groupings. This listing ends duplicate classification of items and will serve as the standard item list for all LSAA market research and statistical reports.

All linen rental products can be included in one specific textile item group. An alphabetical cross-reference listing is included so that you may quickly find the major group listing for a specific item.

Item Groups of Linen Rental Textiles

The purpose of the Item Group Listing is to establish major groups of linen supply textile items for survey and reporting purposes. This listing defines major groups of textiles which are different from one another because of construction, type of processing, pricing or type of customer. These major item groups are defined in traditional linen supply terms and are compatible with the groups listed in the LSAA publication *Textile Rental Merchandise Glossary and Coding Manual*.

These standard major item groups will be used in future LSAA survey work and statistical reports such as the Linen Use Ratio Survey, Representative Price Survey, and the Sales and Replacements by Product Type Report.

The first thirty-three major item groups probably represent over 99% of the dollar volume and the number of pieces produced in our industry.

Further checking will be done to see if the "Miscellaneous" Category has items that represent a significant percentage of either the dollar volume or number of pieces produced for sale.

MAJOR GROUPINGS OF LINEN RENTAL TEXTILES

1. BIB AND BAR APRONS

A utility type apron worn to protect wearer's clothes. Usually tied around the waist, and may have an upper front called a bib. Varies in size, but generally provides wrap-around protection for the wearer. May be in white, colors or striped.

Included in this group are:

Bar Apron
Bib Apron
Butcher Apron
Candy Apron
Coat Apron
Cobbler Apron
Four-Way Apron
Grocery Apron
Hickory Apron
Hickory Striped
  Apron
Hoover Apron
Shop Apron
Waist Apron

2. TEA APRONS

An apron type garment generally worn by women, smaller in size and generally "dressier" than the bib or bar apron. May be in colors to match or contrast with the costume or dress of the wearer. Most often worn by waitresses and retail store clerks.

Included in this group are:

Fountain Apron
Pinafore Apron
Tea Apron
Waitress Apron

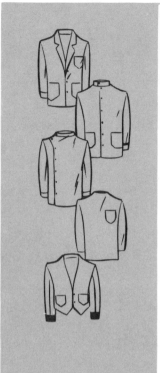

3. SHORT COATS

An outer coat type garment, which may be worn by either men or women, shorter than three-quarter length, generally waist length or hip length. May be worn as the outer garment without a shirt or undergarments, or as an outer garment over other clothing. May be collarless, or have a military type collar, or have lapels. May be fastened in the front, across one shoulder, or be a wrap-around type either buttoned or tied in the back. Short coat-type garments worn exclusively by women are included in the Dresses Category.

Included in this group are:

All coats shorter than ¾ length

Bank Coat	Frock
Barber Gown	Gown
Bar Jacket	Lapel Type Coat
Bus Boy Coat	Manager's Coat
Butcher Jacket	Mess Jacket
Clerk's Coat	Military Coat
Cook's Coat	Phantom Vest
Dental Gown	Side-Button Coat
Dentist's Coat	Smock
Dishwasher Coat	Tuxedo Coat
Doctor's Coat	Vest
Doctor's Gown	Vest Coat
Eton Jacket	

4. LONG COATS

An outer coat type garment which may be worn by either men or women, three-quarter length or longer. Generally, long sleeve, with length and detailing varying with the type of end use. Long coat type garments worn exclusively by women are included in the Dresses Category.

Included in this group are:

All coats longer than ¾ length

Butcher Coat	Lapel Type Coat
Butcher Frock	Long Coat
Clerk's Coat	Lugger Coat
Cooler Coat	Meat Lug Coat
Doctor's Coat	Shop Coat
Frock	Smock
Gown	Utility Gown
Lab Coat	

5. COVERALLS AND OVERALLS

A one-piece outer garment covering both the upper and lower body. Available in various colors.

Included in this group are:

Coveralls
Dairy Suit
Overalls
Unionalls

6. DRESSES

All garments worn exclusively by women, may be worn as an outer garment, or as a covering over other clothing.

Included in this group are:

Beauty Shop Gown
Blouse, Women's
Dress
Fit-All
Frock, Women's
Gown, Women's
Jumpsuit, Women's
Nurse's Uniform
Office Smock
Pinafore
Skirt
Smock, Women's
Waitress's Uniform
Wrap Dress

7. PANTS

A man's outer garment covering the lower part of the body. May be in white or colors. Included are all washable "work-type" pants. Executive slacks, or dress pants, are included in the Executive Slack Category.

Included in this group are:

Cook's Pants
Dishwasher's Pant
Slacks (except
   Executive Slack)
Trousers (except
   Executive Slack)
Work Pants

8. EXECUTIVE SLACKS

A man's outer garment covering the lower half of the body. Distinguished from the Pants Category because the Executive Slack is generally of finer quality intended for "dress" rather than utility or work wear. Includes all dress pants that are dry cleaned and the finer quality polyester/cotton dress type of pants and slacks which may be washed or dry cleaned. Uniforms that are dry cleaned are included in this group.

Included in this group are:

> Dress Pants
> Dress Slacks
> Executive Slacks
> Trousers, Dress Type
> Uniform, Dry Clean Type

9. SHIRTS

A man's outer garment covering the upper part of the body. May be in white or colors, long or short sleeve. Included are all "work-type" shirts. Executive shirts and dress shirts are included in the Executive Shirt Category.

Included in this group are:

> Closed Collar Shirt
> Cook's Shirt
> Work Shirt

10. EXECUTIVE SHIRTS

A man's outer garment covering the upper half of the body. Distinguished from the Shirt Category because the Executive Shirt is not monogrammed, generally of lighter material of finer quality. These shirts may be dress shirts, either long or short sleeve, with button or french cuffs. May be white or colors, plain, striped or patterned.

Included in this group are:

> Dress Shirt
> Executive Shirt

11. PILLOWCASES

The outer covering of a pillow. Generally a pillow slip is used under the pillowcase, as a protective covering for the pillow.

Included in this group are:

> Pillowcase
> Pillow Slip

12. SHEETS

The covering of a bed immediately above and below the sleeper. Include all sheets larger than 40″ x 72″. Sheets smaller than 40″ x 72″ such as hospital and nursing home draw sheets, and specialized hospital sheets are included in the Hospital Linen, Flat and specialty Category.

Included in this group are:

Bed Sheet	King Size Sheet
Draw Sheet	Queen Size Sheet
Full Bed Sheet	Twin Bed Sheet

13. MISCELLANEOUS LINEN

Includes all textile items used on the bed other than sheets and pillowcases.

Included in this group are:

Bed Spread	Pillow
Blanket	Sheet Blanket
Bolster	Thermal Blanket
Bolster Case	Thermo Blanket
Mattress Pad	

14. NAPKINS

A flat textile used at meals to protect the diner and to wipe the lips and hands. Place mats are also included in this category. Common sizes are 18″ x 18″ and 22″ x 22″.

Included in this group are:

Corded Napkin	Momie Cloth Napkin
Dinner Napkin	Napkin
Table Doily	Place Mat
Luncheon Napkin	

15. TABLECLOTHS

An outer covering for the top of a table. Normal weight table tops and banquet cloths are included in this group. Common sizes are 54″ x 54″ and 72″ x 72″. Extra heavy, absorbent, or flannel materials used on table tops between the table and the outer table cloth are included in the Miscellaneous Category.

Included in this group are:

Banquet Cloth
Table Cloth
Table Cover
Table Top
 (Normal weight)

16. BARBER TOWELS

A non-terry flat towel of a narrow, close woven material such as huck, crash, or twill. Usually kept separate in the plant because of processing requirements necessary to remove hair. Common size is 16″ x 27″.

Included in this group are:

Barber Towel
Neck Band
Neck Towel

17. KITCHEN TOWELS

A non-terry flat towel of a narrow, close woven material such as huck, crash, or twill, used generally in food preparation and kitchen areas. Distinguished from other towels because of end use and pricing. May be in white, colors, striped or plain. Common sizes are 16″ x 32″, 18″ x 36″ and 36″ x 36″.

Included in this group are:

Cotton Towel
Dish Towel
Glass Towel
Kitchen Towel
Plain Towel
Tea Towel

18. OFFICE TOWELS

A non-terry flat towel of a narrow, close-woven material such as huck, crash, or twill, used for medical purposes such as doctor's and dentist's office, and for hand drying purposes in offices. Distinguished from other towels because of end use and generally higher quality and pricing. Generally white, may be striped or plain. Common sizes are 14″ x 24″, 21″ x 24″ and 18″ x 36″.

Included in this group are:

> Bank Towel
> Club Towel
> Dental Towel
> Doctor Towel
> Face Towel
> Hand Towel
> Medical Towel
> Office Towel

19. CONTINUOUS TOWELS

A non-terry towel supplied in rolls approximately twelve inches wide and in various lengths. Small size may be from ten to sixteen yards, junior size from seventeen to twenty-five yards and senior size from forty-five to fifty yards in length.

Included in this group are:

> Continuous Towel
> Cabinet Towel

20. BAR TOWELS

A flat towel used primarily for wiping purposes, generally made from a ribbed terry fabric. Distinguished from other towels by fabric (terry) and end use. Generally white. Common size is 16″ x 27″.

Included in this group are:

> Bar Mop
> Bar Swipe
> Bar Towel
> Soda Towel

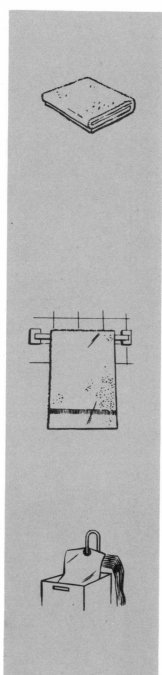

21. MASSAGE TOWELS

A flat towel made from terry fabric with a loop pile on both sides. Included in this group are all terry towels smaller than 20″ x 40″ except school towels, which are included in the Bath Towel Category. Distinguished from other towels because of fabric and size. May be white or colors, striped or plain. Common size is 16″ x 27″.

Included in this group are:

Face Towel (Terry)   Terry Towel
Hand Towel (Terry)   (Smaller than
Hot Towel   20″ x 40″)
Massage Towel   Turkish Towel
Steamer Towel   (Smaller than
                                 20″ x 40″)

22. BATH TOWELS

A flat towel made from terry fabric with a loop pile on both sides. Included in this group are all terry towels 20″ x 40″ and larger. Distinguished from other towels because of fabric and size, and use. School towels, which may be smaller than 20″ x 40″ are included in this category. May be white or colors, striped or plain.

Included in this group are:

Bath Towel   Turkish Towel
School Towel   (Larger than
Terry Towel   20″ x 40″)
  (Larger than
  20″ x 40″)

23. MISCELLANEOUS TOWELS

Includes all towels except those included in the major group categories of: Barber Towels, Bath Towels, Continuous Towels, Kitchen Towels, Massage Towels, and Office Towels.

Included in this group are:

Bowling Towel   Grommet Towel
Burlap   Pullman Towel
Car Wash Towel   Ring Towel
Chain Towel   Roller Towel
Eyelet Towel   (Not Continuous)
Grill Towel   Second-Grade Towel
Grill Wipe   Utility Towel

24. BATH MATS

A flat textile made of heavy terry fabric used as a bath mat or a bath rug.

Items included in this group are:

Bath Mat   Bath Rug

25. WASH CLOTHS

A small, flat cloth made from terry fabric, used to wash the face and other parts of the body.

Included in this group are:

Wash Cloth   Face Cloth
                    (Small Terry)

26. WIPING CLOTHS

A flat absorbent towel used by service stations and industrial users for wiping, cleaning and drying. May be in white or colors, plain or striped.

Included in this group are:

Industrial Towel	Wiper Cloth
Polishing Cloth	Wiping Cloth
Shop Towel	Wiping Towel

27. DUST COLLECTING MATS

A flat heavy mat or rug generally treated with chemicals to absorb and retain dust and dirt.

Included in this group are:

Dust Collecting Mat   Walk-On Mat
Dust Collecting Rug

28. DUST COLLECTING MOPS AND CLOTHS

A flat or tubular textile generally treated with chemicals to absorb and retain dust and dirt. Smaller sizes are flat and may be used for dusting and wiping purposes. Other sizes may be tubular or flat and fit over the handle of a special mop, brush or other holder for sweeping and cleaning purposes.

Included in this group are:

Duster	Dust Towel
Dust Cloth	Dust Tool Cover
Dust Mop	Sweep Cloth
Flat Dust Cover	Sweeping Tool Cover
Dust Treated	Tubular Dust Cover
String Mop	

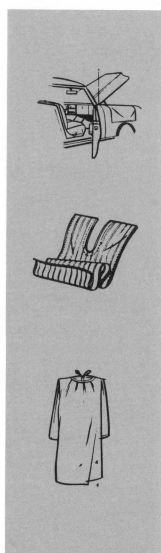

29. INDUSTRIAL LINEN MISCELLANEOUS

Includes all industrial textile items except wiping cloths, dust collecting mops and cloths, dust collecting mats, aprons and garments.

Included in this group are:

> Coverguard
> Drop Cloth
> Fender Cover
> Seat Cover
> Tool Cover

30. HAIR CLOTHS

A large flat cloth with a cut out for the neck, used to protect the wearer from falling hair.

> Hair Cloth

31. HOSPITAL LINEN—GARMENTS

Includes all garments that are exclusive to hospital use. Includes garments worn exclusively within the hospital, such as the operating room and obstetrical areas. Include garments that are not exclusive to hospital use in the appropriate garment category. For example, a nurse's scrub dress is worn exclusively within the hospital and is included in this group. A nurse's uniform may be worn outside the hospital and is included in the Dress Category.

Included in this group are:

> Bungalow Dress
> Bungalow Gown
> Examination Gown
> Isolation Gown
> Obstetrical Garment
> Obstetrical Gown
> Operating Room
>   Gown
> Patient Gown
> Patient Robe
> Scrub Dress
> Scrub Pants
> Scrub Shirt
> Scrub Suit
> Surgical Garment
> X-Ray Gown

32. HOSPITAL LINEN—FLAT AND SPECIALTY

Includes all textile items used within the hospital except for hospital garments and standard linen supply items such as bed linen and bath linen.

Included in this group are:

Abdominal Binder
Baby Bands
Baby Shirt
Baby Blanket
Bed Pad
Bed Pan Cover
Bed Pull
Binders
Breast Drape
Conductive Shoe or
   Boot Cover
Cubicle Curtain
Cystoscopy Sheet
Draw Sheet
   (Smaller than
   40″ x 72″)
Ear Cover
Instrument Wrapper
Lap Sheet
Lap Sponge
Laparatomy Sheet
Legging
Lithotomy Sheet
Mask
Mayo Stand Cover
Nurse's Snood
O. R. Sheet
Obstetrical Linen
Operating Room Cap
Operating Boots
Pack Wrapper
Pajamas
Scultetus Binder
Shoe Cover
Spinal Sheet
Sugical Binder
Surgical Drape
Surgical Linen
Surgical Sponge
T Binder
   (Male and Female)
Table Drape
Wrapper

33. CLEAN ROOM LINEN— FULLY BUTTONED TYPE

Includes all linen and garments used in clean rooms. Generally, clean room linens are synthetic materials to eliminate linting.

Included in this group are:

> Clean Room Coat
> Clean Room Coveralls
> Clean Room Dress
> Clean Room Gloves
> Clean Room Gown
> Clean Room Hood
> Clean Room Pants
> Clean Room Shoe
>   Cover
> Clean Room Smock

34. MISCELLANEOUS

Includes all rental textile items not included in the above categories.

Included in this group are:

Bar Cover	Lobster Bib
Bath Robe	Long Cap
Bib, Children	Meat Shroud
Bib, Adult	Mop
Cap	Neckerchief
Chair Back	Overseas Cap
Chair Cover	Pot Holder
Chef's Cap	Rag
Diaper, Adult	Round Cap
Diaper, Children's	Shower Curtain
Dresser Scarfs	Silver Pad
Gloves	Skull Cap
Hamper Bag	Steamer Rag
Hat	String Mop
Head Band	Table Top
Head Rest	(Absorbent and
Hi-Top Hat	Flannel)
Leg Drape	Window Curtain

Alphabetical Cross-Reference
of Textile Rental Items

Item	Major Group Listing	Item	Major Group Listing
Abdominal Binder	32	Bib, Apron	1
Adult Bib	34	Bib, Child's	34
Adult Diaper	34	Bib, Lobster	34
Apron, Bar	1	Binder	32
Apron, Bib	1	Binder, Abdominal	32
Apron, Butcher	1	Binder, Scultetus	32
Apron, Candy	1	Binder, Surgical	32
Apron, Coat	1	Binder, T- (Male and Female)	32
Apron, Cobbler	1	Blanket	13
Apron, Fountain	2	Blanket, Baby	32
Apron, Four Way	1	Blanket, Sheet	13
Apron, Grocery	1	Blanket, Thermal	13
Apron, Hickory	1	Blanket, Thermo	13
Apron, Hickory Stripe	1	Blouse, Women's	6
Apron, Hoover	1	Bolster	13
Apron, Pinafore	2	Bolster Case	13
Apron, Shop	1	Boot, Operating	32
Apron, Tea	2	Bowling Towel	23
Apron, Waist	1	Breast Drape	32
Apron, Waitress	2	Bungalow Dress	31
		Bungalow Gown	31
		Burlap	23
Baby Band	32	Bus Boy Coat	3
Baby Blanket	32	Butcher Apron	1
Baby Shirt	32	Butcher Coat	4
Back, Chair	34	Butcher Frock	4
Bag, Hamper	34	Butcher Jacket	3
Band, Baby	32		
Band, Head	34		
Band, Neck	16	Cabinet Towel	19
Bank Coat	3	Candy Apron	1
Bank Towel	18	Cap	34
Banquet Cloth	15	Cap, Chef	34
Bar Apron	1	Cap, Long	34
Bar Cover	34	Cap, Operating Room	32
Bar Jacket	3	Cap, Overseas	34
Bar Mop	20	Cap, Round	34
Bar Swipe	20	Cap, Skull	34
Bar Towel	20	Car Wash Towel	23
Barber Gown	3	Case, Bolster	13
Barber Towel	16	Case, Pillow	11
Bath Mat	24	Chain Towel	23
Bath Robe	34	Chair Back	34
Bath Rug	24	Chair Cover	34
Bath Towel	22	Chef Cap	34
Beauty Shop Gown	6	Child's Bib	34
Bed Pad	32	Child's Diaper	34
Bed Pan Cover	32	Clean Room Coat	33
Bed Pull	32	Clean Room Coverall	33
Bed Sheet	12	Clean Room Dress	33
Bed Spread	13	Clean Room Glove	33
Bib, Adult	34	Clean Room Gown	33

Item	Major Group Listing	Item	Major Group Listing
Clean Room Hood	33	Cover, Ear	32
Clean Room Pants	33	Cover, Dust Tool	28
Clean Room Shoe Cover	33	Cover, Flat Dust	28
Clean Room Smock	33	Cover, Fender	29
Clerk Coat (¾ length or longer)	4	Cover, Mayo Stand	32
Clerk Coat (¾ length or shorter)	3	Cover, Seat	29
Closed Collar Shirt	9	Cover, Shoe	32
Cloth, Banquet	15	Cover, Shoe, Clean Room	33
Cloth, Drop	29	Cover, Sweeping Tool	28
Cloth, Dust	28	Cover, Table	15
Cloth, Face	25	Cover, Tool	29
Cloth, Hair	30	Cover, Tubular Dust	28
Cloth, Polishing	26	Coverall	5
Cloth, Sweep	28	Coverall, Clean Room	33
Cloth, Table	15	Covergard	29
Cloth, Wash	25	Cubicle Curtain	32
Cloth, Wiper	26	Curtain, Cubicle	32
Cloth, Wiping	26	Curtain, Shower	34
Club Towel	18	Curtain, Window	34
Coat Apron	1	Cystoscopy Sheet	32
Coat, Bank	3		
Coat, Bus Boy	3		
Coat, Butcher	4	Dairy Suit	5
Coat, Clean Room	33	Dental Gown	3
Coat, Clerk (¾ length or longer)	4	Dental Towel	18
Coat, Clerk (¾ length or shorter)	3	Dentist Coat	3
Coat, Cook's	3	Diaper, Adult	34
Coat, Cooler	4	Diaper, Child's	34
Coat, Dentist	3	Dinner Napkin	14
Coat, Dishwasher	3	Dish Towel	17
Coat, Doctor (¾ length or longer)	4	Dishwasher Coat	3
Coat, Doctor (¾ length or shorter)	3	Dishwasher Pants	7
Coat, Lab	4	Doctor Coat (¾ length or longer)	4
Coat, Lapel Type (¾ length or longer)	4	Doctor Coat (¾ length or shorter)	3
Coat, Lapel Type (¾ length or shorter)	3	Doctor Gown	3
Coat, Long	4	Doctor Towel	18
Coat, Lugger	4	Doily, Table	14
Coat, Manager's	3	Drape, Breast	32
Coat, Meat Lug	4	Drape, Leg	32
Coat, Military	3	Drape, Surgical	32
Coat, Shop	4	Drape, Table	32
Coat, Side-Button	3	Draw Sheet (Larger than 40"x72")	12
Coat, Tuxedo	3	Draw Sheet (Smaller than 40"x72")	32
Coat, Vest	3	Dress	6
Cobbler Apron	1	Dress, Bungalow	31
Conductive Shoe or Boot Cover	32	Dress, Clean Room	33
Continuous Towel	19	Dress Pants	8
Cook's Coat	3	Dress, Scrub	31
Cook's Pants	7	Dress Shirt	10
Cook's Shirt	9	Dress Slack	8
Cooler Coat	4	Dress Type Trousers	8
Corded Napkin	14	Dress, Wrap	6
Cotton Towel	17	Dresser Scarf	34
Cover, Bar	34	Drop Cloth	29
Cover, Bed Pan	32	Dry Clean Type Uniform	8
Cover, Chair	34	Dust Cloth	28
Cover, Conductive Shoe or Boot	32	Dust Collecting Mat	27

Item	Major Group Listing	Item	Major Group Listing
Dust Collecting Mop	28	Hand Towel (Huck, Crash or Twill)	18
Dust Collecting Rug	27	Hand Towel (Terry, Under 20"x40")	21
Dust Tool Cover	28	Hat	34
Dust Towel	28	Hat, Hi-Top	34
Dust Treated String Mop	28	Head Band	34
Duster	28	Head Rest	34
		Hickory Apron	1
Ear Cover	32	Hickory Stripe Apron	1
Eton Jacket	3	Hi-Top Hat	34
Examination Gown	31	Holder, Pot	34
Executive Shirt	10	Hood, Clean Room	33
Executive Slacks	8	Hoover Apron	1
Eyelet Towel	23	Hot Towel	21
Face Cloth	25	Industrial Towel	26
Face Towel (Huck, Crash or Twill)	18	Instrument Wrapper	32
Face Towel (Terry)	21	Isolation Gown	31
Fender Cover	29		
Fit-All	6	Jacket, Bar	3
Flat Dust Cover	28	Jacket, Butcher	3
Fountain Apron	2	Jacket, Eton	3
Four Way Apron	1	Jacket, Mess	3
Frock, Men's (¾ length or longer)	4	Jumpsuit, Women's	6
Frock, Men's (¾ length or shorter)	3		
Frock, Women's	6	King Size Sheet	12
Full Bed Sheet	12	Kitchen Towel	17
Garment, Obstetrical	31	Lab Coat	4
Garment, Surgical	31	Lap Sheet	32
Glass Towel	17	Lap Sponges	32
Glove, Clean Room	33	Laparotomy Sheet	32
Gloves	34	Lapel Type Coat (¾ length or longer)	4
Gown, Barber	3	Lapel Type Coat (¾ length or shorter)	3
Gown, Beauty Shop	6	Leg Drape	32
Gown, Bungalow	31	Legging	32
Gown, Clean Room	33	Linen, Obstetrical	32
Gown, Dental	3	Linen, Surgical	32
Gown, Doctor	3	Lithotomy Sheet	32
Gown, Examination	31	Lobster Bib	34
Gown, Isolation	31	Long Cap	34
Gown, Men's (¾ length or longer)	4	Long Coat	4
Gown, Men's (¾ length or shorter)	3	Lugger Coat	4
Gown, Obstetrical	31	Luncheon Napkin	14
Gown, Operating Room	31		
Gown, Patient	31		
Gown, Utility (¾ length or longer)	4	Mask	32
Gown, Women's	6	Massage Towel	21
Gown, X-Ray	31	Mat, Bath	24
Grill Towel	23	Mat, Dust Collecting	27
Grill Wipe	23	Mat, Place	14
Grocery Apron	1	Mat, Walk On	27
Grommet Towel	23	Mattress Pad	13
		Mayo Stand Cover	32
Hair Cloth	30	Meat Lug Coat	4
Hamper Bag	34	Meat Shroud	34

Item	Major Group Listing	Item	Major Group Listing
Medical Towel (Huck, Crash or Twill)	18	Pot Holder	34
Mess Jacket	3	Pullman Towel	23
Military Coat	3	Pull, Bed	32
Momie Cloth Napkins	14		
Mop	34	Queen Size, Sheet	12
Mop, Bar	20		
Mop, Dust	28		
Mop, String	34	Rag	34
		Rag, Steamer	34
Napkin	14	Rest, Head	34
Napkin, Corded	14	Ring Towel	23
Napkin, Dinner	14	Robe, Bath	34
Napkin, Luncheon	14	Robe, Patient	31
Napkin, Momie Cloth	14	Roller Towel (Not Continuous Topel)	34
Neck Band	16	Round Cap	34
Neck Towel	16	Rug, Dust Collecting	27
Neckerchief	34	Rug, Bath	24
Nurse's Snood	32		
Nurse's Uniform	6	Scarf, Dresser	34
		School Towel	22
O.R. Sheet	32	Scrub Dress	31
Obstetrical Garment	31	Scrub Pants	31
Obstetrical Gown	31	Scrub Shirt	31
Obstetrical Linen	32	Scrub Suit	31
Office Smock	6	Scultetus Binder	32
Office Towel	18	Seat Cover	29
Operating Boot	32	Second-Grade Towel	23
Operating Room Cap	32	Sheet, Bed	12
Operating Room Gown	31	Sheet Blanket	13
Overall	5	Sheet, Cystoscopy	32
Overseas Cap	34	Sheet, Draw (Larger than 40"x72")	12
		Sheet, Draw (Smaller than 40"x72")	32
Pack Wrapper	32	Sheet, Full Bed	12
Pad, Bed	32	Sheet, King Size	12
Pad, Mattress	13	Sheet, Lap	32
Pad, Silver	34	Sheet, Laparotomy	32
Pajamas	34	Sheet, Lithotomy	32
Pan Cover, Bed	32	Sheet, O. R.	32
Pants, Clean Room	33	Sheet, Queen Size	12
Pants, Cook's	7	Sheet, Spinal	32
Pants, Dishwasher	7	Sheet, Twin Bed	12
Pants, Dress	8	Shirt, Baby	32
Pants, Scrub	31	Shirt, Closed Collar	9
Pants, Work	7	Shirt, Cook's	9
Patient Gown	31	Shirt, Dress	9
Patient Robe	31	Shirt, Executive	9
Phantom Vest	3	Shirt, Scrub	31
Pillow	13	Shirt, Work	9
Pillow Case	11	Shoe or Boot Cover, Conductive	32
Pillow Slip	11	Shoe Cover	32
Pinafore	6	Shoe Cover, Clean Room	33
Pinafore Apron	2	Shop Apron	1
Place Mat	14	Shop Coat	4
Plain Towel (Huck, Crash or Twill)	17	Shop Towel	26
Polishing Cloth	26	Shower Curtain	34
		Shroud, Meat	34

Item	Major Group Listing	Item	Major Group Listing
Side-Button Coat	3	Towel, Chain	23
Silver Pad	34	Towel, Club	18
Skirt	6	Towel, Continuous	19
Skull Cap	34	Towel, Cotton	17
Slacks (Except Executive Slacks)	7	Towel, Dental	18
Slacks, Dress	8	Towel, Dish	17
Slacks, Executive	8	Towel, Doctor	18
Slip, Pillow	11	Towel, Dust	28
Smock, Clean Room	33	Towel, Eyelet	23
Smock, Men's (¾ length or longer)	4	Towel, Face (Huck, Crash or Twill)	18
Smock, Men's (¾ length or shorter)	3	Towel, Face (Terry)	21
Smock, Women's	6	Towel, Glass	17
Snood, Nurse's	32	Towel, Grill	23
Soda Towel	20	Towel, Grommet	23
Spinal Sheet	32	Towel, Hand (Huck, Crash or Twill)	18
Sponge, Lap	32	Towel, Hand (Terry, Under 20"x40")	21
Sponge, Surgical	32	Towel, Hot	21
Spread, Bed	13	Towel, Industrial	26
Steamer Rag	34	Towel, Kitchen	17
Steamer Towel (Terry)	21	Towel, Massage	21
String Mop	34	Towel, Medical (Huck, Crash or Twill)	18
String Mop, Dust Treated	28	Towel, Neck	16
Suit, Dairy	5	Towel, Office	18
Suit, Scrub	31	Towel, Plain (Huck, Crash or Twill)	17
Surgical Binder	32	Towel, Pullman	23
Surgical Drape	32	Towel, Ring	23
Surgical Garment	31	Towel, Roller (Not Continuous)	34
Surgical Linen	32	Towel, Second-Grade	23
Surgical Sponge	32	Towel, School	22
Sweep Cloth	28	Towel, Shop	26
Sweeping Tool Cover	28	Towel, Soda	20
Swipe, Bar	20	Towel, Steamer (Terry)	21
		Towel, Tea	17
		Towel, Terry (Larger than 20"x40")	22
T Binder, Male and Female	32	Towel, Terry (Smaller than 20"x40")	21
Table Cloth	15	Towel, Turkish (Larger than 20"x40")	22
Table Cover	15	Towel, Turkish (Smaller than 20"x40")	21
Table Doily	14	Towel, Utility	23
Table Drape	32	Towel, Wiping	26
Table Top (Absorbent or Flannel)	34	Trousers (Except Executive Slacks)	7
Table Top (Normal Weight)	15	Trousers, Dress Type	8
Tea Apron	2	Tubular Dust Cover	28
Tea Towel	17	Tuxedo Coat	3
Terry Towel (Larger than 20"x40")	22	Turkish Towel (Larger than 20"x40")	22
Terry Towel (Smaller than 20"x40")	21	Turkish Towel (Smaller than 20"x40")	21
Thermal Blanket	13	Twin Bed Sheet	12
Thermo Blanket	13		
Tool Cover	29	Uniform, Dry Clean Type	8
Top, Table (Absorbent or Flannel)	34	Uniform, Nurse's	6
Top, Table (Normal Weight)	15	Uniform, Waitress	6
Towel, Bank	18	Unionall	5
Towel, Bar	20	Utility Gown	4
Towel, Barber	16	Utility Towel	23
Towel, Bath	22		
Towel, Bowling	23		
Towel, Cabinet	19	Vest	3
Towel, Car Wash, Terry	23	Vest Coat	3

Item	Major Group Listing	Item	Major Group Listing
Vest, Phantom	3	Women's Frock	6
Waist Apron	1	Women's Gown	6
Waitress Apron	2	Women's Jumpsuit	6
Waitress Uniform	6	Women's Smock	6
Walk-On Mat	27	Work Shirt	9
Wash Cloth	25	Wrap Dress	6
Window Curtain	34	Wrapper	32
Wiper Cloth	26	Wrapper, Instrument	32
Wipe, Grill	23	Wrapper, Pack	32
Wiping Cloth	26		
Wiping Towel	26		
Women's Blouse	6	X-Ray Gown	31

LSAA COST SURVEY RESULTS

OPERATING PROFITS FOR THE LAST TEN YEARS
For All Reporting Companies (with and without laundries)

Year	No. of Companies	Average Profit (Percent)
1968	66	7.92
1967	82	10.05
1966	75	10.75
1965	75	9.25
1964	117	7.83
1963	68	8.48
1962	64	9.33
1961	59	9.09
1960	84	11.15
1959	74	10.44

AVERAGE PROFIT BEFORE TAXES
ALL REPORTING COMPANIES - <u>WITH AND WITHOUT LAUNDRIES</u>

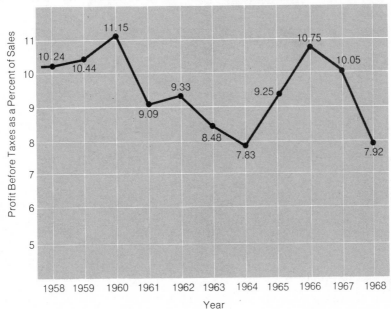

LSAA COST SURVEY RESULTS

COSTS AS A PERCENTAGE OF ANNUAL SALES VOLUME
1964 — 1968

LINEN AND TOWEL SUPPLY COMPANIES OPERATING LAUNDRIES
ALL REPORTING COMPANIES

	1968	1967	1966	1965	1964
PRODUCT REPLACEMENT:					
Flat Linen Replacement Cost	10.5	10.4	*	*	*
Garments Replacement Cost	7.5	8.5	*	*	*
Rep. Cost—Dust Control & Others	.4	NA	*	*	*
Cost of Other Products Sold	2.0	NA	*	*	*
TOTAL PRODUCT REPLACEMENT COST	20.0	19.6	19.2	20.4	19.7
LAUNDERING:					
Productive Labor	19.0	18.6	17.8	18.3	18.0
Productive Supplies	3.5	3.4	3.6	3.6	3.9
Power	3.7	3.5	3.4	2.9	3.8
Overheads—Building & Machinery	3.5	* *	* *	* *	* *
—Building Overhead	* *	1.8	1.5	1.7	2.5
—Machinery Overhead	* *	1.1	1.8	1.6	2.1
Depreciations—Build., Mach., Power Plt.	3.0	* *	* *	* *	* *
—Depr.-Building	* *	.6	.4	.5	.7
—Depr.-Machinery	* *	2.5	2.6	2.1	2.7
—Depr.-Power Plant	* *	.4	NA	.1	.4
Indirect Laundry Overhead	6.1	3.7	2.1	2.7	3.8
Plant Supervisory Expense	1.4	1.6	.7	.9	2.2
Outside Laundering Cost	.8	.4	.5	.8	.7
TOTAL LAUNDERING COST	41.1	37.3	35.1	35.7	39.2

DELIVERY & COLLECTION:					
Routeman's Wages & Comm.	11.2	11.2	10.8	12.0	10.9
Delivery Equip. Oper. Exp.	2.6	2.6	2.4	2.7	2.8
Depr. of Delivery Equip.	.8	.8	.6	.7	1.0
All other Delivery Exp.	1.9	1.5	1.0	1.4	1.1
TOTAL DEL. & COLL. COST	16.4	15.8	14.9	17.0	15.7
SALES PROMOTION COSTS:	3.9	3.3	3.4	3.1	3.2
OFFICE:					
Office Personnel Salaries	3.1	2.9	2.9	2.9	3.1
Bad Debts	.4	.3	.2	.2	.4
Depr.-Office Equip.	.2	.2	.2	.2	.2
Personnel Relations & Welfare	2.1	2.1	***	***	***
General Office Expense	2.9	5.9	9.9	8.1	5.7
Administrative Salaries	2.8	2.5	2.5	2.9	3.7
TOTAL OFFICE COSTS	10.8	13.5	15.9	14.4	13.0
TOTAL OPERATING COST	92.1	89.5	88.8	90.8	92.1
OPERATING PROFIT (Before Federal and State Taxes)	7.9†	10.5†	11.2†	9.2	7.9

*Information not requested prior to 1967.

**In 1968 all plant overheads were combined, all depreciations were combined also.

***Included within gen. off. expense for these years.

†Includes companies which reported a loss.

GENERAL NOTES:
1. The sum of individual cost elements does not necessarily equal the subtotals or grand total. This is because not all companies reported all items and because of the rounding of percentage figures.
2. Prior year's figures are not necessarily from the same reporting companies.

KEY BUSINESS RATIOS FOR LINEN SUPPLY

KEY RATIO	1968-69 Performances		1967 Performances		Ratio Expressed As
	29 Private Comp.	7 Public Comp.	44 Private Comp.	4 Public Comp.	
A PROFITABILITY MEASURES					
1 Operating Profit on Sales	7.3	10.4	7.8	10.6	percent
2 Net Profit After Taxes on Sales	4.0	4.9	5.0	5.4	percent
3 After Tax Return-on-Investment	12.5	15.1	19.5	15.7	percent
B FINANCIAL CONDITION INDICATORS					
4 Current Assets to Current Debt	2.53	2.20	2.46	2.49	times
5 Cash & Rec. to Current Debt	1.73	.98	1.96	1.32	times
6 Net Worth Turnover	3.70	3.10	4.30	2.83	times
7 Working Capital Turnover	6.69	5.86	13.85	8.04	times

C RECEIVABLES						
8 Credit Sales to Total Sales	76.8	—	—	—	—	percent
9 Average Collection Period	39.6	—	40.5	—	—	days
10a Receivables Over 90 days Old	5.5	—	5.2	—	—	percent
10b Receivables Over 60 Days Old	10.1	—	10.0	—	—	percent
10c Receivables Over 30 Days Old	28.7	—	24.7	—	—	percent
11 Receivables to Average Monthly Sales	101.5	—	—	—	—	percent
D PRODUCTIVITY MEASURES						
12 Revenue per Pound Processed	21.3	—	20.2	—	—	cents
13 Revenue per Employee (all)	10786	—	10595	—	—	dollars
E PRODUCTION PERSONNEL FACTS						
14 Employees per Supervisor	26.4	—	—	—	—	employees
15 Monthly Employee Turnover	13.2	—	11.2	—	—	percent

Notes:

(a) 1968-69 figures are not necessarily from the same companies as for 1967.

(b) Public company information was derived from latest available annual reports. Most "publicly owned linen supply companies" are diversified. Linen rental revenue, however, comprises 38% to almost 100% of total revenues of each company used to develop the averages. Each public company reported in excess of $10 million annual sales for their latest year.

(c) Monthly employed turnover (ratio 15) is the ratio of "replaced separations" to average number of production employees during an average month. "Replaced separations" includes only hirings to replace workers who quit or were discharged. Seasonal hirings or layoffs are therefore not included.

KEY BUSINESS RATIOS BY
ANNUAL SALES VOLUME CATEGORY

KEY RATIO	Under $500,000	
	1968-9 10 Comp.	1967 11 Comp.
A PROFITABILITY MEASURES		
1 Operating Profit on Sales	8.1	7.7
2 Net Profit After Taxes on Sales	5.0	5.5
3 After Tax Return-on-Investment	12.0	21.9
B FINANCIAL CONDITION INDICATORS		
4 Current Assets to Current Debt	2.06	2.33
5 Cash & Rec. to Current Debt	2.35	2.39
6 Net Worth Turnover	3.84	5.80
7 Working Capital Turnover	6.48	16.61
C RECEIVABLES		
8 Credit Sales to Total Sales	82.4	—
9 Average Collection Period	35.9	41.8
10a Receivables Over 90 Days Old	7.5	7.3
10b Receivables Over 60 Days Old	12.3	11.1
10c Receivables Over 30 Days Old	37.8	27.1
11 Receivables to Average Monthly Sales	106.4	—
D PRODUCTIVITY MEASURES		
12 Revenue per Pound Processed	—	20.1
13 Revenue per Employee (all)	10543	8178
E PRODUCTION PERSONNEL FACTS		
14 Employees per Supervisor	28.1	—
15 Monthly Employee Turnover	—	15.6

Note: 1968-69 figures are not necessarily from the same companies as for 1967.

$500,000 to $1,000,000		$1,000,001 to $2,000,000		Over $2,000,000		Ratio Expressed As
1968-9 7 Comp.	1967 12 Comp.	1968-9 6 Comp.	1967 15 Comp.	1968-9 6 Comp.	1967 6 Comp.	
5.8	4.9	6.2	9.5	8.4	9.8	percent
3.5	3.8	3.6	5.8	3.7	5.4	percent
9.1	14.6	11.1	22.2	20.3	18.3	percent
2.75	2.36	3.32	2.76	2.04	2.16	times
1.60	1.81	1.38	1.89	1.15	1.62	times
3.31	5.06	2.56	3.07	5.13	2.92	times
7.90	19.92	5.19	7.82	7.69	12.45	times
74.3	—	71.8	—	75.0	—	percent
45.4	32.4	39.8	44.1	40.8	.44.5	days
—	5.8	3.8	3.1	4.3	7.1	percent
—	11.1	8.8	9.9	8.8	11.1	percent
—	25.7	25.7	22.5	22.0	26.2	percent
97.8	—	87.4	—	108.0	—	percent
—	21.6	19.9	20.0	—	18.8	cents
11109	10934	9292	12017	12800	11426	dollars
20.3	—	33.9	—	21.3	—	employees
—	11.6	—	12.1	—	10.1	percent

DEFINITIONS AND APPLICATIONS
LINEN USE RATIOS

Sixty-three members reported data for computing their Linen Use Ratios for the current Linen Replacement Analysis Survey. Forty-eight companies reported linen replacement data for the calendar year 1965; nine for twelve-month divided periods covering portions of 1965 and 1966, and six for parts of 1966. About half of the production volume was divided between each of the past two years.

The **Association Standards** were determined by experience in a well-controlled operation and should be minimum objectives in a well-run linen supply company. An effective linen conservation program should make it possible for you to reduce your linen use ratios to the Association replacement percentage standards and below.

The **Gross Replacement Ratio** represents the number of pieces of new linen put into service for every one hundred pieces produced for service, and it is the average percentage of linen replacement of the reporting companies.

The **Number of Expected Servings** per item is obtained by dividing the Gross Replacement Ratio into 100. For example, with Bib/Bar Aprons, the Gross Replacement Ratio was 4.047; this divided into 100 gives an average of 24.7 servings.

The **Loss Ratio** represents the percentage of items "lost" or not accounted for by ragging. This figure includes additional linens put into service for new customers and for increases in present customers, plus theft, other losses, and inventory adjustments. The Loss Ratio equals the number of new pieces put into service minus the number of pieces ragged, divided by the number of new pieces put into service. Of the Bib/Bar Aprons replaced, 45.2% could not be accounted for by ragging.

The Linen Use Ratios can be used to determine replacement cost per serving and replacement cost as a percentage of sales. To determine replacement cost per serving, divide the cost of the item by the number of servings. For example, if the gross replacement ratio for sheets is 1.9, you can expect 53.6 servings. If the cost of a sheet is $2, the replacement cost per serving is $2 divided by 53.6 or 3.7 cents.

To determine linen replacement cost as a percentage of sales, divide the cost of the item by the number of servings times the rental price. For example, if sheets have 53.6 servings and the rental price per sheet is 20 cents, the total rental income per sheet is $10.72. With a cost of $2 per sheet, your linen replacement cost is $2 divided by $10.72 or 18.65%.

Linen use ratios can be an important tool since they enable you to evaluate your linen replacements by comparing your rates with the Association Standard and the industry average. Large differences warrant careful investigation ...tighter inventory controls...stringent measures.

An effective textile control program should make it possible to reduce your linen use ratios to the Association replacement standards or below.

LINEN USE RATIOS

ITEM	Assn. Standard	Gross Replacement Ratio				Number of Expected Servings		Loss Ratio	
		1966	1962	1960	1959	1966	1962	1966	1962
Aprons, Bib/Bar	3.2	4.0	4.1	3.5	3.4	24.7	24.4	45.2	45.9
Coats, Long	*	4.5	2.9	—	—	22.1	34.5	44.3	30.8
Coats, Short	3.0	3.5	3.1	3.3	3.4	29.4	32.3	42.1	39.8
Dresses	3.4	3.8	3.1	3.1	3.2	26.2	32.3	28.1	32.5
Pants	4.0	5.3	4.6	4.7	5.0	18.8	21.7	50.5	53.2
Shirts	3.4	5.1	4.3	4.4	4.8	19.7	23.3	53.1	53.4
Overalls, Coveralls	*	4.4	4.4	4.9	4.8	22.6	22.7	38.1	43.1
Tablecloths	*	2.7	2.8	—	—	36.8	35.7	55.4	55.3
Napkins	3.1	3.0	3.3	3.4	3.3	33.1	30.3	66.3	59.4
Towels, Barber	2.0	2.6	3.3	2.7	2.5	38.6	30.3	48.5	48.7
Towels, Bath	*	3.1	2.9	—	—	32.8	34.5	87.3	82.5
Towels, Kitchen/Bar	5.2	5.1	6.2	6.0	5.9	19.5	16.1	44.2	50.3
Towels, Massage	3.0	3.4	3.8	3.6	3.6	29.8	26.3	72.6	68.9
Towels, Office	3.7	4.3	4.0	3.6	3.5	23.5	25.0	56.2	59.8
Towels, Continuous	1.4	1.6	1.3	1.7	1.6	61.6	76.9	80.9	57.9
Hair Cloths	*	3.1	3.6	4.4	3.8	32.6	27.8	34.1	35.5
Mats, Dust Collecting	*	3.2	—	—	—	31.5	—	78.4	—
Mops, Dust Collecting	*	3.8	—	—	—	26.5	—	67.9	—
Wiping Cloths	*	7.1	—	—	—	14.1	—	70.7	—
Sheets	*	1.9	2.0	2.3	2.3	53.6	50.0	71.0	66.6
Pillow Slips	*	2.3	2.8	3.2	2.8	42.9	35.7	67.3	77.4

*No Association Standards established.

INDEX